Ella Deloria's *Iron Hawk*

Ella C. Deloria. Ella C. Deloria Research Project.
Courtesy of the Dakota Indian Foundation.

Ella Deloria's
IRON HAWK

Julian Rice

University of New Mexico Press
Albuquerque

Library of Congress Cataloging-in-Publication Data
Deloria, Ella Cara.
   [Iron Hawk. English & Lakota]
   Ella Deloria's Iron Hawk / [edited by] Julian Rice. — 1st ed.
      p.   cm.
   Story in Lakota and English; introd. and critical essays in English.
   Includes bibliographical references and index.
   ISBN 0-8263-1435-X (cl). — ISBN 0-8263-1447-3 (pa)
   1. Oglala Indians—Legends.   2. Lakota dialect—Texts.   I. Rice,
Julian, 1940–   .   II. Title.
E99.03D4513   1994
398.2′089975—dc20   93–10515
                                                            CIP

Contents

Acknowledgments

Vine Deloria, Jr. granted permission to quote from two unpublished manuscripts by Ella Deloria: "Dakota Tales in Colloquial Style," and "Teton Myths" (the George Bushotter collection). Both are housed in the Boas Collection of the American Philosophical Society in Philadelphia.

The South Dakota Historical Society granted permission to quote from the unpublished book, "Camp Circle Society" by Ella Deloria. Marvene Riis, archivist, facilitated access to the manuscript.

Tapes and transcripts from The South Dakota Oral History Center at the University of South Dakota in Vermillion were obtained with the assistance of its directors, Herbert Hoover and Leonard Brughier.

The videocassette of Ben Marrowbone referred in chapter 3 was obtained at the Oglala Lakota College archives with the assistance of its director, Ted Hamilton.

To Agnes Picotte
   for carrying on Ella Deloria's
   memory and work

And to Albert White Hat, Sr., Victor Douville,
   Doris Leader Charge, and Ronald Goodman
   for carrying the Lakota oral tradition
   on into the twenty-first century

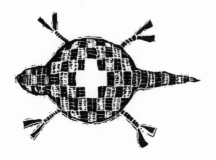

Introduction

This book is the second of three devoted to the bilingual literary art of Ella Deloria. The first, *Deer Women and Elk Men: The Lakota Narratives of Ella Deloria*, focused primarily on her published collection of oral narratives, *Dakota Texts*. The sixty-four stories in that volume were written in Lakota and translated into English. Each story is approximately three to five pages long in each language, the usual length for transcribed folklore. Few students of folklore in any language have come to expect a traditional narrative as long as the story presented here. *Iron Hawk* is almost fifteen times longer than any single story in *Dakota Texts*. At the end of the translation Deloria notes that *Iron Hawk* atypically combines elements from the whole culture hero genre in a single story. As a rule shorter stories supplement each other in creating the Lakota ideal, but *Iron Hawk* contains "all the usual incidents bound up and woven together around one hero" (see chapter 2).

Iron Hawk is one of four unusually long stories included in an unpublished 1937 manuscript, "Dakota Tales in Colloquial Style." The other three will be published in the sequel to this volume. Readers may wonder if Deloria broke tradition by synthesizing episodes that oral narratives separate in shorter versions. In the introduction to "Colloquial Style" she explains that the stories are based on those of various old men, "notably one named Makula [Breast]." She also indicates that she did not transcribe or record the stories while they were told but wrote them down later from memory. In this sense Deloria participated in the storytelling tradition in a unique way. Like the storytellers themselves she told her own versions of stories she had repeatedly heard, but unlike them she set down her versions in written form.

Under his other name of Hokacatka (Left Heron), Makula had contributed six relatively long stories to James R. Walker's *The Sun Dance* (1917). Slightly different versions of two of these and an additional story appear in Walker's *Lakota Myth,* edited by Elaine A. Jahner (1983). Unlike Deloria, Walker did not know Lakota well enough to write without utilizing several interpreters (see Walker, *Lakota Belief and Ritual* 21–23, 32, 34, 283–85 and *Lakota Myth* 11–13). He embellished and rewrote some of the stories he obtained, especially those given by George Sword (*Lakota Myth* 12–15). When Franz Boas sent Deloria to investigate the authenticity of Walker's stories, she observed that those collected from Makula were "all in keeping" with the oral tradition her informants knew, while Sword's stories struck "no responsive chord anywhere" (Walker, *Lakota Myth* 21). Since Deloria did not have the Lakota transcriptions that Walker used for her interviews, Walker's translators must have left Makula's story structures intact. She herself would later restore their Lakota texture.

Makula's work demonstrates that a storytelling performance could be longer than most published stories presuppose. The evidence is strengthened by his substantial contributions to Martha Warren Beckwith's "Mythology of the Oglala Lakota" (1930). Beckwith's interpreter was William Garnett who also worked for Walker, and her collection preserves only the English texts with one exception. She employed Ella Deloria to transcribe and translate Ben Kindle's Winter Count of the years 1759 to 1925 (Beckwith 349–67). This may well have been one of the occasions when Deloria heard Makula tell the story of Iron Hawk. Undoubtedly she read the English version in Beckwith. Deloria's version adds humorous dialogue, vivid characterization, and thematic depth that Garnett's version only begins to suggest. Perhaps Makula imparted these qualities to Deloria more effectively in Lakota, or perhaps Deloria's own literary gifts are responsible. Considering Makula's reputation the stories probably arise from a collaboration of gifted word masters, a dialogic convergence culminating in Deloria's written text. The Beckwith version is reprinted in an appendix to this volume so that the reader can appreciate Deloria's contribution.

Makula was an Oglala of the Gopher band, a group of Cheyenne who had joined the Lakota. His maternal grandfather was one of these Cheyenne, and his other grandparents were northern Lakota. The Gopher band, however, lived in the White Clay community in the southwestern corner of the Pine Ridge reservation. Deloria refers to his having been dead for almost four years in a 1939 letter to Boas regarding the Walker material (Walker, *Lakota Myth* 23). She wrote *Iron Hawk* in 1937 within a year after his death. In "Camp Circle Society" (an unpublished ethnography ca. 1945) Deloria mentions that she knew Makula in his mid-eighties (4). Makula himself said that he was born the year some hunters found the body of an old woman inside of a buffalo cow's stomach (Mekeel 50), or 1850–51 according to Lone Dog's Winter Count (Mallery 1:282). His life spanned the most dramatic events of recorded Lakota history: the Fort Laramie treaty was signed in 1851; by the time of Red Cloud's war and the 1868 treaty Makula was seventeen and by 1876 he was twenty-five and old enough to have fought at Little Big Horn; in the 1890s when the Lakota were adjusting to reservation life Makula was in his forties, and by sometime after 1910 when he told stories for Walker, he was an elder in his sixties. It might also be remembered that he was a dozen years older than Black Elk and that like Black Elk he was a healer (see Beckwith 378–79) and holy man (Mekeel 51), as well as a master storyteller. The storytelling tradition he passed on through Deloria must be at least two hundred years old.

Like Lakota culture itself the stories of Makula are thoroughly imbued with spiritual concepts and metaphors. He told Beckwith how a spider spirit in a dream taught him to identify and ceremonially use a certain weed to stop bleeding. In addition to his skill as an herbalist he employed eloquence to heal the effects of exploitation and betrayal. When the Commissioner of Indian Affairs, John Collier, visited Pine Ridge in 1935, Makula performed the welcoming ceremony. His speech addressed the traditional priorities of Lakota culture and serves here to define the purpose of Iron Hawk and the culture hero ideal:

> Iho! Iho! Iho! Iho!
> Wakan Tanka! tuwa tokanl cekiyepica kacaś.
> Niśnala Ikcewicaśa maka ohiniyan cekiciyapi.
> Wakan Tanka wanmayanka yo!
> Wicaśayatapika tacannunpa kin le iyahpaya ceciciya ce.
> Wakan Tanka waniheyunka kakipeya ca ewagle kte,
> Maka oyate taku wate kin sitomni,
> Peji hinape icaǵeya pawankanl hiyu miciciyiye.
> Waniheyunka kawakipe kin canpaza najin, tona inkpa wate
>   kin ake econ s'e tanin miciciyiye.
> Wakan Tanka onśimala ye oyate maka aicaǵe kin tanyan
>   mawani kte.
> Onśimala ye okpani icaǵe kin wicatakuni śni ye.
> Anpetu kin nupinyan tawe nakicijin.
> Tunkaśila eya miś'eya Wakan Tanka takuwaye,
> Iyapi kin tanyan imicicu ye, mitakoja ob wani kte,
> Inś'eya, Ikcewicaśa maka akan nipi kte.

> Listen and be it so!
> Wakan Tanka! Who else can receive prayer?
> To you alone the people of the earth have always prayed.
> Wakan Tanka look upon me!
> Take hold of this chief's pipe I pray you.
> Wakan Tanka, so that I may come through the winter frost,
> That the people all over the earth may have something to eat,
> That all the grasses may be pushed up, grant me.
> That I may come through the frost, that the tree will stand,
>   that the many sources of food will again appear, grant me.
> Wakan Tanka have pity on me that the people will flourish
>   on the earth I walk.
> Have pity on me so that those lacking strength will not be
>   left wanting.

This day protect both your peoples.
Grandfather has said that I too have Wakan Tanka for my
    relative.
Answer these words well so that I will live with my
    grandchildren.
And the people of the earth will live. (Holy Rosary Mission
    Series 1, Box 2, Marquette University Archives. My
    translation)

Makula speaks of the continuity of the Lakota people, their love
for each other, and their acceptance of seasonal (historical) change
as long as their children's future is assured. He also prays for a
manifestation promising that future, and at the same time his own
words partially answer the prayer by confirming continuity in the
present. Mutual survival, he pointedly tells Collier, depends on
mutual trust. Those who smoke the pipe together will not lie to
one another:

> Kola oyate kin le ilagyapi wicoicaġe k'on cannunpa kin le
> onpa yo, nahan śni owotanla oyate kin wooglake wicaka wo.
> Ogna tokata wicaśa wanji ake u kin le cannunpa kin ilagya
> owotanla taku eyin kte kin on le yuha gla yo.

> Friend, by this pipe the people live. Smoke it with us, and as
> the people speak with absolute honesty [while holding the
> pipe], tell the truth. Present it to the next man who comes so
> that through it something just will be said. Keep it and return
> to your home. (Holy Rosary Mission Series 1, Box 2, Mar-
> quette University Archives. My translation)

Makula's concluding prayer invokes the most sacred object in Lakota religion as the means of maintaining truth in future relations
with the federal government.

Prior to being appointed Commissioner of Indian Affairs by
Franklin Delano Roosevelt in 1933, Collier had proved himself
worthy of trust as the executive secretary of the American Indian
Defense Association, a position he held for ten years before entering government service. During that time he had effectively edito-
rialized and lobbied on behalf of Indian religious freedom and the

protection of remaining reservation lands. Nevertheless, Lakota elders like Makula might well have been skeptical that his reforms would erase the physical and cultural devastations of the preceding fifty years. Makula's call for honesty from the government must have been intensified by personal memories of the whole reservation period. In 1891 General Nelson A. Miles, having little stomach for fighting the Lakota in the "outbreak" after Wounded Knee, reported to the Secretary of War that the tribe had been cheated out of the food rations promised them by the treaty of 1876: "For the fiscal year beginning July 1, 1890, the following shortages in the rations were found to exist: 485,275 pounds of beef [gross], 761,212 pounds of corn, 11,937 pounds of coffee, 281,712 pounds of flour, 26,234 pounds of sugar, and 39,852 pounds of beans" (Mooney 80). Miles also noted that winter clothing was not supplied until the season was "well advanced" (Mooney 80).

In another letter to Senator Henry L. Dawes, author of the infamous Allotment Act of 1887, Miles summarized a situation Makula may have had in mind when he asked Collier to initiate an adherence to truth-telling among federal officials:

> While the Indians were urged and almost forced to sign a treaty presented to them by the commission authorized by Congress, in which they gave up a valuable portion of their reservation which is now occupied by white people, the government has failed to fulfill its part of the compact, and instead of an increase or even a reasonable supply for their support, they have been compelled to live on half and two-thirds rations, and received nothing for the surrender of their lands, neither has the government given any positive assurance that they intend to do any differently with them in the future. (Mooney 80)

The federal neglect that allowed the Sioux to go hungry was the unconscious side of the government's active will to rob them of their land, a will efficiently implemented in Senator Dawes's bill. Through this legislation, Congress forced Indian tribes to divide their lands "in severalty," assigning each individual head of a family 160 acres. The large "surplus," amounting to over half of the existing lands, was thrown open to settlement by whites. The allotments were given only within the then new and still existing reservation boundaries at Standing Rock, Cheyenne River, Crow Creek, Lower Brule, Pine Ridge, and Rosebud. Robert Grey Eagle, vice president of Oglala Lakota College, speaks of the steady "whittling down" of the Lakota land base that continued through the time of Makula's speech and into the present:

> on Pine Ridge alone, we've lost more than a million acres . . . In 1924 Bennett County was opened to homesteading. In Jackson-Washabaugh County, 40 to 50 percent of the land-owners were non-Indians. It's about 20 percent in Shannon County. The land grab continues. By the year 2000, what will we have left? (*The Lakota Times* 19 February 1992)

The effect of the allotments on subsequent generations ought to have been obvious. The fact that it was not illuminates the unre-strained greed of early twentieth-century legislators and their con-stituents. Grey Eagle describes a condition of ownership fraction-alized into uselessness:

> I was told I was a landowner. When I checked, I found that I had $\frac{1}{32}$ of $\frac{1}{4}$ of a quarter section in Hisle, and $\frac{1}{16}$ of $\frac{1}{8}$ of $\frac{1}{8}$ section in Porcupine. In order to put up a fence, plant a gar-den, or build a house, I have to get all the signatures of the owners. If I don't, the bureau (of Indian Affairs) agent can lease it for me. You're left out of the negotiations. If you tell them you don't want it, they just tell you, "Sorry, you're a minority (owner)." So life goes on.
> (*The Lakota Times* 19 February 1992)

The assault on Lakota culture was just as unrelenting as the legal maneuvers to seize their land. The work of Ella Deloria takes on added impact in light of the aggressive ignorance, clerically and governmentally sanctioned, that oppressed Indian people for the half-century preceding Collier. The system of government board-ing schools in which Indian children were regimented into replicas of lower class white farmers, mechanics, and maids has been well documented (see the bibliographical note in Prucha 347; for an extended account of life at Carlisle, see Standing Bear, *My People the Sioux* 133–76; on early Lakota opposition to the schools, see Hyde 308–10, 318–19, 321–25, 328; see also the more recent reminiscence by Mildred Stinson in Cash and Hoover 94–95).

These schools did not close until 1934, and they waged a particularly vicious attack on native languages. In his zeal to promote English for Indians, Commissioner of Indian Affairs J. D. C. Atkins (1885–1888) unintentionally chose a metaphor that reflected his inability to recognize the equality of an oral culture with his own pen and ink world:

> their barbarous dialect should be blotted out and the English language substituted . . . The object of greatest solicitude should be to break down the prejudices of tribe among the Indians; to blot out the boundary lines which divide them into distinct nations, and fuse them into one homogeneous mass. Uniformity of language will do this—nothing else will. (Prucha 199)

Once their specific tribal consciousness has been reduced to a blank slate, Indian children will come to appreciate, as Atkins puts it, "the language of the greatest, most powerful, and enterprising nationalities beneath the sun" (Prucha 200). Indian languages, on the other hand, are "of no use to them" and are "detrimental to their education and civilization" (Prucha 202). Accordingly, Atkins issued an order that "no books in any Indian language must be used" in any government school (Prucha 202).

As a substantial piece of literature in an Indian language, *Iron Hawk* makes an implicit statement against brainwashing Indian children out of their own cultures and languages. The specific content of *Iron Hawk* also recognizes the value of traditional tribal education. In the first section of the story Iron Hawk is expertly raised by his meadowlark grandfather. His development represents the central role of the grandfather in fostering a boy's growth (see Deloria, "Camp Circle Society" 80, *Waterlily* 24, and Mails, *Mystic Warriors* 514) and portrays gently effective guidance in contrast to the harsh militarism of the government schools (on Spotted Tail's rescue of his children from the domineering Captain Pratt at Carlisle Institute, see Hyde 321–25).

Thomas J. Morgan, the Commissioner who succeeded Atkins in 1889, expounded on the government's purpose and method:

> The periods of rising and retiring, the hours for meals, times for study, recitation, work and play should all be fixed and adhered to with great punctiliousness. The irregularities of camp life, which is the type of all tribal life, should give way to the methodical regularity of daily routine. (Prucha 231)

From the point of view of Sid Byrd, a Lakota student for six years in one of the schools, the effect was dehumanizing:

> the white man wanted us to jump through the loops and the hoops like a dog . . . we were controlled by whistles and bugles. A bugle was sounded when we were to get out of bed. We got into formation and we marched to our meals. At the dining room a triangle was used and when the first triangle sounded, we sat down on stools. The second triangle indicated that there was to be complete silence and we were to bow our heads and say our prayers, and at the third triangle we began to eat. ("In the White Man's Image")

Morgan justified this rigid scheme by vividly imagining evils to eradicate. The efforts of Franz Boas, Ella Deloria, and John Collier occurred in a culture that still revives views like that of Morgan. For decades missionary effort has been exerted on behalf of the "helpless" Indian children Morgan impersonated in 1889 at the Lake Mohonk Conference of Friends of the Indian in New Paltz, New York:

> "If you leave us here, what can we hope for? . . . our religion will be a vile mixture of superstition, legends, and meaningless ceremonies . . . We shall have no literature, no accumulated treasures of the past, no hopes for the future . . . Our only hope is in your civilization, which we cannot adopt unless you give us your Bible, your spelling book, your plow and your ax. Grant us these and teach us how to use them, and then we shall be like you." (Prucha 244)

Sid Byrd did not leave the Genoa, Nebraska school until it closed in 1934, the year after Collier took office. His recollection of coming home at the age of twelve keynotes the surging hope that many Lakota people felt at the time Deloria wrote *Iron Hawk*:

My grandparents had been informed, and they were standing waiting at the train station. I practically leaped from the train, tears of joy streaming down my cheeks, and I ran to my grandmother, and she embraced me, and she said, "takoja, takoja, tehantan yagli so" 'my grandchild, my grandchild, you come from a long ways,' and she embraced me; tears were streaming down her cheeks. I suddenly discovered that the people that I loved and longed to be with, I could no longer communicate with these people. And I wept bitterly, and I vowed that I would relearn my language . . . I'll always be a Lakota. They can never change me. ("In the White Man's Image")

In addition to closing the boarding schools and restoring the right of collective tribal ownership to Indian lands, John Collier was a strong advocate of Indian languages and cultural traditions. He had attended Columbia University from 1902 to 1905, ten years before Ella Deloria's attendance, and may well have been influenced by Franz Boas who began his forty-six year tenure there in 1896 (on Boas and Boasian anthropology, see DeMallie, "Afterword" to Deloria, *Waterlily* 234, Krupat 65–67, 75–80, and Murray 98–101). As Commissioner of Indian Affairs Collier emphasized the role of anthropological research in forming Indian policy: "in the ethnic field research can be made a tool of action" (Collier 156). He noted that eighteenth century Danish scholars had "rendered the [Greenland] Eskimo language into written form," thereby allowing that people to be united with the "wider world" (Collier 176).

Certainly this must have been a substantial part of the motivation of Deloria and the other Boasian scholars. Transferring Lakota into a written language makes its study and appreciation possible far beyond the boundaries of the Lakota-speaking community. Many readers of a foreign language are not fluent speakers, but their appreciation of the literature they experience is much enhanced by being able to read in the original. Ella Deloria's *Iron Hawk* is written literature intended for serious readers. Collier envisioned and encouraged exactly this sort of development: "expression along many lines of literature, of the arts, of religion and of philosophy will come into being. The ancient-modern Indian affirmation of the deathless man-nature relationship will flow into poetry and symbolic art" (Collier 187).

Previous federal authorities had believed that Indians were capable only of agricultural, industrial, or domestic labor and had been unable to conceive of their entering into the humanistic study of their own traditions in their own languages. Schools like Carlisle and Hampton had "outing" programs where the students were placed with white families of "the highest type" in order to learn housekeeping and farming (Prucha 226). Many of these students later testified that their hosts had used them as slave labor ("In the White Man's Image"). For over forty years Ella Deloria effectively refuted such assumptions about her people's intellectual capabilities:

> I have a mission: To make the Dakota people understandable, as human beings . . . those who came out among them to teach and preach, went on the assumption that the Dakotas had *nothing,* no rules of life, no social organization, no ideals. And so they tried to pour white culture into, as it were, a vacuum and when that did not work out, because it was not a vacuum after all, they concluded that the Indians were impossible to change and train. (letter to H. E. Beebe 2 December 1952 qtd. in DeMallie, "Afterword" to Deloria, *Waterlily* 237–38).

Vine Deloria, Jr. recalls how his aunt welcomed the introduction of Indian Studies programs into colleges and universities:

> In *Speaking of Indians* which was written during World War II, Ella was afraid that the government would continue its policies of vocational training for Indians rather than expand into academic fields. You probably realize that for decades the idea was that Indians could not achieve a college education be-

cause they were "good with their hands." (letter to Janette K. Murray, 23 April 1974, qtd. in Murray 230)

Collier was probably responsible for much of the impetus that eventually created Native American Studies as an academic discipline, and in 1935 Deloria wrote to Boas of a visit to the Lakota reservations by the commissioner, her impression of his sincerity, and her belief that "he is a real friend" (letter to Boas, 29 November 1935). Unfortunately Collier's programs were not as successful in practice as he had hoped. According to Vine Deloria, Sr. the medical and technical experts sent to the reservations could not or would not communicate with the reservation people: "I do not remember *ever* seeing those experts, who were supposed to be improving the reservation by teaching the Indians, out on the reservation" (interview in Murray 120).

While Collier's dreams of cultural development have been realized among the Lakota through the work of Deloria and the establishment of Lakota studies at reservation colleges, the system of elective tribal government he initiated has come under increasingly severe criticism from some of the most articulate Lakota spokesmen. At a recent traditional elders' forum at Oglala Lakota College, Robert Grey Eagle, vice president of the college, spoke of elective democracy as a white imposition: "It was a way that was adopted in 1934 . . . [traditional chiefs] were not leaders because they were popular or because they went on the campaign trail" (*The Lakota Times* 31 December 1991). Grey Eagle's definition of the traditional leader as willing to lay down his life for the "elderly and the child" is earned by Iron Hawk and by Red Calf (see chapters 3 and 8). In the last episode Red Calf personifies a continuing ideal expressed by Robert Grey Eagle:

"A Lakota warrior was not the one with shades, braids and cool statements, but one who shoveled snow for the elders, one who found an orphan that no one wanted and said, 'Come with me.' It was a hard way to live" (*The Lakota Times* 31 December 1991).

While Grey Eagle rejects the spiritual effects of political competition, he carries through the commitment of Deloria to the Lakota language as the key to cultural survival: "It is part of our thought and philosophy. It is essential to understand. And we shouldn't ridicule those who are trying to learn" (*The Lakota Times* 31 December 1991). And as Deloria preserved Lakota culture by writing oral narratives, Grey Eagle proposes the writing of traditional laws to make them more enforceable and respected:

> Perhaps it is time we changed our outlook on some of the so-called taboos on writing. We are, after all, surrounded by writing, films, recordings, books, and photographs . . . It is time we brought literary recognition to our traditional laws and have them formally enacted as our way of life. We need to codify and write our traditional laws into our codes and ordinances. (*The Lakota Times* 13 May 1992)

Like Grey Eagle, Elgin Bad Wound, President of Oglala Lakota Colllege, affirms Collier's spirit of cultural revival, while condemning his attempt to force Lakota society to abandon its traditional form of government and adopt Western-style democracy under the Indian Reorganization Act of 1934: "The present system, the form of government known as IRA, is alien to our beliefs . . . It becomes the general practice to discredit your opponents . . . to say they are bad people and have made mistakes in their lives" (*The Lakota Times* 8 May 1991. For discussions of the IRA's impact on the Lakota, see Useem and Eicher 9, Macgregor 99–100, Farber 127–28, and Schusky 146). The story of *Iron Hawk* presents a hero who makes mistakes that enable readers to understand leadership rather than simply the achievement of leadership in spite of mistakes. Bad Wound recalls his own divergence from Lakota ideals but attributes his return to early lessons resembling those given by Meadowlark to Iron Hawk. The culture hero's difficult journey is evoked by Bad Wound's acknowledgment that being responsible for others is life's greatest challenge: "I never believed I was a person who could hold together a family. I was very cavalier, adventuresome . . . always in trouble. I was very independent. Not the family type" (*The Lakota Times* 11 December 1991). But Bad Wound endured the trickster diversions of the dominant society to become a father of three sons and the administrative guide of over 1,000 students per year at Oglala Lakota College: "Looking back I could've been absorbed by mainstream America. But I'm glad I didn't do it. I credit that to my upbringing. My parents brought me up with a strong sense of identification, and the practices instilled were so strong I never lost them" (*The Lakota Times* 11 December 1991).

By going to Columbia Ella Deloria helped to bring future generations back from the government school of thought and into the state of mind fostered by educators like Bad Wound. Although she taught her younger students to be sympathetic with those who live strictly by Lakota tradition, she did not insist that there was only one way to be Lakota: "Our heritage is rich and good . . . Use it, respect, and be sympathetic with those who still live entirely by it" (Interview with Kenyon Cull, headmaster of St. Mary's School, 15 March 1974, qtd. in Murray 151). She herself was not a traditionalist in the sense that Black Elk was. She performed expertly in the non-Lakota profession of ethnological scholarship, employing her academic tools to return sustenance to the Dakota and Lakota nations in strikingly innovative ways. With subtle linguistic features, such as exclamations or compound words, that she wrote down for the first time, she supplied the emotion, humor, or irony that many folklorists have felt only oral performance could convey.

Paul Manhart, S. J., in his introduction to the Lakota language volume of stories, *Lakota Tales and Texts,* collected and edited by Eugene Buechel, S. J., makes a case for the performance-is-best approach: "a story does no good written in a book unless people tell and retell it in fact" (ix). For Manhart the written text is valuable primarily as a guide to help new narrators "check on the essentials" before retelling the story in their own words (x). Whether or not its readers vocalize the texts, Buechel's collection contains 104 valuable literary and ethnographic documents, including stories, historical reminiscences, descriptions of ceremonies and customs, and autobiographies. They may, as Manhart hopes, stimulate readers to emulate the creative ideal he observed in Frank Kills

Enemy, who adeptly adjusted differing versions of the same story to different audiences and situations (ix). But the Buechel stories might also be rewritten by Lakota writers employing Deloria's multifaceted technique.

While Buechel's method of collecting stories was essentially scientific, Deloria's practice resembled that of the storytellers themselves. Buechel taught Lakota adults to write their thoughts or to record others in a syllable-by-syllable method that they could quickly learn. In most cases the accounts he received left out everything but actors, actions, places, objects, and events. Although Buechel rewrote the monosyllables in words and paragraphs, he did not restore elements of tone and emotion that the original method of recording had necessarily omitted (see *Lakota Tales and Texts* xxviii–xxix). Deloria never depended on recordings or shorthand notes but composed the stories entirely out of her memory and imagination. In the introduction to "Dakota Tales in Colloquial Style" she apologizes for remembering some stories more thoroughly than others, but she includes *Iron Hawk* as one of those she heard "often enough" and "systematically enough" to retain the conventional "set forms" and "small details." In other instances her memory is either nearly perfect, or her empathic appreciation of what she hears is so complete, that she reproduces whole sequences of dialogue, including even the subtlest forms of wordplay (see Appendix 2).

Although Deloria initiated the use of written Lakota as a creative art, a substantial body of Dakota and Lakota work preceded hers. Two Minnesota missionaries, Stephen R. Riggs and Thomas S. Williamson translated substantial parts of the bible into the D dialect beginning in 1839 and continuing on for several decades. The sum of their efforts eventually became *Dakota Wowapi Wakan* (Dakota Holy Book) a complete bible published in 1914. Minnesota missionaries also produced a smaller body of ethnographic texts that refrained from proselytizing or did so only indirectly. Letters written in Dakota to Riggs and Williamson by residents of the Santee agency were translated by Deloria in 1937. And in 1941 she edited and translated forty one "ethnographic and folkloristic" documents that Gideon and Samuel Pond transcribed in 1839.

None of this Dakota work has been published, although eight stories collected and translated by Riggs can be read in the 1977 reprint of his *Dakota Grammar, Texts, and Ethnography* (83–149), originally published in 1893.

In the twentieth century few books of secular content have been published. Seven fine bilingual children's books by Emil Afraid of Hawk and Ann Clark did appear between 1942 and 1954 (see Works Cited), but apart from Deloria's work the potential for Lakota writing has yet to be fulfilled. In a bilingual newspaper column, Ivan Star Comes Out advocates and demonstrates the value of the written word:

> Iblukcan kin he Lakota iyapi kin le wowapi el ecela owa ungluhapi kte tokata.
>
> Oyate tankaya owanjila. Lakota iyapi kta wan unkpatitanpi hantan ecela ake kini kte.
>
> Wowapi kin lena Lakota iya owapi kte na oyate kin iyapi kin le tokahe kiyapi kte.

> I think we will be able to retain our language only in written form in our future.
>
> Together, as a nation, we must push our language to a national language stature and only then will it survive.
>
> Books must be written in the language to make it our first and only language. (*The Lakota Times* December 25, 1990)

Deloria has already written many of the books Star Comes Out envisions, but surely some of her readers will write more. She generally wrote for thoughtful adults rather than for children. *Iron Hawk* encompasses questions of social value, spiritual identity, and verbal purpose. Beckwith defines the genre by mentioning the hero's acquisition of supernatural power and his use of it to create ceremonies "of traditional value for the preservation of the group" (340). Elaine Jahner has extended this definition to include the basic elements that occur in *Iron Hawk*: the hero's unusual birth, his "journey to the world's western quadrant," a "humiliating challenge from the trickster" and "a show of power in a camp other than one's own" ("Cognitive Style" 44). *Iron Hawk* also includes the hero's vulnerability, a characteristic that Jahner finds distinctively Lakota: "Among the Skidi-Pawnee, the Blackfeet, the Arapaho, and the Gros Ventres, Blood-Clot Boy's actions are at all times self-assertive and generally lack the Lakota element of temporary immobility" ("Cognitive Style" 48–49). After overcoming their enemies the heroes of these tribes return to their celestial homes, while the Lakota hero "simply . . . continues to live as an adult contributing member" of society ("Cognitive Style" 49).

Iron Hawk is symmetrically structured in four sections: 1) the hero's adoption and upbringing by the meadowlarks; 2) an encounter with the trickster, Iktomi, and his extrication from that predicament by new grandparents followed by his achievement of marriage and leadership in his wife's camp; 3) a second near disastrous loss of self in his seduction-abduction by the Rock woman, his son Red Calf's journey to the sky to rescue him, and his resumption of heroic identity in introducing horses to the tribe; 4) Red Calf's journey to bring the meadowlarks from the eastern edge of the world to their grandson's camp in the west, and the promise of continuity in the birth and naming of Red Calf's son, Rattling Deer Hooves.

The episodes follow the general pattern outlined by Jahner and confirm her observation that the Lakota hero is vulnerably human rather than a god. Deloria sharpens the genre outline as if to answer a major thematic question—what are the fundamental Lakota beliefs and how are they most frequently expressed? In having Red Calf recover the grandparents in the fourth and final episode, Deloria shows that the Lakota past, its consciousness and wisdom, is never lost, although individuals like Iron Hawk, and even Red Calf very briefly in the last episode, may occasionally forget the priority of cultural endurance. While the individual characters are only human, the "hero" is actually anyone who "wears" the Lakota virtues when the people need them. The virtues, represented by the hawk cap and the name "Iron Hawk" are immortal but not transcendent. They have power only when a human being enacts their meanings, but no human being is a hero in and of himself; at the same time Lakota culture is heroic when its people earn its clothes and live up to its "name," i.e. its symbolic consciousness.

In this book the commentary that follows the story emphasizes Lakota symbolism in *Iron Hawk*'s literary text, its linguistic texture, and its cultural context. Two chapters of literary criticism (3 and 4) precede a series of ethnographic discussions: on child rearing, the impact of speech on reality, and the meaning of meadowlarks (chapter 5); on the related associations of the sun, fire, and the color red (chapter 6); on the social and spiritual connotations of clothing (chapter 7); on the structuring effect of directional symbols in culture hero narratives (chapter 8). While the journey to the West is crucial in individual development, the return to the East reflects collective purpose. In bringing the grandfather from the East to Iron Hawk's camp, Red Calf brings the past to the present and completes the heroic circle.

Deloria assigns fulfillment to the hero's son rather than the hero himself, since the story concerns the consciousness of the whole *oyate* (tribe). The four generations of Meadowlark, Iron Hawk, Red Calf, and Rattling Deer Hooves help to define each adult as a temporary container of power. Even heroes are humbly expendable. By focusing on Red Calf rather than Iron Hawk in the last episode, Deloria demonstrates the purpose and reward of individual effort. As a landmark of literature and scholarship, *Iron Hawk* too will stimulate varying forms of work. Its unique elaboration provides opportunities for both academic criticism and narrative emulation. Rattling Deer Hooves is anonymous in the "Iron Hawk" Makula gave to Beckwith. Although Deloria notes that she did not hear enough of his subsequent adventures to repeat them (see Chapter 2), she did give him an infancy and a name. Perhaps some future reader will write the rest of his story.

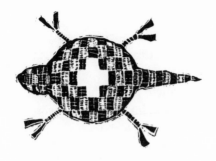

Iron Hawk: Oglala Culture Hero

The Lakota Text

1. Wiyohinnape cin ekta kal heceś oyate-cikalala wan wicoti ke'.
2. Yunkan hocoka kin itohanyankel kal wakeyala wan ciscila iśnala han ca el wicahcalala wan winunhcalala wan kici tila śke'.
3. Ho, nunpin oyate-cikala wan etanhanpi k'eyaś isanp lila cik-cikapila k'eyaś blihecapila nan winyan kin iyohahcin śpulakeśni ke'.
4. Heceś hingnakula kin anpetu wan tima pel-śniyan yankin nan cannunpahela ke'; iśtogmus wiyukcan yankela nan tohanlśna yablu-iyeya kakel yanka ke'.
5. Tankal tateyanpa ca tawicula kin wipa-apiyahin nan ungna tiyopa el paiyuksa ahiyokas'in nan heya ke':
6. "Wichaca, ito cank'in-mninkte; tokśa htayetu kinhan wagli nan wakal-wayinkte," eya yunkan tunwe-wacinśni hecena, "Ho, iyaya yo, cin toke," eya ke'.
7. Heceś wikan kakśa yuha wana canyatakiya luźahela canke kinye s'e tuwela kin sipa acakikśin-manika ca yin nan canmahel iyaya ke'.
8. Yunkan ungna patak-inaźin ke, taku wanyaka canke—Yun-

kan lece kal leca-mnitan kin un peżi-śaśa kin iciyuwiya psa-
owinża s'e yunkan ca el cokaya hokśicalala wan heceya-tunpila ca
t'ehowaya naġalġatela ke'.

9. Cekpa kin nahanhcin ikoyak hpayela canke "Hina! Hina!
Mitakoża, mitakoża!" eya cinktakta canha wan opapun kin ogli ca
icu nan un cekpa wakiciksela nan icu ke'.

10. Yunkan ayaśtan iyeyela canke heya ke': "Hinun takoża,
tuwa wanakihme-wacin lel t'eniyinkta kecin ihpeniyan he?

11. "Tka takoża nit'inkeśni ye! . . . Peżi-śaśa kin he wakan ye
. . . akanl le yahpaye cin, tokel nit'inkta he?" eyaya kignala ke'.

12. Hecenaś, canlekta waśteka, ataya ektunżin nan hokśicalala
k'un yuha tiyatakiya inyanka ke'.

13. Kiyela ku kin hehanni żahela s'e pan inyanka canke wicahcala k'un hinapa.

14. "Wicahca, mitakoża awaku we! . . . Tuwa wanakihme-
wacinhcin manil ehpeya tkaś awaku we . . . eś he t'eye-wacin
k'eyaś wanaś taninyan epe: T'inkteśni ye, mitakoża!" eya ke'.

15. Wicahcala k'un iś ektap iś'oś'oya etkiya u ke– "Miciku!
Miciku! Miciku!" eyaya ayuġal yin nan icu ke'.

16. "Ha o, ha o, takoża, anpetu-ahanzi nan cante maśica can
iśniś taku imakiblezinkta hunśe!" eyaya yuha timahel kigla ke'.

17. Htayetu wana wi mahel iyaya yunkan hokśicalala k'un
ceya ke'. Canke tunkaśitku kin wase keya waśin icicahiya iyutan
nan un tancanla kin sitomniyan śaya apawintin nan kohan heya
ke'.

18. "Mitakoża tawoyute-cola k'eyaś icahwayinkte lo. . . . Takoża, itokaġata anpetu wan iyakitaninśni ca hokśi-kigna ukte lo;
ca takoża, niye ko nignakta ce; tanpastusteśni opakas'in nita-
wakta ce. . . Wiyohinyanpatanhan iś wicaśa wan wicitowancaya
wanyak hinapa ca tuwa unśika wanyaka:

19. "'Ka unśika ca ituśe ni unkte,' ecankin nan eya can he icaġe
cun wicotapi kin icignuniyan wiwaniciyake cinhan wicoicaġe sutaya luhakte, takoża!" eyaya tansinl apawintahe ceyaś ehanihcinś
wana iśtinmela ke'.

20. Hinhanna canke anpowanka winunhcala k'un kikta nan
wana cetikta yunkan ungna hingnaku kin inahni-yuhicin nan
heya ke':

21. "Wicahċa, kikta nan takoża wanyanka nan ito," eya canke ikpapakas'in yunkan hokśilala k'un e ca iyotakehan yankin nan tima tiyokśankśan wakil yanka ke'.

22. Tośu-hute kin etanhan wankatakiya wanyak ayin nanśna tice ekta iciyakaśkapi kin ekta ehunni hecunhan ke'.

23. Canke, "Hecetu we lo, takoża, tanyan wakita yo. . . letu ca itimahel oinicaġinkta ce, iyekiya yo!" eyaya yunkan okahniġela s'elececa ke'.

24. Ake htayetu wi mahel iyaya yunkan ceyinktehcin canke ake wana wicahcala k'un wase waśin icahiya tansinl ataya ikiciun nan eyakeś iyapi k'eya un wokicíyake c'un hena ecekce eyin nan yaiśtinma ke'.

25. Ihinhanna canke winunhcala kin cetikta ca can icukta-inapin nan tioġeya hingnaku kin yuhica ke'.

26. "Ma keya, takoża el etunwan, le tokel nunke, wicahcala!" eya canke unśtinma kikta iyotaka yunkan lece takożakpaku k'un wana hanskela ca iyecinka inażin nan ticokaya takuni igluzeześni nażin ke'.

27. Hecena wicahcala k'un iyuśkin ita heya ke': "Hunhe, hunhe, takoża! hecutu we lo! Maka kin le tuwa takuye-inahni nan ecala alikta cin canśna iye pilaic'iye lo! Hecel wicoicaġe sutaya yuha ye lo, takoża; pilamayayin na pilaniciye lo, takoża!" eyaya wiyuśkinyan howaya ke'.

28. Ake htayetu yunkan wi mahel iyaya hanl hokśilala kin cinktakta canke kunśitku kin tokel okuwa-ka nuntka k'eyaś sam iglaececa na hankeyaś ceya ke'.

29. Canke ake wana tunkaśitkula k'un wase waśin icicahiya iyutan nan un tansinl śayela iyun nan heya ke':

30. "Ho, iśtinma yo, takoś, iśtinma yo!" eyin nan eyakeś woki-ciyake c'un hecehcin ake eyaya tancanla kin pawintahin nan yuiś-tinma ke'.

31. Ihinhanna yunkan hihanahcin hokśila k'un, "Tunkaśila, unci, kiktapi nan hinapapi ye!" eya un canke ehas tukte-unma tokeya inapinkta taninśni kicipatitan inapapi yunkan hokśila wan wana hanskela ca tankal okśankśan etunwan iyokipiyehcin nażin ke'.

32. Heceś tunkaśitku k'un heya ke': "Hunhe, hunhe, takoża,

takoża, hecetu we lo! oipazica hena ocaicuyayinkta ce, yanunik-
teśni ce tanyan wanyakin nan iyekiya yo!" eyaya ke'.

33. Wana ake htayetu yunkan wanaś hokśila-hanske sece c'un,
ceya ke'. Canke tunkaśitku kin tansil slayin nan śayela wiyun nan
heya ke': "Ho, ito le wana ehanke takoża wase wecicunkte lo."

34. Heceś tansinl wiyun nan kohan eye s'a k'un ecekce ake
eyin nan wana le htayetu-icitopa yunkan heya ke':

35. "Ho, wicaśa wan he wiyohinyanpatanhan hinapin nan wicitowancaya wanyak hinape cin he tuwa unśika wanyaka can unśila, nan, sam cinka can toiyoyanpa un iśnala opemni na atokan-
yan egle can he tuwe kin okitaninyan icaġe c'un tunkin heca-niun
ni!" eya ke'.

36. Heceś wocekiye un tohanni kin hehan okitaninyan unkta
ca wakicunza ke'.

37. Ihinhanna yunkan hokśila k'un tunkaśitku tankal kipan
canke inapin nan kici maka kin wanyakapi ke'.

38. Yunkan hehantu ca wana waunspekiya ke, takożakpaku
kin. Taku tona wakanyawakte c'un hena ecel okiyakin nan heya
ke':

39. "Ho, takoża, kakiyotan wiyohpeyata eciyape lo. . Heciya
Wahupakoza kin ti ce kiksuya yo.

40. "Nan he tawowaśi kin tate ca kici anpetu can makoce kin
awanyakape lo. Kahintapi nan tanyan yużażapi canke hecel un
wicaśa maka akantu kin zaniyan tate-waśte cuwi-mahel iwicayaya
un ikiblezapi kin e yelo.

41. "Kakiyotan iś waziyata heci oyate-luta kin ounyanpe lo.
Hena ikce-wicaśa wowicak'upi un oyate ni unpe lo.

42. "Kakiyotan iś wiyohinape kin ee ca etanhan wicaśa wan
wokokipeya hinapin nanśna wicitowancaya wanyak hinapin nan
tuwa unśila nan iyokalya can he waś'ak.

43. "Kakiyotan iś itokaġata kin ekta wicakigna wan un ca he
tohanl hi nan wamakognaka kin kigna kilowan can iśtinme lo.

44. "Wankata kin ekta iś taku wan wakanyan yanke cin he
maka kin le ataya itancanyan yuha yanka ce; nan ohlate maka kin
he iś ina-unyanpi kin e ca icah-unyanpe lo.

45. "Ho, takoża, wiconi kin le iyekiya yo, he wakan ye lo." eya
ke'.

46. Hecel unspekiyin nan hehanl he-anpetu kin kiyuśka ke'; anpetu wan el tuwa maka akanl icaġa can iśnala iyaye cin he el i kin he un; ecin tankake cin ohinni wakanheźa gluswicaunpikte cin he hecetuśni; eya cik'apila kin el ecela; ho, tka wana tohanl oic'ihipi can hehanl iśnala iyayapi; hecel wicoicaġe uye lo.

47. Heceś wana ihinhanna yunkan wicahcala k'un tokiyotan iyayin nan tehan-gliśni ke'.

48. Tannake gli yunkan tatanka tucuhu wan yuha gli nan tona-can yuwaśtehin na yuśkopya eyuśtan yunkan itazipa ca kaġa ke'.

49. Hokśila kin he itazipa wan wakanyan kicaġin na hehanl canpa-hu kin etan wanhinkpe ko kiyuśtan nan wase un yuhopho-pin nan k'u ke'.

50. Hecun nan hehanl iye pa kin etan pehin wan san ca lila hanska gluźun nan yutitan yuzin nan o-śi ke'.

51. Canke hokśila kin wacin-ksapyehcin apaha naźin nan iyay-eya yunkan wicapehin k'un woslel iyeya ke'.

52. Yunkan he wantanyeyinkta wakicunza canke hetanhan tunweni śutinkteśni ca kaġapi.

53. Canke wana hokśila kin wipe-yuhalaka ca wayeyinktehcin nan iyaya ke'.

54. Anpetu ataya tokah'an yunkan htayetu hanl maśtinska wan agli na tunkaśitku kin k'u ke'. He wiyohpeyata i nan heciyatan-han maśtinska kin agli ke'.

55. Canke wicahcala kin tokel-okihika iyuśkin itin nan heya ke': "Ha o, ha o, takoźa, hecetu we lo! . . . Le wicaśa kin tunweni hustakeśni k'un; tunweni iyanka-okikpaniśni k'un! . . . ho, ta-koźa, hanke yuta yo, hecel niś eya hustakeśni, huhu-wayazanśni ecel nikankte. . . . Pilanic'iyin nan pilamayaye lo!" eyaya ke'.

56. Ihinhanna yunkan ake waye-iyaya ke'. Hehanl waziyata-kiya iyayin nan anpetu ataya un yunkan htayetu hanl maka wan cep-iyakapa ca agli ke'.

57. Canke wana ake wicahcalala k'un iyuśkin it'a heya ke': "Ha o, ha o, takoźa, tanyan ecanun we lo. Le wicaśa kin waun-śpenic'iye lo. Hanhepi, anpetu ko opta wiic'igni nan wamakaś-kan-swula kin iyuha tawoyute canke takuni śupe iyokiśiceśniyan un k'un, unyutinkta ca tanyan zaniyan takuni śupe iyoki-śiceśniyan unk'unkte lo!" eya ke'.

58. Ake hinhanna yunkan waye-iyaya ke'. Hehanl wiyohin-yanpatakiya iyayin nan htaiyakpaza hanl glihunni yunkan hoka wan agli ke'.

59. Canke ake wicahcala k'un hecel eś cikiye c'un ecehcin oh'anyan canke un itomnila s'e howaya ke'.

60. "Hunhunhe, takoźa, wicaśa kin le maka kin iyotanhcin ta-wayelaka maheta-kiya ti ye lo. Le-anpetu kin wicaśa kin le unyu-tinkta canke un maka kin lila kiyela takuunyinkte lo!" eya ke'.

61. Naic'it'eśni ecanl awaśtelaka canke "Tunkaśila, ake waye-mni?" eya yunkan "To, to, he le waunśpenic'iciye cin, tokel he tiyatani winyan s'e nakinktelaka? To, ninkte lo! Tokśa hecanun-han unhanketa woyute-tokapa kin ayaglikte," eya canke wana ka itokaġatakiya iyaya ke'.

62. Htayetu yunkan tahca wan k'in agli canke wicahcala k'un pal iyeyin nan heyaya śkan ke':

63. "Hunhi, hunhi, tanyan wagli yagli ye lo, takoźa, wicaśa kin le iyotan waśte k'un! . . . le tuwe kin peźi nan can-inkpa-nunuźela, oyul-waśte kin hena kahnih-pahi yute lo.

64. "Wah'anic'ila ye lo, le tuwe kin, hena woyute maka eciya-tanhan hinape cin ece-cin ye lo, hena un waś'akin nan luźahe cin akibleze cin un; talo kin hanke unyutinkte lo, takoźa, kinhan unkiś-eya waś'akya cehpi-waśteya unk'unkte lo," eya ke'. Canke hetanhan hokśila kin waskuya, nan maka-mahel waicaġe cin hena, woźupi koko, woyuteya unśpe ke'.

65. Wana he tatiye topa kin iyuha ekta waye-i nan hecekce agli canke henala seca yunkan ake icizaptan-iyayin na waziyatanhan ptehincala wan agli ke'.

66. Mila ikikcu nan iye iyunkala niġe-wablas iyeyin nan tapi kin nahanhcin ni ca naknakin nan kate cin hecena tunkaśitkula kin k'u, nan, "Tunkaśila, le yuta yo," eya canke iyahpayin nan cantokpanihca yaptapta yute c'eyaś taku waśte iyehanyanśni ke'.

67. Taśiyaka kin nakun icu nan k'u canke "Ho, winunhca, le e śpan-makiya yo," eya canke śpankiya ke'.

68. Heceś wotin nan igluśtan yunkan lila wowiyuśkin oźula canke inila yanka okihiśni ke'.

69. "Winunhca, lila cante mawaśte ca ito eyawapahakte lo," eya canke, "Tuki, cin toka ca!" eya ke'.

70. Hecena ṗahala wan aḱanl inaẓin nan ototanlaḣcin maku zi-yela naẓinla nan heya ke': "Ptehincala pi naṗin!" eya ke'.

71. Yunkan ehanḱec'un he taśiyak-nunṗa-wicaśala ca hokśilala wan icaḣyela ke'.

72. Ca lehantuḱe ceyaś wana wetu canśna glihunnila nanśna hecena wowiyuśkin un eyaṗaha can, "Ptehincala pi naṗin!" eye s'a caś nayah'unpi kin.

73. Wanaś hece takoẓakpaḱu k'un waoka canḱe un wicaḣcal-ala kin lila wiyuśkin un ehaś tokel eḱaǧeċa nun tka, nan wana ḣtayetu canḱe hokśila kin iśtinma-ḣṗaya yunkan el inaẓin nan waceḱiya ke':

74. "Hunhunhe, mitakoẓa, cewinś owanyaḱ-waśte ke! . . . Ho, taḱu wakan, tunki hinhanna yunkan mitakoẓa wana kośkalaḱa nan waś'akya hanskin nan owanyaḱ-waśte-iyakapa nan wokoyaḱe waśteśteḣca ece hokśicalkiyapi tawa ece lel ḱiciyanḱa ca ayanṗa ni!" eya ke'.

75. Heceś iyunḱapi nan ihinhanna anṗao yunkan wana waḱi-cunzapi k'un ḱikta nan "Tunḱaśila, ḱikta nan wanmayaḱa yo! Wan le taḱu wamiyecunze c'un iyuha iyenic'iċetu welo!" eya canḱe wanyaḱa yunkan ke un akotanhan iyecetu ke'.

76. "Ha-ye, ha-ye!" eya ke'; "Takoẓa, lena ecekce ḱic'un wo! oyate hena-wicaḱeca k'eyaś etan tuwa lecel takoẓa-tun ḱa!" eyaya ḱic'un kin oḱiya ke'.

77. Hecun nan anṗetu-hanḱeyela eyaṗaha nan heya ke': "Ho po, oyate maka sitomniyan hiyeye cin, maka aḱal taḱu śkanśkan-yan toni gluha un kin, nah'unpi ye!

78. "Le anṗetu kin mitakoẓa tawoyute-cola icaḣ-waye c'un, manil t'inkta cinkiya ayuśtanpi ca mniyosloslo ya yunka tka wag-logli k'un,—he lehanl caẓe yukin-kta ce, naḱiciḣ'unpi ye!

79. "Wacinḱa yunkanś iḣṗeyapi ewaḱiyinkta tka he iyomaḱip-iśni ca ito eyaś Cetan-maza ewaḱiyinkte lo!" eya maka owancaya hoyeya canḱe ataya ho-naḣ'unpi nan Cetan-maza anṗetu-hanḱe-yela ocaśtunka śke'.

80. Waoḱa canḱe tanyan wana tipi nan lila el wicaipi canḱe woimaǧaǧa iċakiẓeśni unpi yunkan ungna kośkalaḱa k'un heya ke':

81. "Tunḱaśila, icaḣmayayin nan pilamayaye cin un ohinni

wacicio ena waunkta wacin k'un, lehanl towaś ománi-wakinica ye
lo," eya ke'.

82. Yunkan, tunkaśitkula kin itogna apehca lila cante śica ke:
"Hehehe, takoża, canku ogna wowicaśaśni yunke c'un, tanyanś lel
zaniyan yaun k'un!" eyaya iyokiśni can ake iyenaye ca keś ake
omaniktehcin ke'.

83. Yamni-iyokiśni yeśan ake icitopa-eya canke hehanl wana
tunkaśitku kin iyowinyan ke'.

84. "Ohan, takoża, yakitan ca ito ninkta ce," eyin nan mila-
wakan wan taku k'eyaś waksa iyececa ca e nan wapośtan wan
cetan-tanka-śaśte num aikoyaka ca hecel k'u ke'. "Waktaya omani
yo, taku wakan yunke lo, takoża," eya ke'.

85. Canke wana he kic'un nan mila nan wa ko gluha kakena
yahan ke'. Tehan hecel iśnala ya yunkan ohanketa kośkalaka top
iś eya lila wakanyan owanyak-waśtepi ca op ecipa ke'.

86. Itokakin iha ayuta unpi nan wanżi heya ke': "Hunhi, maka
opapun kin ekta kośkalaka wan hokśicalkiyapi ca Cetan-maza eciyapi, ocaśtunke c'un! K'eyaś tuwaś lehank yela wanunyakapikta
keuncinpiśni!" eyapi ke'.

87. Heyapi nan iyuśkinyehcin itkokipapi ke'. "Ho wo, kola,"
eyapi, "Tokeśke le omayani huwo?" eyapi yunkan Cetan-maza iha
nan "Wan, eya ci le walemacetu kin iyuha winyanpaya ece-
tawacinpi ca miś eya heca un le omawani sece lo," eya yunkan,
"Hunhi, kola, tanyan ye lo; wan unkiś eya le heca un icimaunipe
lo," eyapi ke'.

88. Akeś wanżi, "Hoye, cin tokel abeya yepica ka, iyayapi ye,
owanżila-unyawkte," eya canke Cetan-maza: "Ha o," eyin nan op
ya ke'.

89. Wana heceś hopyakel yahanpi nan tohantu yunkan ble
wan tanin canke ekta-kiya cankuyapi nan wana el ihunni ke'.

90. Yunkan mni-aglagla peżi-hinkpila owaśtecaka wan el tiska
wan iśnala han ke'.

91. "Ho, letu we lo," eyapi ca wana el yapi k'eyaś wonaġicun-
sya tiwokśan wicahu sekseca enana hiyeya ke'.

92. Hececa k'eyaś nunġe wanil el yapi yunkan winunhćala
wan sakye-kitun hinapin nan wanwicayak-nażin ke'.

93. Kiyela inażinpi yunkan, "Hinun, hinun, mitakoś wana nipe

le! . . . Hinapapi, taku leniceca wanniyak-hipe!" eya yunkan ti-
mahetanhan wikoškalaka keya hopapi cinla hinapapi nan wistece
s'e kana inazinpi ke'.

94. "Ihopi, takoš, lena eepe, hiyupi—eya ašihtinpike c'eyaš!"
eyin nan apatan pacekcek hiyuwicaya ke'.

95. Canke koškalaka kin yusiwicacupikta ca unma toktok
iyayapi keš wana ihunnipikta canšna winunhcala kin sakye awica-
paha canš ena ožužun wahe s'e glihpayapi ke'.

96. Wana iš hehanl Cetan-maza el ye c'eyaš wana taku okahniga canke waktaya yin nan kakel wicincala wan ayugata yunkan
hecena wana ake winunhcala k'un sakye yuwankal glou tkaš
oh'ankoya iye tokeya kute nan wan-wakan wan tunkašitku ki-
cage c'un he un o yunkan ataya kpanyela wobleca ke'.

97. He tunkan-winyan canke wakan-wakapa hel un tkaš Cetan-
maza kte ke'.

98. Hecena inikagin nan takolaku k'eya t'e s'e hpayapi k'un
iyuha wicayukini nan winyan wicak'u canke tokiyotan awicaki-
yaglapi ke'.

99. Yunkan leyalaka henakehcin wakinyan-wicašapi canke
iyoha anunkatanhan wakagli yuglakšikšan hukutakiya ceca ouya
hpayi nan si kin ekta okižalya okiwanžila iyehyehya hanke, eca-
han ke'.

100. Nan ištihanke kin eciyatanhan nakun wakangli hiyu nan
hena iš isto-ounya yin nan nape kin akanl okižata ca hena iš eya
eca-iyehyehya han ke'.

101. Iyayapikta yunkan itokap Cetan-maza wokiyakapi ke':
"Ho wo, Cetan-maza, Nitaoyate—niyate, nihun, nitunkašila, ni-
kunši, niciye, nitanhanši, nihakata, nicinca hena iyuha owicaki-
yaka yo, letanhan niho kin he ituya yeyayinktešni ce;

102. "Nakun maka-mahel nunkin nan houyaye c'eyaš
naunh'unpi nan ekta uniyanpikte ce;

103. "Oglaka yo, le-anpetu kin wakinyan kin takuyaye lo,"
eyapi ke'.

104. Ho, yunkan wicakapi ca Cetan-maza tohan-ni k'un hehanyan tohanl iyotiyekiyin nan wakinyan kin awowicaglaka
canšna išnalaš oh'ankopi canke aškan s'e hihunnipi nan okiyapi
ke'.

105. Hetanhan waziyatakiya icimani ke'. Yunkan wicaśa wan manil akipa k'eyaś tuwe kin hanśkin nan lila woimnaka ke'. Ṫanyan igluzin nan owanyak waśtehca ke'.

106. Tahakalala-ogle wan ziyapi ca un nan eya toketuke c'eyaś lila aiglupi ke'.

107. "Hunhi, hunhi, kola Cetan-maza he niye huwo? . . . Hunhi, wan, kola, tokeśke le omayani he?" eya canke wana ake wiyapaya-omani keya-oglaka yunkan heya ke':

108. "Hunhi, kola, wan, miś eyá le hecel un omawani ca sakiṗ unyinkte lo," eya canke wana yapi yunkan wicoti wan oiyokipiya el wicaśkan ca wanyak iyahanpi ke'.

109. "Ho, kola, ḳatu we lo," eya ke'. "Ka cokaṗ tipi wan he cin hetu ca le hokśicalkiyapi wan winyan waśteṗ cila ca ti k'eyaś atḳuku kin lila glonica nan lel kiyela tuktel makohloḳa-mahetuya wan ekta kanpeska ota ca etan tuwa kagli hantanhanś ecela winyan k'ukta ḳeye lo.

110. "Lila mahetuya nan kanpeska kin oicu-śilya hiyeya ca tuwa iyuta keś ektani ohinhṗayin nan ot'e lo," eya ke'.

111. "Hunhi, kola, taḳu weś le iyutapi kin, iwiśkaś oicu-tehiḳa nacece ce," Cetan-maza eya, yunkan hecena, "Hoḣ, aoś'akelaḳe lo, wan. Ho, k'eyaś yacin hantanhanś sakiṗ unyin nan ito iciyokiheya unḳotḳin nan etan icu-wauncinkte," eya canke "Hoye," eya ke'.

112. Wana el ipi k'eyaś waśun wan mahetaḳiya otanḳaya k'eyaś tiyoṗa-ḳahya ohloka kin etan taḳuni iali-picaśniyan han ke'.

113. Wana wicaśa kin, "Ho, kola, matete kin lel sutaya yus zezeya otḳe-mic'iyinkta ce amaliḳel kutḳiya yin nan si el omayuspin nan kohan naṗ-sani iyohiyaya hantanhanś kanpeska kin tonakel icu wo.

114. "K'eyaś hayapi waśteśte nun we lo, gluślokin nan hacola ecun wo, hecel ośkinciye-niwaśte kte; agna waśteśte k'un yagluhlecinkte sece," eya canke iyuha ecel ecun ke'.

115. Wana wicaśa k'un hansḳelahcaka canke hukutaḳiya zezeya otḳe eyaś cete kin ihunni nun s'e hehanyan ke'.

116. Heceś Cetan-maza wana oskaṗya oslohe-ic'iyin nan si kin naṗ-sani un oyuspi nan naṗe-unma un panḳeska tonakel wana icu nan wicaśa k'un eya hecel ecunśi ca tahunsḳa el oṗatica ke'.

117. Wana iś hehanl etan iíc'ikcukta ca yuġal-iyeye ḣcehanl ungna wicaśa kin nagwagwakin nan nahtahtaka canke naṗ-akaśpeyaya nan ayuśtan ca ceteta glihṗaya ke'.

118. "Kola, toka huwo?" eya un keyaś ecanl el nunġe yuześni waś'aka canke tokaśniyan glinapin nan Cetan-maza tahayapi k'un iyuha ecekce un nan iyaya ke'.

119. "Ḱaġi-mayan tka! . . . Nakeś wana okablaya wicawoha-mninkte," eyaya ehank'un wana ake Ikto he e ca wana hokśical-kiyapi-igluzin na hocokatakiya ya ke'.

120. Iś oyate ognaye-waśtepi s'a ke cin, el ye c'un hehanni iki-kopi nan "Cetan-maza he e ca u we lo, hokśicalkiyapi wan maka oṗaṗun kin eciyatanhan otanin k'un he e ye lo!" eyaya icinatanpi nan yus wicaśa-yatapi ti kin el akipi ke'.

121. Kanṗeska k'eya hunskatanhan iḱikcu nan wicaśa-itancan kin k'u canke hecena lila ḱicilowanpi nan ohitiḱe-kiyapi; ecin tu-weni heca icu oḱihiśni tka canke he un.

122. Hecenaś winyan k'uṗi canke kal anṗetu-hankeyela wica-woha-eti ke'.

123. Tawicu kin lila teḣilapi nan yuwah'anic'ilapi canke tan-yan hingnatun-ic'ila itan un ehaś oh'an-śica ke'.

124. Tankaḱula wan wicincala wana iś eyaś wikośkalaka cik'ala ca cuweku hingnatun-eti kin el ya canśna itkop kiśica ke'.

125. "Ako gla na! . . . ektan wicaśa wanmakiyaḱ-wacin, iśta-waśteka ca!" eya-ośtegla canke toketkiya ceya iyaya ke'. K'eyaś hokśi-haḱaktala canke tuweniḱel el etunweśni, cuweku hingnatun kin ecela un iḱik'opi ke'.

126. Kohan he makoḣloka wan ekta Cetan-maza yanke c'un hel ikiyela wicaḣcalala wan tawicu ḱici manil tipi ke'.

127. Yunkan he winunḣcala kin e ca canleya keyin nan oḣloka kin ikiyela hiyaye ḣcehanl tokiyaṗ hokśicala wan ceya naḣ'un canke ena ṗatak inaźin nan tan-anaġoptan yunkan heciya cete kin ekta ca tuwa ceya canke blaska-iyunkin nan eyokas'in ke'.

128. Ṫan-wanyaḱeśni, iśta-aecetuśniyan wawanyaḱela nan agna oḣloḱa kin oiyokṗaze c'eyaś wanaś he wakanheźa kin slolya canke heya ke': "Hina, hina! Ṫaku sam tawacin-hinyans awicaye! Oyate kin le eca taḱupika ca!" eyaya ceya iyaya ke'.

129. "Hinyanḱa, taḱoźa, tokśa icicukte!" eya inyankyanḱ kig-

nin nan itaṗ sata hanska wan wikan wan ikantunyan ahi nan ku-
takiya gliheya ke'.

130. "Ho, takoża, inihunni hecinhan, wikan kin hel ogna ihin
nan can kin kaskita yus un, toksa ciyuslutinkte!" eyin nan wana
wankatakiya aku k'eyaś tkelahcaka ke'.

131. Yuakanl, agligle yunkan lece hoksilala wan nażute hlila ca
unśiyehcin ececala ke'.

132. Hecena kic'in, aki yunkan wicahala kin iyuśkin it'in nan
"Ho, winunhca tanyan ecanun we lo; . . iśniś takoża imaġagamay-
inkta hunśe . . . Kan amaye cin ecel cante maśice s'a k'u!" eyaya
yutima icu ke'.

133. Iyecala hoksila kin heya ke': "Tunkaśila, takan etan wacin
ye lo," eya canke, "Hunhi, tokcanunkta he, takoża? . . . wan, takoża takan la ye lo, winunhca!" eya canke etan mahel wiyakapanla
wan ogna yuha ca ikikcu nan k'u ke'.

134. Hecena tunkaśitku kin takan kin hena ṗagmunkiyin nan
un cangleska iyuskiskiya kaġin nan timahel otkeya ke'.

135. "Ho, tunkaśila, unci kici ṗaha-aisinyan yapi nan heciya
owanżi yanka po, toksa ekta ciupikte," eya canke, "Toka huwo?"
ecinhca tawicu kici iyaya ke'.

136. Heceś iśnala tima tokeśkeśke wakan-h'an nacece c'eyaś
wanyakapiśni, itohantu yunkan ekta wicahiyoi canke kici glipi
ke'.

137. Yunkan tima zitkala yul-pica kin heca ece, maġaksica na
iś maġa-śaṗa obe kin oyas'in tima okinyan unpi ke', śiyo koko. Si
kin tuktektel ikoyakapi'.

138. Żakyaṗ s'e hena iyuha hotun unpi canke nunġe wicayak-
papi nun s'e lececa ke'.

139. "Ho, wicakte po na owicahan po," eya canke tunkasitkula
ku takolaku oṗ wakanwaśteya zitkokuwa śkanpi nan iyuhahcin
wicaktepi ke'. Pa kin hena si kin iyayustastak egnak-wicaśi canke
ecunpi yunkan hehanl mniyohutata iyuha ai nan "Ho, iyayapi nan
igluota po!" eya-hingla mniyokahlol iye-wicaya canke tokeya wik-
cemnamna nan hankeya opawinġeġe ośṗayetuntunya mni p'oyela
iyayapi ke'.

140. "Unci, ceh-ololya yo, ito oyate wotapikte," eye c'eyaś lila
winunhcala kin tawat'elyelaśni ke'.

141. "Taku, wana tehan manil wati ca wimaśtece c'un. Tuwa ceġa owakilotin naś omak'upi ka!" eyaya nahlal un k'eyaś "Takoża tokel eye cin ecel ecun ye, iś takuhca yake! . . . Hokśila wan wakunpi s'e wakan ca iyeunkic'iye cin el lehahe lo!" eya iyopeka canke wana ka śina ikikcu nan kicunniyehcan iyaya ke'.

142. Yunkan winyan wan tiihanke el ti canke el i nan okiyaka yunkan waśtecake canke ceh-ok'u nan kici gli ke'.

143. Okiya can hena iyuha iyohpewicayapi k'eyaś sam ota aya canke tokeni h'unhiye-picaśni ke'.

144. Hingnaku kin ihakap hi nan wana kal Cetan-maza tunkaśitkula kin kici kat'eyetanka iyotakin nan opaġipi tkaś ecanl heya ke':

145. "Wan, tunkaśila, tohantuka keś cannunpapi ye, wan, le woyute wanica ca wicoti kin ataya wotapikte; eyapaha ye!" eye canke kakena eyapaha-iyaya ke'.

146. "Hopo, ka manil tipi wan he cin hel ape lehanl wayatapikta ce, el hiyayap! el hiyayap! Tiwepa nakitakapi nan u po!" eya howokawinh glihunni k'eyaś ehanniś wana hocokatunyan topa-owecinhan ahiyotaka ke'.

147. Yunkan Cetan-maza hcihcika tokeya hihunni nan cokap owinśkicatunpi canke el iyotaka ke'.

148. K'eyaś ecin slolyapśni ca hece, wicaśa-yatapi wan tunkanye c'un he pakanpika c'un lila yuonihanpi nan wicaśa tona okśan wiyeya talo hanke waśpa yuha nażinpi, yatapi wanżi kipiya.

149. Unma toktok tohanl ceżi naslulkiya canśna talo hanke el egnakapi ke'. Hecetu canśna h'anhiyehcin yamahel icu nan owohinsko yatahan can kohan unma kin ape nazinpi ke'.

150. K'eyaś hehanhunniyan tunweni iśta-kablayeśni, naitunkap yeya wah'anic'ila yanka canke oyate kin apepi kin kohan k'ok'oya tahnakipcapi ke'.

151. Wana eyaś wicayuślahcin nan hehanl "Wana imapi ye lo!" eya canke hehanl nakeś wakpamni kin wicegna iyayapi nan woyute kin ecekce wicakikpamnipi ke'. Heceś oiyokipiya wicawota ke'. Wana lila hokśila kin wakankiyapi.'

152. Ake itonacan yunkan hehanl cangleśka wan kaġin nan tunkaśitku kin pacangleya hiyuye-kiyin nan leyekiya ke'. "Takoża, ptewot'oġa inca wan he gle!" eye-kiya canke eya canśna wiyeya

wan apaha nażin canke el iyeya can pte-cepa wan kaġmigma gliḣpeya ke'.

153. Topa-akigle hecunpi nan wana pte kin ecaśni s'e top t'a ḣpayapi canke hehanl tunkaśitkula kin mila glumin nan wapata-imnaic'iya ke'.

154. Yunkan ungna wocet'unglaya cokaṗ-ti kin tankakula k'un he e ca hocokatanhan unhin nan tima hiyu nan iyotaka ke'.

155. Cetan-maza hokśila-kaġin nan yanke c'un el ṗat'a nun s'e iyotaka canke kunśitkula kin: "Takoś takoża wase ececa ca iniyutatakte iḣeyapaya yankin ye, eya yunkan "Etanś tokaka," eyin nan śiyute el egnaka ke'.

156. Heceś yuha yankahan canke kohan winunhcala k'un talo-waśtehca ece iyohpeyin nan wok'u ke'. Can-wakśica wan ogna etan yuha glekiya caś le kiglehce un itehan hanl wicahcala k'un ekta etunwan nażin nan heya ke'.

157. "Hunhi, wikośkalaka wan letanhanś canl-waśteya kigle c'un, wanka makotahena comniglakel nażin ye lo: "Taku iyokip-iśni huwo? Waśte yak'uśni hecinhan wohinye sece," eyaya ke'.

158. Etan tohantu yunkan ake wicincala k'un hi nan he wak-śica ahi keya ke'.

159. Canke winunhcala kin heya ke: "Takoś, yakiyagle un he-han kal śil-nayażin s'e lececa ye, he toka he?" eya yunkan.

160. "Han, he cuwe un hecel canśilya naważin ye," eya ke'; "Hingnatun canke śic'e-waya ca wancala eśa ite wanyak-wacanmi canśna itkop makiśice c'un, nake he woyute mayak'u k'un hena hingnaku cinkiye c'eyaś awakśiża canke itogna amaṗa ca waceye," eya ke'.

161. "He, takoża, takole k'u iyeyayin nan ake yau śni, lena-kehcin tuwa hena yutinktelaka:" eyaya ake talo-waśtehca ece ihan nan wakśi-śkokpa nun ṗakiya akiyecel ognakin nan "Ho, nicuwe le unma kagla, takoś," eyin nan k'u canke akiyagla ke'.

162. Hinhanna yunkan eyaṗaha wan hiyaya ke': "Hopo, ita-ziṗa gluwiyeyapi nan wanhinkpe glaowotan po! Sunġila kin ake hiyayinkta ce; tuwa he o hantanhanś cokaṗ-ti yuzinkte lo unke-yap s'a tka k'un, wana hingnatun ca tuwa sunġila kin he o han-tanhanś ha kin yuha nan iye ti el pawoslal iyekiya ece-kte lo!" eya ke'.

163. Oyate kin hutiyuhpa ś'a s'e ikik'opi nan nakeś wacinksap-kic'un wiyeya paha nażinpi ke'.

164. Tohantanke cin he hiyaya can o-wacinpi keś tokeśke aogin-wicaye s'e lececa, wana sam iyaya canśna kicipapi nan "Toka yunkan yao śni?" eyaya kicicuwapi ke'.

165. Ake wana wahuwatayapi ca hokśilala k'un iyeśtuka kat'iyeya canke tunkaśitku kin inyankin nan ha yuzin nan kicicaki ke'.

166. Ake wi coka hiyaye hcehanl eyapahapi nan "Wana ake u we lo, wanbli-luta k'un, śehanśtuka waktaya nażinpi nan wanżih-cin o-wacin po!" eya hiyaye c'eyaś wokokipeya u ke'.

167. Kuciyela kinyan canke wankal etunwanpi can iśta sapyela owohinyansyela awicayuta ke'. Heceś tansak t'api nan tuweni o śni, ca hokśilala k'un iśnala el iyeyin nan wohpa ke'.

168. Hecena tunkaśitku kin iyayin nan wiyaka kin iyuha yu-żun nan taku luta iyececaśni ca agli nan kal otkeya ke'.

169. Ho, k'eyaś cin manitu canke oyate kin takuni oslolyeśni iyopekiciya-hanpi ke'.

170. "Unci, ceh-ololya yo," eya canke eyak'eś he tanka wan ok'u ca ekta i nan ake agli nan wana ota el unpi canke hena oki-yapi ca ptetan, nan taku wocantokpani kin oyaś'in spanyanpi nan wol-wicayapi ke'. Yunkan Cetan-maza-hcihcike c'un ake tokeya hi nan el owohinsko hopahan ke'.

171. Ihinhanna kin el winyan wan wicotitanhan uhan canke winunhcala kin ekta etunwan ape yankahan yunkan hi nan heya ke': "Ścepan, wahośi-umaśipi tka lilakel wau we, talo waśteśte yagnaka ca ito etanhan wawatinkte sece, ecanmi nan," eya owe-hanhan ke'.

172. "Hinun, tanyan yahi ye, ścepan, le woyute otalahcake cin cin hena tuwa tepya okihika. Tima iyotaka waśpanciciyinkte," eyin nan wana tohantu ka yunkan woekigle canke imnayehcin wotahin nan igluśtan k'unhan heya ke':

173. "Ho, ścepan, le hośi-wahi ye: Hokśila wan luhapi kin he hiyowahi ye; he cokapti tankaku kin hingnayinkta cin ca," eya yunkan hecena winunhcala kin ite-ececaśni . . Tehan inila yankin nan ohanketa heya ke':

174. "Ścepan, tuwa akakśa . . . mitakoża eya wowakan yuhala

k'eyaś nahanhcin wakanheźa k'un. . . . nakun wicaśa-śicela ye śan, tokeśke he hingnayanpikta iyecetulaśni . . . ścepan, oweunhahapi sece?" eya ke'.

175. K'eyaś hokśila kin nakih'un yanka canke heya ke': "Gnin nan oyaka yo: U nan mitokap lel kawinh-kignin nan 'Cico-wahi ye,' eyinkte lo. Kihunni wal-iyehanl ekta mninkte. . . el wai yeśan iyemakiyeśni nan omayutanśni hantanhaś wakukte . . . topa-micohi nan miś eya topa ekta mninkte. . . nan ataya tunweni iyemakiyeśni hantanhanś iho po, ecaś, tunweni kici waunkteśni ye lo," eya ke'.

176. Canke winyan k'un he yuha kignin nan oyaka c'unhan wicaśa-yatapi ti kin ekta lila ikik'opi nan wanaś unihan ti-ska wan waśte ca pawoslal iyeyapi canke tokiyap oyas'in, "Ma! he taku to-kunpi huwe?" winyan kin eyapi can hunh wanaki-hunhunpike s'a k'un hena "k'eya, man, he hokśila-wakan k'un winyan k'upikta ca wicaśkan ye, taku slolyayeśni!" eyapi.

177. Kohan hokśila k'un tunkaśitku, kunśitku ko tankal yewi-caśi, nan paha-akotanhan apepikta keya canke wana cin taku eye cin oyas'in ksapya eye cin un, "Toka huwo?" eyeśni iyayapi.

178. "Heci yanka po! Tohanl cihiyowaipi naniś tohanl ektana waun kin hehanl ecaś ku po," eya ke'.

179. Wana hecacakte c'un wicaśayatapi-cuwitku-hakakta kin aigluhopi nan u canke iś tima catku el otaninyan yanka yunkan wana inilahcin timahel hiyu nan kawinh-iyaya "Cico-wahi ye!" eya ke'. Canke "Ha o," eya ayupti nan hecena ena yanka ca kigla ke'.

180. Wana kihunni-iyehanyan canke ektakiye c'eyaś wakan-yan tan-kitun nan ya ke'.

181. Wana kiyela ya canke wanyak naźinpi yunkan glihpe-ic'iyin nan icaptanptan-kic'un nan inaźin yunkan he-hota, he-hloġeca wan waśte-iyakapa ca waniyetu-nunpa-wahecetu inaźin ke'.

182. Hecena katinyeya maka k'ak'a ya canke wayuś'inyeya ca abeya kiyukanpi yunkan yin nan wicincala k'un atkuku kici na-źin ca itelake el iyaye c'eyaś ecanl ceya iyaya ke'. . . . kokipin nan ite nakihma canke hecena kawinh-glicu nan tiyata kiwicaśa nan kiyotaka ke'.

183. Yamni-akigle hecehcin ecun k'eyaś iyena kokipin nan

oyutanśni ke'. Inunpa k'unhan heśluśluta-ic'icaġin nan iyamni
k'unhan tatanka-tanka k'eyaś he-kaġiṗa ewicakiyapi can heca śke'.

184. Iciyamni-kicunni k'unhan wicincala atkuku kin iyopeya
ke'. "Cunkś, teciĥila taku iyuha ičakiżeśni icaĥ-ciye c'un, lehantu
kin oyate wawapilayayinkta yunkan oyakihiśni ye lo.

185. "Hokśila kin le wowakan ikoyaka ca wacinye-pica yeśan
lugnayinkte cin ogna yaśkan ye lo.

186. "Kiksuya yo, cunkś, le ehanke-ukta ce, ake yuzinakinkte
cin oyakihiśni hantanhanś iyeś nit'e cin he waśakala nan le e wo-
teĥiwalakte lo, oyate wacin niyanṗe śan wawicayakiĥtami kinhan"
eya yusyus iwahoya canke wana wiyeya nażin ke'.

187. Yunkan ake hokśila k'un u nan kiyela hel icaptanptan-
kic'un nan tatank-ehani wan hehutela ca wokokipeya inyank hiyu
ke'.

188. Wicincala k'un paunka-nun s'e atayela u k'eyaś atkuku
takeye c'un hecela kiksuyin nan iśtogmus yuġal-hingla iyaya
yunkan tuktel oyuspa ke'.

189. Hecena taku toka taninśni-hingnin nan hehanl iyuha
wacin-ksaṗapi yunkan hokśilala wan hunkelaśni ca pat'a-iĥṗeya
canke pawe hiyu inażinla ke'.

190. Heceś wana hokśila-wakan k'un winyan k'upi canke ti-
ska k'un unpi.

191. Itankal wotapi wan tanka takuni iyehanyanśni kaġapi ca
tuwe kin oyas'in el opapi'.

192. Nan hokśila kunśitku k'un iś eya woyute waśteśte el ai
canke nake-kici-yuzapi kin tima yankapi nan wotahanpi yunkan
cuweku kin hehanl eś waĥ'anic'ilahe śni, nake woyute iyutan un
tipi kin el eyokas'in inażin ke'.

193. Yunkan iś ehankela tankaku kin kiśicin nan "Hiya, cuwe,
tankani keś un, nahanĥcin unśaṗapi nan heyounṗuzapi
nacece. . ." eya canke ceya kigla ke'.

194. Tokiyaṗ iśtam-nihanpi oyaĥe-kiyin nan atkuku kico
canke ti el i ke'. "Toka huwo, cunkś?" eya yunkan, "Ate, tohantan
kin hokśi-waśte mayagluha kehe s'a k'un nan mitankala ee haka
kta kin un iś hece icaĥ-ic'iye c'un, otaninyan hingnatun nan hetanhan lila waĥ'anic'ila nan owemahaha ye'.

195. "Hinhanna kinhan kośkalaka wikcemna wati el u-

wicayaśikte. Hena mihingna kin waluta makagli ca pawoslal iye-
miciciyapikte, oyate wanmiciyakapikta ca," eya canke atkuku kin,
"Ho, tokśa ecamunkte lo, cunkś, cante siceśni yo, nitankala na-
hanhci cante t'insya yankeśni ca hecun we lo," eya ke'.

196. Yunkan iyecala iś eya wicincala wan hingnatun k'un atkuku wahokiya ca el i ke'. Yunkan "Ate, hinhanna kipan wicaśa
zaptan uwicaśi ye," eya canke atkuku kin ecunkta keye ke'.

197. Wana htayetu yunkan hokśila-wakan k'un iś ehankela
kunśitku wahokiya canke ekta i ke'. "Toka he, takoża?" eya yunkan, "Unci, he cokap-ti wan hu zizi kin he el yin nan, 'Iktomi,
Cetan-maza hayapi wahokiye, wana eyaś tehan-yakiun ca,' eya
yo," eya ke'.

198. Canke winunhcala kin tokel wiyukcan taninśni etkiya yin
nan tiyopa el inażin yunkan tima wicaśa ota tilehanyank ipi ca op
yankin nan cannunpahan ke'.

199. "Ake gla na, tase lel yaukte ca caś!" wana ake Cokapti e ca
eya-kiśice c'eyaś ecanl, "Iktomi-Huzizila, Cetan-maza hayapi wahokiye, eyaś wana tehan-yakiun keye," eya ke'.

200. "Hunhun! tokeśke takeye! . . . Winunhcala-witkotkoka
wan!" eyayapi k'eyaś ecanl Ikto ihaha, "Ho, iyekiciciyap! iyekiciciyap!" eyaya hayapi-waśteśte k'eya u tawicutu k'u hena iyuha
winunhcala kin iyekiciciya canke agli nan timahel eyaya yunkan
lece takożakpaku hokśilala wan nażute hlihli ca makohlokatanhan
yuslute c'un eśni s'e ehank'un he Cetan-maza e hunśeca, hopyakel igluecetu nan cannup-yankahan ke'.

201. Ecekce kic'un nan tawicu kin kico ke': "Nicuwe ekta yin
nan uśi yo," eya canke lecaś kici okiciyuśice c'eyaś ekta i nan
"Cuwe, nico we," eya canke ekta hi ke'.

202. Wana tima hiyotaka canke heciya ke': "Ho, hanka, wi-
coiye tanyanśni nun nan nitankala nakun ecehcin aniyupte c'un,
otehi-nic'ila nan nitankala iye ikpaganla canke le kici waun we lo.

203. "Hecannikte sece; wana śic'e igluwankatuya ca makiyu-
śekte le, ecannikte sece; ungna hecanni ki lo;" eya ke'.

204. Heceya cante-śica-un hunśe, heya yunkan lila nakeś nablayin nan wiyuśkin ke'; ecin tiwahe ena okiciyuśicapi can iyotan
otehike cin he un.

205. "Ho, iyayin ye, manil unyinkte," eya canke tawicu kici i

ke'. Yunkan heci tuweni owanyakeśni, kul iyunk-kiyin nan yuto-
keca canke pte winyela ca inazin ke'. Yunkan iś eya icaptanptan-
kic'un nan hehutela ca inazin ke'. Yunkan hehanl cinca-kicagin
nan ake wicaśa-kahya kici gli ke'.

206. K'eyaś pte-ouncage yuhapi ecel heya ke': "Ho, yukśankśan tahin yuśnaśna omani yo," eya canke pte-winyela wan waśte
eyapca ca yukśankśan omani nan gli canke hehanl kici kul iyunkin nan icaptanptan-kic'unpi nan iglulakotapi ke'.

207. Wana wicaśa wikcemna cokap ti el ipi canke hingnaku
taku agli kin wicak'u ca yublecapi yunkan yaśle ha wan hakte-
iteya hin kin kunlkuntahan ca e nan kangi-wiyaka k'eya nakun
waśtehceśni ca hecel yuataninpi canke eya hecel eyapika ca ticeta
tośu wan aiyakaśkapi nan kiglapi ke'.

208. Yunkan iś eya wicaśa zaptan Cetan-maza ti kin el ipi
nan tawicu kin wopahta wan wicak'u canke yublecapi yunkan
śungila-wakan wan luta ca opitktehcin keś iyakcunnipi s'a k'un
he ha kin e ca yuataninpi; nan wanbli wan wayuś'inyeyal un k'un
he tawiyaka kin śayela we oputkap s'e yuataninpi ke'.

209. Canke hena ticeta eiyakaśkanpi ca tokiyatanhan kin
oyas'in wanyak-ahi nan tipi kin itankal ohli s'e han ke'.

210. Hehanl ake Cetan-maza heya ke': "Ho, wanhinkpe luhapi
kin iyuha wacin ye lo," eya canke mnakiyapi nan kahipi yunkan
hehanl tunweya nunp yewicaśi ke'.

211. He toka pahata yewicaśipi eyapi kin ecunpi śke'.

212. Tanyehcin wowicak'upi nan wipipi hanl tunweya-
yewicaśipi canke yapi nan paha wan otaninyan tehanl yanka
canke ekta iyahanpi nan nazinpi ca tiyatanhan wanwicayak yankapi ke'.

213. Yunkan ungna kakśankśan inyankapi nan śina wankal ye-
kiyapi nan hehanl lila iyank glicupi nan glipi ke'.

214. Wana glipi yunkan Cetan-maza op cannunpin nan hehanl
heya ke': "Ho, kośkalaka, makokignake aipazica kin hena ohinni-
yan ocaicuyaye c'in, tukte-wanzi etu ca taku waśte wanlaka hecinhan omakiyaka yo. . . . nan mayagna yeśni hantanhanś napahunka un epazo wo!" eya śke'.

215. Yunkan napahunka un epazopi nan ka paha kin akotanhan ataya śina akahpap s'e pte hiyot'inza keyapi ke'. "Pilamayay-

ape lo!" Cetan-maza eya ke˙. Hetanhan ca pteoyakapi kin wicaka-
pihca ca napahunka u epazo au kišto.

216. "Ho, iyuha lel owanži yanka po!" eya canke wana tokeni
oiye apsil-picašniyan un canke anagoptanpi nan ena yankapi˙.

217. Heceš iye tawicu kin e nan koškalaka wikcemna iye hena
wicapahi nan wanhinkpe mnaye c'un hena yuha-wicakiyin nan
henakeca ekta yapi.

218. Yunkan ainap hel oškokpa wan el tawicu kin iyunk-kiyin
nan pte-ha wan akahpa ihpeyin nan ohlate icaptanptan-kic'un-ši
ca ecun yunkan pte-winyela wan wašte ca inažin ke˙.

219. "Ho, iyayin nan pte unpi kin wicegnagna omani nan hehanl el maku nan miyohomni iyaya yo. Topa-hecun wo, kohan
lena milazata wanhinkpe yuha wiyeya nažinpikte," eya ke˙.

220. Canke wana wicegna iyayin nan omani kin ecel pte kin
owanži nažinpšni ikikiyela hiyupi nan glicu yunkan ihakap ahi-
kawingapi ke˙.

221. Topa-hecun canke iyena sam kiyela upi nan icitopa kin
ehanl hecena kici glipi nan ataya owancaya icipahaya unpi ke˙.

222. Canke koškalaka wikcemna wiyeya ewicagle k'un hena
k'un hena wana tokel okihi iciyokiheheya kutepi nan wancala esa
sutešni. Iyohila un pte wanži ktepi ške˙. Iye he ehanni tunweni
šutinktešni-wakicunzapi canke hecun-wicaya ške˙.

223. Yunkan hehanl wanhinkpe kin pahi-wicaši canke ecunpi,
nan taceži kin hena nakun. "Miš kohan wagninkte lo," eyin nan
tawicu kici glicu ke˙.

224. Heceš kihunni nan "Ho, wanase-ya po!" eya canke oyate
kin šika talo yukan can hel lila wiyuškinpi s'a canke wana ake lila
wicaškan nan iyuha ekta eyaya ke˙.

225. Maka amanipi canke talo henakehcin akupi kin wok'inke
c'eyaš kitanyekel eš talo yukan canke šina ogna akiyuha aglipi
nan wancahcin imnapi nan akap yuhapi ke˙.

226. Anpetu ataya talo tokšupi nan hanhepi oiyokpaza hanl ig-
luštanpi nan hehanl wotapi nan oiyokipiya wacipi ke˙.

227. Ake iyecala winyan k'un manil hingnaku kici i nan heciya pte-winyela ouncage ogna hpayin nan nagwakahin nan ptehincala wan tun ke˙; ptehincala wan ihankeya wašte ca tun ke˙.

228. Cetan-maza he cinca yunkan hokśilala lila iyuśkin-itin nan caś-kitunla ke'; taśiyaknunpala wan tunkaśila-ye c'un he tokel caś-tun nan yaotanin k'un he ecehcin ecun ke'.

229. Ptehincala wan hinśa-hinzila ca ćisćilala kin hehanni śpukeśni oiyankela canke oyuspin nan gluha nażin nan tuweni unśni k'eyaś eyapaha nan heya ke':

230. "Ho, po, taku maka sitomniyan hiyeye cin, maka akanl taku śkanśkanyan toni gluha un kin, wahupakoza kin koya, nah'unpi ye!

231. "Le-anpetu kin hokśila wan micitunpi ca imatan nan ibluśkin nan lehanl wana caże yukinkta ca "Ptehincala Luta" eciyape lo! Tuktel wanmiyecilakap nan iyotiyekiya-iteka can unśimicilapi ye, kola!" eya ke'.

232. Hecunpi nan ake kilakotapi nan wakanheżala wan waśte nahanhcin tunwelaśni ca glokipi canke okśantanhan wanyak ahi ke'.

233. Wana tanka ayela kin ecel tunkaśitku wan Cetan-maza waśun tanhan icu k'un he el hi nan gluha yankela s'a ke'.

234. Wana hpecaśniyan śkehanhanlaka yunkan wicahcala kin heya ke: "Takoża, nitunkan wana ehantan takożakpaku topa ye lo. Hena Iktomi-hu zizi cinca ca aśihtinpila k'eyaś takoża-wicaya canke wicayuhakel un ca miś le mitakoża waunspewiciyinkte lo," eya canke "Ho wo, niś he niye ye!" eya ke'.

235. Canke mani-unspekiyin nan ia-unspekiyin nan śkal-unspekiya ke'.

236. Wanhinkpela k'eya kicagin nan wakute-unspekiya canke lila ohinni tunkasitku gluhlaganlaśni ke'. "Takoża wana han-skinkte lo," eya yunkan ecetu ke'.

237. Hecel unpi k'un ungna Cetan-maza hocokatanhan gli yunkan tilazata tawicu kin wahatkahan canke el glinażin ke'.

238. Yunkan hokśila k'un wana hanskela ca wanhinkpe yuha oinyanka canke kico nan heya ke: "Ho, cinkś, tunkaśila wan maka-opapun kin ekta icah-maye c'un he lena mak'u we lo, wapośtan kin le, nan mila kin le, nan wanhinkpe, tatucuhu-itazipa kin le.

239. "He tunkaśila kin caże-ociyake c'unhan namah'un ca

lena un iyeniciyinkte lo. Ṫanyan iyeḱiya yo, nan tukte ehan toka-
munḱa eśa lena icu nan ekta ya yo," eya ke'.

240. Yunkan tawicu kin iyokipiśni nan, "Iś taḱu! . . . wakan
tka! . . . he taḱowe tonikakta he?" eyaya iyokteḱa ke'.

241. Eyaś ecanl iḣat'in nan, "Wan, okata ca nunwe-unyinkte
lo, wana eyaś henala ecun ye," eye c'eyaś wicalaśni, "E, le wana
niśḱoyela ihewakiya ca wi mahel iyayeśnihanni wagluśtankta tka!"
eya ke'.

242. Yamni-iyunġe c'eyaś wicalaśni canḱe icitoṗa k'un han
posḱisḱi-yus yeape ke'.

243. K'eyaś he eka yeś wiyoḱihiśni ca hecetukeś "Ho, eca miś-
nala keś mninkte lo," eyin nan iyaya ke'.

244. Mni kin tanyan ḱaluzin nan otankayaḣceśni k'eyaś eyaś
otohanyan copa yapi keś ungnahanla ohipiśni k'un hececa ke'.

245. Mni kin iyosni un iḱibleza canḱe waś'aḱya nunwanhin
nan hehanl ohutata wi aḱanl-ic'iya gliyotaḱin nan asniḱiya yanḱa-
han ke'.

246. Yunkan ungna tuwa tokiya cażeyal-ḱiṗan ke'. "Cetan-
maza!" eye c'eyaś winyan ca lila ho-waśtelaḣcaka ke'.

247. Paḱas'in owotanlaḣcin iyotaḱin nan anaġoptan yunkan
ake eya ke'. "Cetan-maza, tehantanhan wanciyak-wahi ye, leci
uwa na! Ocaśtunpiḱa cinla yaun ca le ekta cihi ye!" eya yunkan
mni kin kowakatanhan ca he panhan ke'.

248. "Wan, śma ca toka-wauśni ye lo!" eye c'eyaś ake eya
canḱe canzeze hotanin nan "Śma ca toka-wauśni ce epe lo!" eya
yunkan ake ḱico ke'.

249. "Hunhunhe, otawat'eśice lo! . . . heceḣcin wanmayalaḱa
yacin kinś toka niyeś yau śni?" eya yunkan toka-hiyuśni keya ke'.

250. Canḱe hehanl, "Ociciyake lo! tokel yahilu oyakihiśni hecinhan miś'eya iyemaceca ye lo!" eye śan ake icitoṗa-ḱico canḱe
"ohan," eyin nan ośkokṗa wan el iċaptanptan-ḱic'un yunkan
hehutela ca t'inze s'e inażin ke'.

251. Hecena mnil iḣṗeic'iyin nan mniitancan kin waś'aḱa
canḱe tatanka kin ekta yeś lilakel śkinciyin nan iyuweġa ke'.

252. Yunkan hel peżi-hansḱasḱa-egna wikośkalaḱa wan pce-
cela nan puḣ'iḱe c'eyaś lila winyan waśte ca iḣa wanḱal ayuta nażin ke'.

253. "Ho wo, miyeco ca le wahi ye. Ṫokel unkiyuweġinkta heci eya yo," eya. Yunkan, "tokśa paġoh'aṗe el aḱan ciyanḱin nan cankahu el pażoya niye cin hel ḱaġe ciyuzinkte," eya canḱe, "Howo," eya ke'.

254. Canḱe wana ake k'in mnil iḣṗeic'iyin nan nunwa gnin nan wana mni coḱan glapi hanl ungna yuwanḱal aya ca aḱibleza ke'.

255. Ṫokel oḱihi śkinciya ic'ibleblel tkeic'iye c'eyaś winkcekce yuze s'e yuwankataḱiya aya ke'.

256. Hanḱeya ḱinyanpśni k'eyaś maḣṗiyataḱiya yapi ca ecel makoce kin sam ćisćila ayin nan hanḱeya otaninśni, nan heci wanḱal oḣloḱa wan tak wokitan ogna maḣṗiya-makoce kin ekta aki ke'.

257. Wana oiyokṗaze c'eyaś tiyata kiśni canḱe hokśila k'un cinktakta atkuku iḱigni ke'.

258. "Inila yanḱa, cinkś, tokśa niyate nunwe-iyaya ca tohanl igluśtan ḱinhan glikte," eyahe c'eyaś hanḱeya iye ko nihinciyin nan hanḱeya oyaka canḱe oiyokṗazeḣce c'un heca-hanhepi ca can slayapi nan ileya yuha mni-aglagla olepi ke'.

259. Oyate kin yucik'a s'e hanhepi ataya ḱiṗan olepi k'eyaś iyeyapśni ecel anṗa ke'.

260. Toḱa ektaś iyecinḱa ḱiṗan amani nan ayupteśni canḱe gli nan "Hiyupi na! Wicaśa wan toki imakiyaye! Mni-makit'e sece!" eya caś olepi k'un wana iyuha tiyata kiglapi ca ake iśnala "Cetan-maza! Ṫoki ilala he?" eya ceyaya iyaya omani ke'.

261. "Mni t'e lo," eyapi canḱe ceyahe c'eyaś kohan cinca kin heya ke: "Ina, tukte iyehantu ca ate nunwe s'a hecinhan ekta amayin ye!" eya canḱe ekta ai yunkan hel tahanṗe nan hayapi un k'un iyuha peżi-egna hiyeya ke'.

262. Yunkan hokśila kin ena iyotaḱin nan, "Gla yo, ina, lel ate iyawakipekte," eya canḱe hunku kin nihinciya, "Hiya, cinkś, ni-yate le mni t'e. Niśnala lel nanḱe c'eyaś tunweni kukteśni ecel taḱunl niś eya ayakipakte!" eya wicalaśni ke'.

263. Ṫoṗa-akigle iyokiśni k'eyaś nah'unśni ḱitan canḱe han-ḱeya, "Howe, eca, eyaḱeś miye wacin kin ogna yunkan lececa k'un," eya iśna woglaglak nażin ke'.

264. "Ho, eca cinkś, waktaya lel yanḱa. Ṫokśa ake waukte,"

eyin nan kigla canke iśnala k'unhan wapośtan-wakan kin he
kic'un nan mila-wakan, wan-wakan ko gluha inażin nan heya
ke':

265. "Howo, tunkaśila, wiyohinyanpata toki nanka hecinhan,
namah'un wo! Niye lena ate yak'u nan iyayustak wowaś'ake woo-
kihi yak'u k'un hena lehanl iwacinciyin lo! Lena ate ena ayuśtan
nan tancan ecela tokiyaya ca owakilekte lo!" eya ke'.

266. Hecena iglucetan-tanka nan owotanlahcin wankatakiya,
ehaś owanżi nażin s'e yin nan mahpiyata ohloka-ćisćila k'un he
ogna mahel iyaya ke'.

267. Hena hel hocokatunyan oyate tanka wicoti ca ikiyela i
yunkan eciyatanhan wicaśa wan nata kin sapa igluskitin nan itkop
u ke'. Yunkan hena śkibibila oyatepi ca heya ke:

268. "Hunhi, hokśila, niyate lel aglipi ca oyate kin wanyakape
lo. Lehantu hcin pazopi canke okśan mimeya wawanyaka kin
ahinażin ca ena oye ihpeyape lo. Tka hehantan wana napciyunk-
can ye lo," eya ke'.

269. Hecena hetanhan ya yunkan ake wicoti wan el ihunni
ke'. Yunkan hetanhan iś wicaśala wan cantku kin ataya cehnaga
un sapkiyela ca el itkop u nan heya ke':

270. "Hunhi, hokśila wan atkuku okile keyapi k'un he le niye
huwo? Ho, niya lel agli-pazopi ca oyate kin yumimeya wawanyak-
imnaic'iyapi na hehanl akiyaglape lo. . . k'eyaś hehantan śaglogan-
can yelo!" eya ke'. Yunkan hena iś zitkala k'eya Cantku-sapa ewicakiyapi k'un hecapi ke'.

271. Ake wicoti wan el i yunkan wicaśa wan el u ke'. He-oyate
kin iś zitkala k'eya. Iśta-nica-tanka ewicakiyapi ca wetu cansna
ecala agli nan tokeya "makitasakinkte sece" ecinkeśni witka tun
iyeyapila k'un hecapi ke'. Nata nan tahu opta sapapila nan tansinl holhotapila k'un hena epila.'

272. "Hunhi, hokśila, niyate lel aglipi nan pazopi ca oyate kin
wanwayak-aikpablayape lo. . . leś oye kin yumimeya ihpeyapi
kin. . . tka hehantan wana śakowin-can ye lo," eya ke'.

273. Ake wicoti wan el ihunni yunkan hel iś zitkala k'eya
Hupahu-wanblila ewicakiyapi ca waniyetu ataya ena unpila k'un
hecapi ke'. Wanżi el u na, "Hunhi, hokśila wan atkuku okile

keya-otanin k'un, he niye iteka lo. Ho, niyate lel agli-pazopi canke tunweni wicaśa-akantula wanzi wanyakapiśni ca icipaha-hape lo . . . k'eyaś letan akiyaglapi hantan wana śakpe-can ye lo," eya ke'.

274. Hecena hetan inyankin nan wicoti wan el ihunni ke'. Yunkan he iś zitkala k'eya lila čikčik'apila ca zitka-tola ewicaki-yapi k'un heca-oyatepila ke'.

275. Eciyatanhan wicaśa wan toic'iyin nan u ke'. "Hunhe, hunhe, Cetan-maza cinca wan atkuku okile-ukta keyapi k'un! Ho, lel niyate aglipi ca oyate kin iśta-waśeca-ic'iyape lo. K'eyaś hehantan zaptan-can ye lo," eya ke'.

276. Canke ake ya yunkan wicoti canke ikiyela asnikiya ke'. Eciyatanhan wicaśa wan śa-ic'iyin nan u ke'. Yunkan he oyate kin Śunluta ewicakiyapi k'un hecapi ca etanhan u ke'.

277. Ake iś eya ecekce eyin nan, "hehehe, wana letan niyate eyayapi hantan topa-can ye lo," eya ke'.

278. Wana sam kiyela ka ayapi canke bliheic'iyin na ake ya, yunkan ake wicoti wan el atayela ihunni ke'.

279. Yunkan hena iś śiśokapi ke'. Zitkala k'eya śa-zipi ca tapetu holya ececapi k'un hecapi'. Yunkan hena iś, "Niyate letan akiyag-lapi hantan yamni-can ye lo," eyapi ke'.

280. Canke ake iyayin nan wicoti wan el i yunkan he-oyate kin lila i waśicupi ca takeya taninśni wakinice s'e howayapi ke. Eyaś zitkala k'eya to-sapapi ca wagmeza-owożuta iglonicapi s'a k'un hecapi ke'.

281. "Hunhi, hunhi, kola tanyan yahi ye, ena un ye!" Eya yus unpi ke'. K'eyaś inahni-iyayinkta keya yunkan hehanl "O, eca, ni-yate lel agli-pazopi hantan nunpa-can ye lo," eyapi canke hetan lila iyaya ke'.

282. Oyate wan pasu tankinkinyanpi nan iśta totopi ca tanśil sap-ic'iyapi ca aogluteyapi ke'. "Niyate lel ahipi k'eyaś ake eya-yape lo, hehantan wanca-can ye lo. Lila ilala hantanhanś yakigle-ginkte sece lo," eyapi canke hetan ake iyayin nan oyate wan el wicai ke'. Yunkan hena unkce-kiha-oyatepi ca itkop nipi na aglapi ke'.

283. "Hunhi, hokśilahce san ksisya omani ye lo!" eya imna-

pihca ke'. "Ho, kola, le niyate oyakile ca slol'unyape lo. Lel aglipi
k'eyaś pcelyela-pazopi nan ake hecena akiyaglape lo. . . . Hinhanna nakeś le hecunpi ca wawanyaka peźi inastopi kin nakeś
wana he ecel kiglewacin naic'iowotan ye," eyapi ke'.

284. Canke hetan wotin nan ake ya yunkan oyate wan tanka
ca wicaśa nan winyan kin mimamapihce s'e lececa ke'.

285. El yinkte c'eyaś cokata taku lila ikik'opi nan iś watuka un
t'inkte s'e toka-yeśni canke kal capunpun-okiźata wan el iyunkin
nan h'unt'a un ceyahan ke'.

286. Yunkan winyan wan ikiyela hiyaya hunśe, "Hinun, hokśila wan le ceya he. Eyaś tośtoś mitakoźa lel hpayin nan ceyahe
ca!" eyaya nan icu ke'.

287. He winunhcala ca tiyatakiya leya agla ke': "Takoźa, hocokata wicaśa-ksapa kin mniciya pe. . . . Hena lecala hukuya winyan
wan wocantiheyeka ca yeśipi yunkan itap gli ye.

288. "He wohinape kin ekta wicaśa wan Cetan-maza eciyapi,
ca wakan un canke tokeśkekel gnayin nan akuśipi yunkan wiyeya
kan yanke s'e itap agli ca ikik'ope.

289. "Ehanni he tohunwel leciyatanhan-winyan wan kte ca un
nakun wayaka yuza pe. Hel yuha yankapi nan hinhanna wi cokan
hiyaye cinhan ktepikte; ca tokehcin oyate wicota k'eyaś tokśa tapi
kin hanke yatinkte. Oyate henawicakeca k'eyaś iyuha yutapikta ca
kpanyela waśpuśpupikta keya pe," eya canke ceya yunkan, "Inila
yanka, takoś, tokeśa tapi yatinkte!" eyaya kigna ke'.

290. Anpao yunkan eyapaha wan heya hiyaya ke: "Le ehanke
Cetan-maza wanlakapi nan hehanl ktepikta ce; wi hinape cin kici
el naźin po; ikpahicapi nan cin-cokśu yucik'ayela hiyaya po!"
eya ke'.

291. "Iho, iho, takoźa, kikta, he ociciyake c'un ecehcin eye.
Tiyatani yanka, tokśa tapi kin hanpe cicakukte," eya-yuhica ke'.

292. "Hiya, unci, unyinkte lo!" eya canke, "Hiya, takoźa, lena
oyate-ikce-kapiśni, lena wakan pe. Ikce-ikicicahtak ya iyayapi keś
ko ksuye-kiciyapi ca woinape ke, ce tiyatani keś yanka!" eya ke'.

293. (Yunkan lena wakan-wicayuwipi can el takuśkanśkan
keya hinhpayapi nan wowaśipi k'un hecapi śke'.)

294. Topa-akigle yinkta keya canke hecetu keś kici hocokata

wana kata wicahan canke ekta ipi nan wawanyaka kin pazanzan winunhcala kin takożakpaku kic'in yin nan otaninyan inażin ke'.

295. Yunkan cokatahce cin hel wikośkalaka wan lila winyan waśte k'eyaś winyan-wicaśaśni-iteya iha yanka ke'.

296. Kablaś yanka canke cana kin el tatanka wan nisko ot'ins iyotakehan yanka ke'. Nan wikośkalaka kin pagoh'ape kin opta sutaya yus yanka canke toka-inażinśni ke'.

297. K'eyaś hokśila kin he atkuku kin e ca iyekiya ke'. Tatanka k'un kakel ahitunwin nan hecena gloglo canke oyate kin kahektakiya napa-kinażinpi k'eyaś Ptehincala Luta iye he atkuku kin ia-nakih'un canke leya ca okahniga ke:

298. "Hehehe, cinkś, takowe-yau huwo? Miyeka yeś le anpetu tahena makte-pikte lo." eya gloglo ke'.

299. "Unci, kiya emagle ye!" eya śkinc'iye c'eyaś winunhcala kin pipiya śina ayut'inzin nan heya ke: "Hiya, takoża, Oyate kin lena ihanhan-iwokicitopi keś ko untunkiciyapi ce epe!" eye c'eyaś lila kitan nan wana unnihan tope-eya canke "ho eca, milazata na- żin," eyin nan kuya egle ke'.

300. Hecena atkuku tawanhinkpe k'un wanżi ekta egle nan winyan wan Cetan-maza akśiś yanke un he apaha ke, kunśitku unpi kin etanhan.

301. Yunkan wanglakin nan," Oyuspapi, maktekte! —tuktiye- cel tuwa eyinkta ca!" eyin, na tatanka kin inap iyaya ke'.

302. Topa-iyute c'eyaś heyin nan ainap iyaya ca oyate kin he tuwa kecin ignipi keś tokeni hokśila wan niśkola nażin kin e- kiyapiśni canke wana itopa tka hecena wan iyayeyin nan atkuku kin oh'ankoya ektaśniyan ihpeic'iya canke winyan k'un o yunkan wokpan wobleca ke'.

303. Inyan-winyan canke iswula kin wasu śekse napsil yeya canke oyate kin iśta iyayapikta-ikopapi un abeya napapi ke'.

304. Hecena tatanka k'un nażin hiyayin nan gloglo cinca kin anakitan nan kic'in napa canke oyate kin ihakap inyankapi ke'.

305. K'eyaś wicahcala k'eya kal anunwap cannunpahanpi ca el ikiyela kuwa awicayapi yunkan iyowicakipiśni'. "Awicayuśtan po. He Cetan-maza cinca wan Ptehincala Luta eciyapi kin kicica ca tunweni owicayakihipikteśni ye lo.

306. "Ptehincala Luta cik'ala k'eyaś wakan yelakaś Tunkan
Hetun-win eka yeś iwokpan ye lo, śehanl eś taku inihunkapi ka!"
eyapi canke kawingapi ke'.

307. Heceś iglulakotapi nan hecena wicaśa kin hokśi-kic'in inyanka ke'.

308. Wana wicoti wan el glapi yunkan he unkcekiha-oyate
k'un epi canke wanżi inyank itkop wicau nan hecena inyankapi
ca wicisakip niyaśniśni "Hokśila, inażin ye! Tokel niyate yaglogli-
yaku kin oyaglakinkte, oyate kin wanah'un cantokpani pe lo,"
eyaya inyanke c'eyaś "Ate, cinkta hecena iyaya yo! Inażinśni yo!"
eya yanka canke atkuku kin iyopteya glicu nan ake wicoti-ici-
nunpa k'un el ku ke'.

309. Hena kangi-oyate k'un epi ca pasu niskosko iśta toyela
unśiśiiya patak wicaśipi tkaś hecena ake iyopteya glicupi nan
wicoti-iciyamni wan el kupi ke'.

310. Ake inażin-wicaśipi k'eyaś hecena glicupi ke'. Hehanl
śiśoka-wicoti kin sam glicupi nan hehanl śunluta-wicoti kin sam-
glicupi ke'.

311. Hecena kupi nan, kupi nan kupi nan zitka-tola-oyate kin
epi nan hupahu wanblila kin epi nan hehanl iśtanica-tanka kin
epi nan hehanl cantku-sapa kin hena iyuha ceyaya inażin nan
woglak wicaśipi keś nawicah'unśni glicupi ke'.

312. Zitkala kin hena kowicakipapiśni k'eyaś Tunkan-oyate
kin wicakigleġapikta kokipapi ke'.

313. Wana unhanketa wicoti wan el Ptehincala Luta toka ektap
ihunnila k'un hel glipi ke'. Hena Śkibibila-oyatepi'. Zitkala kin
hena wetu canśna tokeya nahanhcin wa śkanśni kin hehanni gli-
pila nanśna ohotunyankel unpila'.

314. Can ehanke-icamna nanśna tonana cuwitat'apila k'eyaś
nunġe-wanil aglihunnila s'a'.

315. Ohakap iśe unmapi kin nakeś glipi.'

316. Wana eyaś hehanyan wicakigleġapikteśni-iyecetu canke
hel asnikiyapi ca lila wicayuonihanpi nan wowicak'upi ke'.

317. Nan heyapi: "Ho, lel tonacan asnikiya po, lila wanitu-
kape. Kohan nitunkaśila mniciyapi nan tokel gleniyanpikta hecinhan iwanyakapikte lo," eyapi ke'.

318. Yunkan wicoti wikcemna k'un hena eciyatanhan wanżik-

żila tukte iyotan wiyukcan-wopika yuhapi kin he glaḣniḣ-uyapi ca hena witaya wakiya-iyotaḱapi ke'.

319. Ṫaḱu kapi ca tipiyokiheya wan el heyahanpi nan unhanḱeta wanżi u nan Cetan-maza cinca ḱici wicaḱico canḱe el ipi yunkan heyapi ke':

320. "Ho, nitunḱaśila lecel winiciyukcanṗe lo: Ognaḱe wan nicaġapikta ca he ogna kuya yaglapikte lo. Tka taḱu wanżila iceniciyapi kin he le e: Maka kin ekta ayahanpi ḱinhan ognaḱe kin he makiċaḣtaḱapi nan hehanl ikan kin yutiktita po.

321. "Hececa ḱinhan yuwanḱal unḱicupikte. Ṫaḱu Wakan kin nicaġapi nan unkiś eya unḱaġapi k'eyaś otakiya śkinciya canḱe eunktunżapi nan leciyana unkayuśtanṗe lo.

322. "K'eyaś le ognaḱe kin makiċaḣtaḱe cinhan hecel unglapikte lo," eyapi ke'. Hecena zitkala kin iyuha wowaśi ecunpi nan taḱu wan iśnala ihanḱeya ḱaḣwopikapi k'un heca wan lila tanka waśte ca ḱaġapi ke'.

323. Coḣ-wanżica-swula un ḱaġapi nan hehanl mahetanhan iye wiyaḱa-tawapi ocaże kin iyuha un wogligleya panśyela waśte yuśtanpi ke'.

324. Hehanl coḣ-wanżica hu k'eya lila hansḱasḱa ca yusleslel sunpi nan wahoḣpi-tanka kin toṗakiya ikanyanpi nan hankeya ikan toṗa kin hena owanżila iciyugmupi nan wiyeya gnakapi ke'.

325. Wana iyehantu keyapi nan Cetan-maza cinca ḱici ekta iyotaḱ-wicakiyapi k'eyaś lila tanka canḱe oḱacaglaya ekta yanḱapi ke'.

326. Heceś mni-c'api mahetaḱiya ceġa yeyapi s'e hukutaḱiya uwicayapi nan wana tohantu yunkan makata asasyela gliyotaḱapi canḱe glicupi ke'.

327. Ṫuwa wanwicayaḱin nan oyaḱa canḱe maka glakinyan anawicatanpi k'eyaś Cetan-maza iyowicakiśni ke'. "Mitaḱuyepi, towaś ako nażin po, kola pilamayanpi k'un iś ehanḱela pilawicawayinkta ce," eyin nan yuwakanyeḣcin wahoḣpi kin makata iwotoya iċaḣtaḱin nan hehanl ikan kin el yutiktitan yunkan maḣṗiyatanhan yutitanpi nan wahoḣpi k'un yuwanḱal glokiyaglapi ke'. Ihinhanna yunkan zitkala-oyate kin wikcemna ataya wahoḣpi k'un ożula naṗogna wicayuzapila s'e yankapi nan hukuta hipi nan makowancaya iyayapila śke'.

328. Nakeś hehanl Cetan-maza oyate kin ekta wicagla yunkan tunkanku wicaśa itab k'un wana wicahcala ca el u nan "Ha o, ha o, takoś, iśnikal eś, iśnikal eś" eyaya yustosto nan heya ke: "Takoś, nitawin, nikun, nikunśi, nitunkaśila, nitunla ko iyuha ceya-iglat'api nan waśiglape lo. Tanyan yagli ye lo!" eya.

329. Canke Cetan-maza tianakitan yunkan tawicu kin iśta napopoyela itkop u canke poskiskin gluzin nan, iś winyan kin cinca zaniyan wanglake c'un un ceya.

330. Nan ihakap oyate kin icak'oyela wanyak-inahnipi un au ke'.

331. Yunkan hehanl winunhcalala wan unciye c'un he el cinktakta śil-woglak-hi ke'. "Takoźa, tokanih'an canke Ikto el wai nan unśiśi-iya hepe: 'Takoźa, sunkala tokeśke iyeye-pica heci iyukcan na ecel ecun-wicakiyin ye,' epa, yunkan 'Iś hece witkotkoka ca tokah'an kin tokel iyomawaźa ka. Wicaśa wanźila taninśni wan wotanka ke!' eye, takoźa, nan pacekcek iyemaye!" eya ke'.

332. Canke Cetan-maza "Hu-zizila aku po," eya canke aglipi yunkan kakiyana u kin hehanni ia au nan "Hunhi, hunhi, misun, tanyan yagli ye lo, oyate kin ataya wahpani-wicayaye c'un, canke ceya-iglat'api k'un. Wicaśa kin ceyapi un t'api yunkanś iśe lehanl wana okanheya munka tka ye lo!" eyaya u ke'.

333. Canke heceś Cetan-maza iyopeye-wacin k'un iyenaya ke'. "Iś ektanhcin, taku-wahteka ca un tuwaś iglucanze ka! He Ikto ee nacece cin!" eya ke'.

334. K'eyaś kunśitkula k'un sakye gluha naźin nan Ikto el iyaya yunkan kabloblo nan hecel un canl-asni-ic'iya ke'.

335. Yunkan hehanl eyapaha wan hiyayin nan "Hopo, woyute waśte yagnakapi kin Cetan-maza kau po! Wotinkte lo!" eya canke wiyeya yuha yankapihca wasna koko kahipi ke', nan papa pusyapi kin wokpan oźukźula koko. "Ehaś ota nacece c'eyaś tokśa tawicu nan kunśitku kin kicignakapikte cin," eyapi ke'.

336. Heceś oyate wol-wicakiye s'a k'un iś ehakela wol-kiyapi canke wicoti kin ataya kata wicahan ke'.

337. Heceś hokśicalkiyapi-oti kin tima yankin nan wotahe hcehanl tuwa tilazata hinaźin nan tiogeya "Cetan-maza, hinapa yo!" eya canke inapa yunkan wicaśa wan tokiyatanhan hi nan hel naźin canke "Toka huwo?" eya yunkan heya ke':

338. "Hehehe, kola, heceyaś yagli-otai ca naġi yeciye-wakapin k'eyaś leci wiyohṗeyata nitunkaśila wan wahoniye lo.

339. "'Takoża ecelaś wacin-waye, kicoya po,' eye lo. Tehiya waakipa ca iyotiyekiya yanke lo," eya ke'.

340. "Ho, gnin nan tunkaśila kin okiyaka yo, tokśa wahi-yukte," eyin nan tima glicu ke'. Canke ka wana wiyohṗeyatakiya kigla ke'.

341. Oglaka yunkan tawicu kin ceyaya iyokiśni . . . Hiya, ninkteśni ye, kitan ecinyelaś le yagli k'un!" eyaya k'eyaś cinca kin heya ke: "Hiya, ina, heyeśni yo, ate tokiyaṗ wacinyapi ca ekta yinkte," eyin na wapośtan nan mila, wan ko wakan k'un hena kicu canke iyaya ke'.

342. Yunkan he wahṗa-tanka ca kico hi śke'.

343. Canke kigle c'un ecel yin nan wiyohṗeyata maka-oṗaṗun kin ekta tipi wan wi u kin ektakiya etunwan han yunkan tima wicahcala wan okate eyaś śina pamahel icoma yanka ke'.

344. Canke tima iyayin nan, "Ho, tunkaśila, miyeco ca le wana wahi ye lo, toka huwo?" eya yunkan lila ite ekta cante śicela ca tanin ke'.

345. "Hehehe, takoża, mni kin kowakatanhan oyate wan yan-kapi yunkan etan wicaśa k'eya azumayanpi nan nata wamaśpapi nan akiyaglapi ca le tehiya makakiże lo.

346. "Canke tunkin ṗaha kin he tokeśkekel iwekcu yunkanś, ecincin le mankin nan waceyahe lo," eya ke'.

347. Heyin nan śina kazamni yunkan nata kin ataya śayela śtaśtaya ececa ca lila owanyak-śica ke'.

348. Cetan-maza hnahna nan inapa ke'. "Wahteśni śicapi kin . . . hinyanka yo, tunkaśila, tokśa waglikte," eya canke lena "Haye, haye!" eya-niya tkaś hecena iyaya ke'.

349. Otohanyan yin nan hehanl wapośtan wan cetan-tanka śaśte ikoyake un he kic'un yunkan cetan-tanka-hingla canke kin-yan yin nan wicoti kin aokawinġa ke'.

350. Iwakcipi ca hocokata oiyokipiya wacipi canke hukuciyela kinyan yunkan canwakan wan cokaṗ glepi ca heciya wicahcala nata-ha k'un he ikoyaka ke'.

351. Canke waape unhin nan wana hehanl takapsicapi ca can-wakan k'un hetan oeyaye kaġapi nan wana akoketkiya inyankapi

canke wawanyaka kin iyuha etkiya etunwanpi hanl kinyan hiyu
nan yupsak icu nan yuha glicu canke woza-wica hingnin nan ku-
wapi ke'.

352. Yunkan wanżi wicahcala-ksapa ca heya ke: "Tunweni
makaheyayapikteśni ye lo, ayuśtan po! Cetan-maza eic'iye c'un he
e ye lo!" eya ke'.

353. Canke wana yuha ku nan iglulakota nan wicahcala k'un
ti el gli ke'. Ecel unkiciciyinkte eyaś lila tate-kapuzin nan yugmu-
sya suta canke toel spayeyin nan wana eyaś śtaśta nan zikzica
canke ecel iyaskap-kiciciyin nan asniyan ke'.

354. Canke wicahcala k'un lila cante waśte ke'. "Haho, haho,
toka yelakas takoża, ciglahniġin nan wahociye c'un! Ho, takoża,
wacicukte lo. Taku ikpahela-pilamayayeca caś.

355. "Ako hel wikan wikcemna kakśa otke lo; wanżi kahniġin
nan icu wo," eya canke wanżi waśtehceśni ihankeya otka ca icu
ke'. Yunkan hehanl heya ke: "Ho, takoża, tankal śunka-wakan
wikcemna nażinpi ce wanżi oyuspa yo, he nitawakte lo," eya
canke inapin nan wanżi acik'alaka ca hinzila ca kahniġa ke'.

356. Tunweni hecunśni k'eyaś wikan kin iteha-kahya yuiyape-
han icu yunkan śunka-wakan kin hotuntun el u nan pa ogna iyekiya canke kal kaśka egle ke'.

357. Hecun nan tima ki nan "Ho, tunkaśila, śunka-wakan wan
iwacu we lo," eya yunkan, "To, tanyan ecanun we lo, takoża.
Miye le śunka-wakan wakaġe lo. Maka un wicawakaġin nanśna
can huye-wicawakiyin nan iwaśtela hektatanhan patan iyewica-
waya can manipi nan śunka-wakan ca ni iyayape lo. Lecala s'e le
iyecinka ic'icaġahanpi ca pilamayanpe lo.

358. "Minape un lena wakaġe c'un etanhan tokśa tukte ehan
maka sitomniyan śunka-wakan yukanpikte lo.

359. "Tokeśke he tokeya wakaġa yunkan elahcin iyacu we lo,
hecetu we lo, takoża," eya ke'.

360. "Ho, le yagle c'eyaś hakiktaśni gla yo. Ehanke blo wan el
iyaya he cinhan hehanl nakeś hakikta yo. Tokaś ohpe wanżi ni-
hakap yapikte sece. Hecetu hantanhanś hena nitawakte lo," eya
ke'.

361. Canke hetan glicu nan hinzila kin ecela gluha ku k'eyaś

hakiktaśni ku nan wana ehanke bloya wanka ce el iyahin nan akotanhan wicoti kin otaninyan glinazin canke nakeś hakikta yunkan
śunkakan eyapila kin blaye kin ataya ihakap ahinazin ke'.

362. Hunh cincala iyowaś'iya unpi ca kakel-inazinpi kin hecena azin inyankapi ke'.

363. Sunkakan waśteśtepi canke awicaki-inahni k'eyaś tikiyela
gla yunkan tuwenihcin unśni ke'.

364. Nakeś wana hokśila wan mayatanhan inyank ku nan "Ate,
he niye k'eyaś ozuye ca watakpe-upi keyapi nan iyuha napape lo.
Miye ko owapa k'eyaś nake, 'Ate hee yelo,' epin nan inyank wagli-
yaku k'un," eya ke'.

365. Canke Cetan-maza iyuśkinhca, "To, tanyan ecanun we lo,
cinkś; ho, ekta yin nan 'Tunkaśila, ate gli nan taku k'eya awicagli
ca iyuha yakupikte lo,' eya yo," eya canke mayatakiya inyankela
ke'.

366. Oyaka canke oyate kin taku wanyakapiktehcin un lila
aglihunni nan tunweni śunka-wakan wanwicayakapiśni nakeś
lena tokaheyapi canke okśan itunpa wicanazinpi, yunkan Cetan-
maza heya ke':

367. "Ho, ihankeya nazin kin he hiyukte lo," eya canke hiyu
yunkan śunka-wakan kin wanzi oigluspe-kiyin nan hehanl iyo-
kihe kin he ecun nan hecel ayin nan ecel iyuha wanzi yuhapi ke'.

368. Ake piya okawinh-gli nan ake, nan ake. Hecel wana wi-
casa iyuha śunka-wakan top wicayuhapi śke'. Heciyatanhan ca le
wicoh'an kin u keyape lo. Wicaśa wanzi unśiya icaga keś wana
tohanl śunka wakan top okihi canśna hetanhan wicaśa-kiyapi kin
he.

369. Hecena ota ena unpi canke hena Cetan-maza cinca kici
gluhapi ke'.

370. Hehanl Cetan-maza heya ke: "Cinkś, pahata unyankinkte
lo. Taku wan lila tkeya awacanmi ca nayah'unkte," eya canke kici
iyahin nan wana ekta yankapi yunkan wiyohinyanpatakiya etunwan yankapi canke hecetkiya epazo nan heya ke':

371. "Ho, cinkś, kakiyotan maka-opapun kin ekta imacage lo.
Wicahcala wan winunhcala wan kici icahmayanpi nan lila temahi-
lape śan ihawicawaktaśni omani-wahiyu we lo.

372. "K'eyaś tokśa tohanl icimani-wakapin k̇inhan ekta wica-wagninkta kepa ca lehanhunniyan amapepi k'eyaś wicawagnaye lo.

373. "Hehehe, tunk̇aśila ahitunwan yank̇ahela sece lo, cinkś. Ca oyak̇ihi nan tawat'elyaya hecinhan ekta ninkte lo. Nan leci oyate-tanka el imatancan nan henak̇eh̄cin wacinmayanpi cank̇e ih̄peya iwicaglabla owak̇ihiśni ca olakinkte lo.

374. "Nan nitunk̇aśila iyeś leci uwicayaśikte lo. T̄okśa le-anṗetu kin śunka-wakan maka owancaya oblubleca ca tohanl hena ekta ihunnipi k̇inhan hu-ya upikte lo. Lena un iyeniciyinkta ce yuha nan iyaya yo. . waktaya omani yo, cinkś, canku ogna tak̇u wakan yunk̇e lo," eya cank̇e wana k̇a iyaya ke'.

375. [Nakunś leya keyaṗ śan weksuyeśni'.] "Cinkś, wiyoh̄pe-yata oyate wan la-namah̄unpi ca hena tak̇uwicawaye lo. T̄ohanl oteh̄i wanźi el nawaźin canśna hena omak̇iyaṗe lo. Ca niś eya wonihinciye nihiyagla hantanhanś 'Cetan-maza atewaya ca Pte-hincala Luta emakiyaṗe lo,' eya yo, tokśa hihunnipi nan oni-ciyapikte," eya śke'.

376. K'eyaś hokśila cank̇e k̇atinyeya yeśni ke'. "Towaś waziya-tak̇iya s'e yukśanyan wahiyayinkte, makoce wanblakinkta ca," eyin nan heceś yahan ke'.

377. Yunkan wicoti wan k̇akiya otanin cank̇e wana ecetkiya cank̇uya yunkan kuśeya woheśma-mahel cawegna nan wikośk̇a-lak̇a wan lila winyan waśte ca iśta kin ehaś asin-sloyapi s'e, haco-cola makik̇ceya h̄paya cank̇e ali tka-ke'.

378. "T̄okeśke le nunk̇a he?" eya yunkan "Niyate k̇ici woyag-laka ca nawah̄'un nan letkiya yaukta k̇ehe c'un he nakun na-wah̄'un we.

379. "Nan atayela wicotita yai hantanhanś tunweni wanciyak-inkteśni kin slolwaya ca le kuśeya munk̇e. Ena un na, tokśa miye tok̇eya wagnin nan ehank̇ela yaunkte, tipi wan tiihank̇e el han ca he wati ye," eya ke'.

380. Cank̇e hena k̇ici un nan itehan yunkan winyan kin iśnala kigla ke'. Ohak̇aṗ iś eya ekta i yunkan tipi wan ke c'un hel hokśi-cala wan nakeś-tunpila-iteya ho-kinśyela ceyela cank̇e tima i ke'.

381. Hokśilala wan watoketuka ca hokśicalala wan lila ćiśćila ca awanyak̇ela k'eyaś nunpin locinpi cank̇e ceyahanpi ke'.

382. "Ťoka huwo?" eya yunkan "Tanke canmahetankan gli yunkan le ikpi-gnak gli nan tun nan ihpeya iyaya ca le awanblake lo. Hanhepi ake wicaśa wan kici iye lo," eya ke'.

383. "Hunhi, hecetu hecinhan le micinca ye lo. Ce tanhan tanyan awanmiciyanka yo" eyin nan inapin nan wakinyan kin hoyewicakiya ke'.

384. Yunkan agna yankeśni s'e wakinyan agli nan huhuġahe sekse hiyuyapi ca tahca wan kiktepi canke patin nan taśaka kin he lolopyin nan wahanpi-kaġa ke'.

385. Nan heya ke: "Ho, tanhan, tacantoġe kin icu nan pahlokin nan etan wahanpi kin le nitunśkala ażin-kiya yo. Nan tapi kin śpanśni cikciscila waśpuśpu nan k'u wo. Ťokśa napcinkte," eya canke hokśila k'un tunśkakula kin awanglaka ke'.

386. Yunkan ungna anpetu wan el hokśila k'un tiyoceyahan canke Ptehincala Luta el eyokas'in yunkan heya ke: "Tanke gli nan leya lo: 'Cewinś kiwakanyeś le icahye-wacani ke!' eyin nan nunpin iciyaunpapi ca ksuyeunyanpe lo," eya ke'.

387. Canke wicakigna nan "Ehankel e he taku-winyanka ca magnaye lo!" ecin ke, nan śteic'ila ke'.

388. Ake tahca wan wakinyan ktewicakiyin nan agli yunkan hokśila kin taśaka kin hena iciyakaśkin nan pusya otkeya ke'. Nan wana wakanheżala kin śkehanhanla yunkan taśaka kin hena napokaśkela kin el iyakaśka ke'.

389. Hecun nan eya tanhanku kin hecel eyeśi canke, paha wan akanl tunśkakula kin gluha inażin nan heya ke: "Iyuha nah'unpi ye. Tanhan unspemakiye cin ogna waepinkte! Mitunśkala iyotiye-kiya icahwakiye c'un, hunk-cola k'eyaś bluicaġela k'un, he nakicih'unpi ye.

390. "Letanhan tokatakiya caże yukinkte lo. Taśaka-Yuślaśla eciyapikte lo. Ca wicacaże kin he oyate egna otaninyan unkte lo!" eya yunkan wakanheżala kin nah'unla s'e śkehanhanla nan taśaka ślaśla-hingla śkanla śke'.

391. Yunkan tankeku-witkowin k'un ake tokiyatanhan glihunni nan "Lowacin ye. Tahca yatahanpi kin toka ca omayak'u śni. Ecanl le ece yuha yaśkan nan caże ko laotanin ye. Tantanyan-icaġeca ca!" eya ke'.

392. Hecena ake tokiyotan iyaya canke Ptehincala-luta lila can-

zeka ke'. "Nituńśkala ikikcu nan kakiya can-wakan kin hel oḣlate inażin yo. Kola awowicawaylakinkte!" eya canke ecun ke'.

393. Yunkan wakinyan kin iśiksin-agli nan maḣpiya-glakinyan ataya oile s'e okiwanżila tunwanpi ke'.

394. Canke hokśilala k'un tunśkaku kici iśtogmus oiyanicapila yunkan wana kaska iyaya canke wanyakapi yunkan tankeku wan winyan-witkowin k'un he ticokaṗ kablaś t'a ḣpayin nan ikiyela wicaśa wan hehanl kici un yunkan he iś eya t'a ḣpayin nan oyate-unmapi kin iyuha tokaḣ'anpi ke'.

395. Yunkan ehank'un hena igmun-tanka-oyatepi ca maka owancaya abeya napapi nan hehantan tunweni inunpa witayela ośpayetunyan un-iyowinwicakiyaṗśni ke'. Ecakel ocin śicapi kin he un.

396. Hokśilala wan tunśkaku nikiyela k'un hecela wowakan k'upila canke waokihiya ula ke'. "Nituńśkala awanglaka yo. Tokśa lel wagli nan aciglapikte," eya ke'.

397. Hetanhan wana yin nan tunkaśitkula wan taśiyakpnunpa-wicaśala k'un he ti kin etkiya owotanla nakeś ya ke'.

398. Wana kiyela ihunni yunkan pażola wan akanl tuwa iśnala holyela yankahan canke tokeya wiyunk-wacin el ya ke'.

399. Kiyela ya yunkan he wicaḣcalala ca wiyohṗeyatakiya etunwan yankin nan ceyahan ke'.

400. Anaġoptan inazin yunkan heyahan ke: "Takoża, yaglikta kehe cik'un. Toki ilala huwo? A-hun-hun! A-hun-hun!" eyin nanśna wana tehan-heyelayelaka awicakehanhan-caokit'a ke'.

401. Canke el i nan "Tunkaśila, ayaśtan yo. Ate wahośi-umaśi ca le wanciglak-wahi ye lo.

402. "Ate leye lo: 'Tunkaśila okiyaka yo: tohanl icimani-im-namic'iye cinhan waglikte lo, epa tka leciya oyate wan tanka awanwicablaka canke toka-wakuśni ye lo.

403. 'K'eyaś le-anṗetu kin śunka-wakan k'eya maka owancaya wicabluobleca ca tohanl tunkaśila taoyate kin ekta ihunnipi kin-han hena hu-ya ekta maku kte lo, taoyate oṗ,'—ate heye lo, tun-kaśila." eya ke'.

404. Yunkan śika wicaḣcalala kin wana tunweni iḣaśni ceyapi ece ecunla k'un kitaḣcin wiyuśkin nan yuśinśinyela iḣa canlwaś-teya kici ki ke'.

405. "Winunhcala, mitakoża Ptehincala Luta le e ca gli ye lo. Takoża Cetan-maza le cinca caś eyaś glaotanin k'un, le e ye lo! Nakunś takoża, lecala Taśaka-yuślaśla eic'iya wan nicinca keyapi ca nawah'un we lo," eya ke'.

406. Heceś kunśitkula k'un cancan s'e wokihin nan wok'u canke wotin nan asnikiya hpaye cin el okśantanhan wanyak-ahi ke'.

407. Śunka-wakan ahikta oyaka canke lila ikik'opi nan wanwi-cayak-inahnipi ke'. Nan iyuhahcin wiyohpeyata Cetan-maza taoy-ate kin ekta wicayapiktan nan heci eca-unpikta keyapi śke'.

408. Wana akiyagla canke iśtinmapikta yunkan, kan kin iś heyaps'a ke cin, wicahcalala kin iglaśicela ke'.

409. "Takoża, lila tanyan tuweni tokayeśni waunca yunkan le-cala s'e toka wan tehiya makuwa ye lo.

410. "Hankeya wacin yewayeśni nan 'Hinyanka yo, tokśa tak-oża micigli kinhan kici ecanunkte!' epahe c'eyaś niyate toki iyaya taninśni canke wana lehan-i ihaha-makuwa ye lo," eya ke'.

411. Canke, "Tokaśni ye lo, tunkaśila. Ate tawowakan kin munkta-iyowinmakiya lo. Ca tokśa hinhanna kinhan el mninkta ce, iśtinma yo," eya ke'.

412. Wana hinhanna tkaś ekta i yunkan he toka k'un he sinte-hla ca tuktel taśiyaknunpa wahohpi-glepi can peżi-egna canke ekta kakśa iyunkin nanśna witka kin wicakiyahuge s'a ke'. Ho, k'eyaś wakinyan wicakipan canke hipi nan kte-ihpeyapi ke'.

413. Yunkan wanaś śunka-wakan k'un wiyohpeyata paha wan glakinyan yanka yunkan he hiyahanpi canke Ptehincala Luta iyuha awicagli nan wicakpamni ke'.

414. Heceś oyate kin ataya iglakapi nan wana h'anhiya wiyoh-peyatakiya yapi k'eyaś kohan Ptehincala Luta oh'ankoya kigla ke'.

415. "Ate, wana tunkaśila taoyate op upe lo," eya canke ya-otaninpi ca wiyeya oyate kin yankapi ke'.

416. Yunkan wetu hanl hinhannahcin wanżi tokeyalahcin hi-hunni nan pażolala wan akanl hinażin nan eyapahala ke: "Ptehin-cala Pi Napin!"

417. Yunkan Cetan-maza tunkaśitkula k'un he e ca iyekiyin na gliyoi ke'.

418. Onaḣ'un-waśteya hotaninla canḱe oyate kin iḱiblezapi nan wiyusḱinyan itḱokipapila ke'.

419. Ho, hetanhan ca le wetu can wana tohanl taśiyaknunpa kin maku ziyehċin aglila nan hotunpi nan "Ptehincala pi naṗin!" eyapila can ake piya wicaḱini ye lo.

Susan Mabel Deloria's drawing of the basket made by the bird nations. *Courtesy of the Dakota Indian Foundation.*

Iron Hawk: Oglala Culture Hero

The English Translation

1. Where the sun emerges, there in a certain yonder spot was a camp of small people.

2. And some distance from the circle, there stood a little tent alone, and there a little old man and a little old woman lived.

3. Now, both were of a naturally small nation of people, but they were even smaller, yet they were very energetic, and the woman was especially quick and alert.

4. So one day her husband was sitting indoors beside a dead fire and smoking; with eyes shut he was meditating, and now and again he puffed on his pipe, and so he sat.

5. It was windy outside, so his little wife was adjusting the tipi-flaps, and she happened to appear, just her head thrust inside the door, and she said:

6. "Old man, I think I'll go for firewood; by and by, when it is evening I will return to cook." So, without any attempt to open his eyes he said, "Very well, then; why not!"

7. So with thong-rope coiled she was going as if flying, so fleet she was, a little somebody characterized by her tendency to walk pigeon-toed; and disappeared into the wood.

8. But suddenly she stopped short; she saw something . . . and there where the recent floods had matted down the red grass like a ground covering of straw, in the midst of it a newborn babe lay howling and kicking.

9. It lay still attached by its cord, "O! O! My grandson! My grandson!" So saying, half-crying, she took up a piece of bark with an edge like a sharp blade, and with it she cut his cord, and then took him up.

10. And the little thing stopped his howling instantly, so she

57

said, "Well, Grandson, has somebody, to hide her shame, left you here thinking you would die?

11. "But you shall not die, Grandson! . . . red grass is sacred . . . lying on it thus, how could you die?" In such words she comforted him.

12–13. Immediately now, formerly so seriously intent on wood-gathering, shrilly she ran shouting, so the old man came outside.

14. "Husband, I bring our grandson home! . . . somebody trying hard to hide her shame left him in the wilds but I bring him home . . . she thought to cause his death but I have already spoken it out loud, 'He shall not die, my grandson!'" she said.

15. As for the old man, enthusiastically he went towards them, "Come mine! come mine!" In such words he went reaching out for him and took him.

16. "Hao, hao, Grandson, when days are overcast and I am gloomy, is it possible after all that I shall have something to cheer me up!" Saying it he went into the tipi bearing the babe.

17. It was evening, the sun was now set, and the infant cried. So his grandfather mixed red paint and fat together, and with it he went all over the little body, anointing it and rubbing it, and saying at the same time:

18. "My grandson, though he is without his natural fare, yet I shall raise him . . . Grandson, to the south is a day, indistinct, which shall come to soothe little children; so, Grandson, you too he will soothe; yours shall be a morning's rising without body wearied by pressure (on the hard ground); then from the east a man emerges who sees the whole world face to face at once; and when he sees some pitiable one he says:

19. "'Ah, the poor thing! but just for that, he shall live!' When he thinks thus of anybody, that one does live and grow up; now then, when he sees you somewhere lost in the crowds of men, may he think thus of you, so that you may have a firm hold upon life, my grandson!" So saying he rubbed his body all over until he was asleep.

20. In the morning at dawn the old woman rose and was about to build the fire, when she hurriedly wakened her husband,

21. "Old man, get up and do look at our grandson!" so he pushed himself into a sitting position, and there was the grandson, sitting up and looking intently about the interior.

22. Starting at the base of each tipi-pole, he followed it upward with his gaze to where it ended in the cluster of poles tied together.

23. So, "That is right, Grandson, you do look about well . . . it is here that you are to grow up inside this place, so get acquainted with it!" he said and the little thing appeared to understand him.

24. Again it was evening, and the sun had set and the child was inclined to fret, so once more the old man mixed red paint and fat and rubbed it all over his body and used the same words as before, talking in the boy's behalf; and so he put him to sleep with his voice.

25. It was again morning, so the old woman got up to build her fire and went out to get firewood, and then through the tipi-walls she wakened her husband.

26. "Why say, take a look at Grandson, why do you lie there so, old man!" she said, so still in his sleep he sat up and there was his grandson, now a tall little thing, having stood up by his own power, he stood in the midst of the tent, with nothing to support him.

27. Instantly the old man, most delighted over it, said, "Well, well, Grandson, that is the way! He who is so eager to be a relation to this earth that he wants to step on it at such a tender age does himself a favor! . . . For in that way he will get a firm hold on life. You give me and yourself something to be grateful about, Grandson!" So saying, happily he talked on and on.

28. Again at sundown in the evening the little boy was fretful, so his grandmother was hard put to find how to quiet him, but he made himself more and more fretful, and finally he was crying.

29. Again his grandfather mixed red paint and fat, and with it he anointed his whole body till it was all red, and he said:

30. "Now, sleep, Grandson, sleep!" and he said such words in the child's behalf as he had spoken on previous evenings. All the while he soothed him by rubbing his body, and so he put him to sleep.

31. It was morning again, and very early the boy said, "Grand-

father, Grandmother, get up and come outside!" He repeated this continuously, so the two crowded each other in an effort to get out the door till it was hard to say which was going out first; and the boy was now tall and he stood looking over the surrounding country with satisfaction.

32. So the grandfather said, "Well, well, Grandson, Grandson, that is right! You are going to use the hills (spots where it is pushed and stretched upward) as your step-taking places, so, that you may never lose your way, get acquainted with the land!" he said.

33. Again it was evening, and now the boy would seem to be tall enough (too big to cry), but he did cry. So his grandfather anointed him all over, applying red on him, and said, "Now for the last time shall I apply my grandson's red paint for him."

34. So while putting ointment all over his body, he said what he had been saying before, and now on this, the fourth evening, he said this:

35. "Now, the man who comes out of the east and appears, looking into every face at the same instant, and spotting a pitiful one he has compassion on him, then if he further pleases to, he singles him out to wrap him in his light and sets him apart, and such a one lives a life of fame; would he would do so to you!" he said.

36. Thus, with this prayer, he decreed for him a life of prominence.

37. Next morning the boy called his grandfather outside, so he went and together they looked upon the land.

38. It was then that he taught him, his grandson. He told him the various things that he must hold sacred and said:

39. "Now, Grandson, that is called the west. There somewhere live the winged-ones, so remember that.

40. "And their helper is Wind, so each day they attend to the world. They sweep and carefully wash it, so that thereby men of earth live healthy with fresh winds entering their bodies to revive them.

41. "Over there is the north; there live the ceremonially red people, their work is the food men of earth, that is why they exist.

42. "As for that direction, that is the east, and that is where the man appears, fiercely, and takes in everybody face to face at one glance, and whom he pities and warms is strengthened thereby.

43. "Over there is the south, there lives a soother, and when he comes and sings to soothe the contents of the world, then they sleep.

44. "Overhead is where something sits holy, and he chiefest of all sits holding the world; and underneath is the earth our mother who nourishes us and makes us grow.

45. "Now, Grandson, get acquainted with this life, for it is holy," he said.

46. Thus he taught him, and then on that day he set him free; all who grow upon this earth must go forth alone one day; and that was why he did this; for the elders cannot rightly hold onto their young forever; of course when they are small, only; but now when they can help themselves, they go alone; that is the way life comes.

47. Then in the morning the old man disappeared, and long after he had not returned.

48. Then very much later he did return, and he brought a rib bone from the buffalo-bull; and for some days he was improving it and finished by bending it into a bow; and he had made a bow for shooting.

49. He had made a sacred bow for the boy, and then from chokecherry wood he fashioned arrows, and with red paint he ornamented them.

50. Having done so, then from his own head he took out a very long hair by the root, and stood holding it stretched tight and instructed him to shoot it.

51. So the boy with his wits alert stood aiming, and sent it and he split the hair in two.

52. And thus he had decreed for him that he should be a perfect marksman, so from then he was made to never miss his aim.

53. So now, so armed with weapons as it were, he wanted to go hunting and went away.

54. All day he was missing, and at evening he brought home a jackrabbit and presented it to his grandfather. It was to the west that he went and brought home the rabbit.

55. So the old man was as happy as could be and said, "Good, good! Grandson, that is right! . . . This man never gets tired in his legs; never does he give out in running . . . Now then, eat a piece of him, so that you too may not tire in the legs, that without aches in your legs you may live to the end . . . You have done yourself and me something to consider well!" (To be grateful for), he said.

56. It was again morning, and he went hunting. This time he went north and stayed all day, and when it was evening he came home with a skunk that was surpassingly fat.

57. Once more the old man, very happy, said, "Good, good, Grandson, you have done well. This man can teach you something. Throughout the night and day he forages for himself and has for his food all the smaller living beings, and so nothing hurts his intestines as he lives; we are going to eat him, so well and healthy, nothing upsetting our intestines, we shall live," he said.

58. Again it was morning and he went off hunting. This time he went towards the east, and at twilight he got home with a badger.

59. [This unit was omitted from Deloria's translation. The editor's translation follows]. Because the boy had once again accomplished exactly what he had been taught, the old man cried out as if delirious with joy:

60. "Well, well, Grandson, this man must have a special claim on the earth, for he burrows deep into it for his home. Today we are going to eat this man, so thereby we are going to be closely related to the ground," he said.

61. Instead of tiring his feet out by walking, he grew to like it the more, so "Grandfather, may I go hunting again?" he said, and "Certainly for thus you are training yourself, why should you remain at home like a woman? Certainly you shall go. Later by your continuing, finally you will bring home the chief of all food." So this time he went south.

62. In the evening he brought home a deer, so the old man fell to butchering it and talked as he worked:

63. "Well, well, it is good you have come home bringing game. Grandson, this man is especially fine . . . This somebody picks and chooses the tender grasses and the tips of trees, which are good to eat.

64. "Fastidious is this man, he chooses only food that emerges from the earth, he knows thereby he is strong and swift. We shall eat his flesh and then we too shall live with good flesh and strong." So from there the boy learned to eat fruits and whatever grew from the ground, any thing planted too, that kind he learned to use for food.

65. Now he had finished the four directions and from each had brought game, so it seemed he was through, but he went a fifth time toward the north and returned with a buffalo-calf.

66. Taking his knife, he personally ripped open the belly and took out the liver still twitching with life and warm, and gave it to his grandfather, and "Grandfather, eat this," he said, so the old man fell upon it and with great desire he tore it to pieces with his mouth; but it was comparable to nothing for its goodness.

67. He took out the pylorus also and gave it to him, "Now old woman, this you must cook for me," he said on taking it, so she did.

68. So he ate, and upon finishing he was so full of joy that he was unable to keep still.

69. "Wife, so happy I am that I think I will herald it forth," and she said, "Well, why not!"

70. At once he stood on a small knoll and with his body very straight upward, appearing so yellow of breast, he cried "Buffalo-calf liver, rich to taste!"

71. And it then appeared that after all the little man who raised the child was a meadowlark-man.

72. So to this day, even now when spring comes, he arrives and at once with joy he heralds, "Buffalo-calf liver, rich to taste!" Such have you all heard.

73. Now that his grandson was such a skillful hunter the old man was so happy he hardly knew what to do, and one evening as the boy lay asleep he stood by him and prayed:

74. "Well, well, well, how handsome is my grandson! . . . Now then, Great Spirit, may it be that tomorrow my grandson shall be a young man, strong and tall and surpassingly handsome, and may child-beloved clothing be lying here for him when dawn breaks on him!" he said.

75. Then he retired, and in the following dawn he for whom it had been prayed got up and said, "Grandfather, get up and look at me! Here what you decreed for me has all come true!" So he looked and saw that it was even beyond what he had asked.

76. "Thanks be, thanks be!, Grandson, put these on! Of all the men of earth where has anybody such a grandson!" So saying he helped him to dress.

77. Then the same day he heralded forth saying, "Now then, all peoples all over the earth, all that have life to stir on earth, hear ye!

78. "This day my grandson whom I raised without his natural food; who lay slimy in water having been left out to die but that I brought him home—that one today is to have a name, so hear it!

79. "Had I chosen, I might have called him the abandoned one, but that does not please me, so he shall be called Iron Hawk!" So all the world heard his voice, and all in one day Iron Hawk was famous.

80. He was such a good marksman that they lived well and had many visitors and did not lack for enjoyment, and then the youth said,

81. "Grandfather, you raised me, and I am grateful, and thought to live here always, hunting for you; but now for a time I have the urge to roam."

82. And the old grandfather was suddenly saddened, as if the boy had struck him in the face. "Alas, Grandson, there is falseness on the way; well enough you did live here!" So he forbade him, but though he seemed to give up for a time, invariably he again wished to travel.

83. Thrice he forbade him, and when he asked a fourth time, then the old man permitted him to go.

84. "All right then, you insist, so now you shall go," he said and gave him a holy knife and one that could cut through all dif-

ficulty it seemed, and also a cap to which two little end-claws of the great hawk were attached; and he said, "Go cautiously, there is *wakan* in the way," he said. (bad magic, in this case.)

85. So he took the presents and put on his cap and started off. Long he travelled alone, and then at last four young men, also supernaturally handsome, met up with him.

86. Smiling, looking into his face, they continued, and one said, "Well, there was a famous young man at the eastern edge of the earth named Iron Hawk! But who would have thought we would see him at this close range!"

87. So they talked, and happily they greeted him, "Now then, friend, what is your errand?" Iron Hawk, smiling, said, "Well, of course all men of my age are interested in women; so I too am traveling with such in mind, perhaps." "Well, friend, how fine; for we too are doing the same!"

88. Another said, "Come on, what is good about going our separate ways, let's all go as one!" so Iron Hawk was willing and went with them.

89. So they went along, all so handsome, and after a while they saw a lake, so they made their way thither and arrived.

90. And there along the water where the grass was short and soft, a solitary white tipi stood.

91. "Now, this is the place," they said; so they approached it, but uncannily around the tipi lay here and there human skeletons.

92. Even so, paying no heed, they went and an old woman using a staff came out and stood regarding them.

93. As they came near and stood she said, "Well, so my sons-in-law have come! . . . Come on out, such as you are, you have visitors!" And from within some very beautiful girls came out and stopped, as if very shy.

94. "Come then, Sons-in-law, these are they, do come on—to be sure," and she pushed them staggering towards the men.

95. So just as the young men would take them by the hand, one after another, as they reached them, fell crumpling to the ground when the old woman pointed her wand at them.

96. It was Iron Hawk's turn, but he was aware what was hap-

pening so he went forth alert, and as the old woman raised her staff upon his reaching for the maiden, suddenly he shot first, and with his sacred arrow his grandfather had made for him he shot her, breaking her into countless pieces that went scattering.

97. She was a Rock woman, so she lived there with more magic than everyone else, but Iron Hawk had killed her.

98. Hurriedly he made a sweat bath and revived his friends who lay as if dead, and gave them all wives, and so they took them off to their homes somewhere.

99. And lo, all of them were Thunder men, so from either side of the mouth lightning in a wavy line ran down their legs and ended in forks over their feet, and was in continuous play, shining and flashing.

100. And from the outer corners of their eyes other lines came and ran down their arms and forked at their hands; and those too were flashing constantly.

101. As they were leaving they talked to Iron Hawk: "Now, tell all your people, your fathers and mothers, your grandfathers and your grandmothers, your brothers and cousins, your female respect relations and your children, tell them all, from henceforth you shall not send forth your voice in vain.

102. "Though you lay under the earth yet we shall hear your voice if you call, and come to you.

103. "Tell it then, this day you are related to the Thunder!" they said.

104. And they spoke truthfully, so that as long as Iron Hawk lived, when he faced trouble and called on the Thunders, they being the only really speedy beings, were instantly there to help him.

105. From there he went northward and met a man out in the wilds, a tall and very distinguished looking man, well-dressed and handsome.

106. He wore a buckskin coat, heavily fringed and tanned a bright brown, and in every respect he was very well gotten up (by his own efforts).

107. "Well, well, friend Iron Hawk, is this you? Well, why say,

friend, how come you are traveling?" So again he confessed to his interest in women and the man said,

108. "Well, friend, why I too am on a similar errand, so let's go together." So they went and came up over a hill beyond which appeared a thriving tribal circle.

109. "Now, that's the place, my friend. That center-tipi is where a very handsome child-beloved lives, but her father withholds his own and says he will surrender her only to the man who can bring him a certain type of abalone shell that is found in the bottom of a pit nearby.

110. "It is very deep and the shells lie very inaccessibly, so whoever tries invariably falls in and dies there," he said.

111. "Well, friend, there is nothing but what can be attempted; how utterly hard to get they must be indeed!" Iron Hawk said, and so, at once the other said, "Well, but really it *is* a task, you have no idea! But if you wish let's go there and perhaps we can hang joined to each other, and we can try that way to get some shells." [Iron Hawk] agreed.

112. So they went to the pit, very deep with a large chamber inside, but what answered for an entrance was a hole near which there was nothing to get a footing on.

113. The man said, "Now then, I will hold tight to the edge of the opening here, and hang suspended from that, so sort of step down me as if to ease yourself downward, and have hold of my feet with one hand while you reach down with the other, and if you reach them, get a few of the shells.

114. "But you are wearing fine clothes; leave them here and try it naked; thus it will be easier for you to move, and, too, you will not tear your fine clothes." So he did exactly so.

115. Now the man, who was extra tall, hung suspended from the mouth of the pit, but though his feet seemed to reach the bottom, not quite.

116. So Iron Hawk climbed down his body, sliding down it, and with one hand grasped the feet of the man, and with the other he took up a few shells, and as the man had instructed, he tucked them into his leggings.

117. Now he was about to get some for himself, so he reached downward when suddenly the man struggled and kicked and made him weaken his grasp on the foot, so he let go and fell to the pit's bottom.

118. "Friend, what is wrong?" he called, but not holding ear to it, the man was so strong that with no trouble he eased himself out and donned Iron Hawk's clothing and went off.

119. "He did cramp my movements . . . now at last I shall go forth to be a son-in-law, without being hampered," he said; and come to find out, this was again Ikto so dressed as a child-beloved, and [he] went towards the camp.

120. And how gullible people are! As he approached, men came out to meet him, "It is Iron Hawk who comes, the child-beloved from the edge of the world, so famous from there!" Saying, they crowded each other and leading him honorably, they took him to the chief's house.

121. He drew some shells out of his leggings and presented them, so men and women sang his praises and called him brave; for he had done what nobody else could, apparently.

122. So they presented him with a wife, and all in a day he was established as a son-in-law.

123. The wife, so long pampered, was rendered vain and proud, so thinking herself well wed, she grew too mean.

124. She had a younger sister, a girl now in early womanhood, so when that one would approach her sister's home, just then she would order her off.

125. "Go away! Why must she insist on trying to glimpse my man, as if her eyes were worthy!" So she called her names, and the girl went crying somewhere. But being the youngest, nobody much looked out for her, all too preoccupied with her elder sister's marriage.

126. Meantime near the pit where Iron Hawk lay lived an old couple.

127. And the old woman, going by to hunt firewood, suddenly heard a child crying, so she stopped and listened more carefully, and verified that it was actually from the pit's bottom that someone cried out, so she lay flat and looked in.

128. Not able to see well, being poor of eyesight, and because the pit was black, yet she knew it was a child, so she said, "O dear, O dear, how more and more heartless people are growing! What is the matter with these people indeed!"

129. "Just wait, Grandchild, I will get you out!" So saying, she ran home and very soon brought a long pole with a rope tied to it and let it down.

130. "Now, child, if it is within your reach, place your foot inside the loop of rope, and hold close to the pole, I will pull you out!" So now she brought him upward, but he was very heavy.

131. She brought him up on top and saw a little boy with sores in the nape of his neck, pitiful and neglected.

132. At once putting him on her back she took him home, and the old man was overjoyed and said. "Now, old woman, well have you done . . . Can it be that Grandson will amuse me! . . . as I grow older so I am often sad, but now!" So he led the boy inside.

133. Soon afterward he said, "Grandfather I want some sinew." So, "Well, well, just what use have you for it, Grandson? . . . Say, our grandson asks for sinew, old woman!" he said, so from a small parfleche bag she took out sinew that she had.

134. So he instructed his grandfather to twist the sinew, and he crisscrossed it over a hoop, and hung the hoop indoors.

135. "Now Grandfather, with Grandmother go beyond the hill and stay there, by and by I will come to you," he said, so "Why?" he thought, as with his wife he went away.

136. Thus all alone inside in some mysterious ways he must have worked magic, but they did not see it; some time later he went after them, so they came home with him.

137. And inside were all the birds that are good for food; ducks and geese of all kinds, and pheasants too, fluttering about; but their feet were caught by one string or other.

138. With a jumble of sound they all called out, so they all but broke the eardrums of the people.

139. "Now, kill them and cook them," he commanded, so his grandfather with his friends had a great busy time chasing and killing all those birds. He ordered that the heads and feet of the birds should be laid by, which was done. He took these to the

bank, and standing there "Now, go forth and make yourselves
many!" he said as he threw them into the water, so first tens and
then hundreds in groups went with water foaming behind them.

140. "Grandmother, go and borrow a kettle, the people shall
feast," he said, but the old woman was reluctant.

141. "O dear, for so long now I lived out, I am shy. Whom
shall I borrow a kettle of and who would lend it to me!" So she
held back, but her husband spoke sharply to her: "Do as he says;
what are you saying! Here is a boy possessed with power, as though
it were an idle wish, and such we were lucky to find for our-
selves, and yet you are saying that!" So she took her shawl and
went very haltingly forth.

142. A woman lived in the end tipi, so she went there and told
her wants, and the woman was very agreeable and lent her a kettle and came home with her.

143. She helped, and they cooked all those fowls, but they
seemed to grow in amount, so it was impossible to take care of
them all.

144. The woman's husband followed her, and when Iron Hawk's
grandfather and this old man started to settle down to smoke, he
said to them:

145. "Why Grandfather, smoke any other time. Here food has
been so scarce, so now all the people shall feast; go and cry out
the invitation. So he went off, proclaiming a feast.

146. "Come now, out in the distance where a tipi stands, there
on this day you shall feast. Go there; go there; fasten your door-
ways and go there!" So he went round the circle and got back
home, but already now the people had come and sat down in
four concentric circles.

147. And lo, The Ragged Iron Hawk, as it were (the pseudo-),
arrived first, and a mat was laid out for him in the center, so he
sat there.

148. But of course they did not know, he being related as son-
in-law to the chief, he was respected, and much honored, and
several men stood round him, each with a small piece of meat
ready, enough for one chewing.

149. One after another, when he stuck out his tongue, pieces

of meat [were] placed on it. Then very slowly he took it in, and with complete deliberation he chewed on while the others stood waiting.

150. Not once did he open his eyes, with his back straight so he seemed to bend backward, with pride he sat; so the people waited while they loudly gulped down only saliva, so hungry they were.

151. After he had worn them out (practically plucked them, feather by feather), then "Now I am full!" he said, so at last they passed food out and going in among the people, they gave it out to each as they ought. So they feasted happily. By now they regarded the boy as very powerful.

152. After a few days he made a hoop and caused his grandfather to send it rolling, saying, "Grandson, there goes a buffalo!" Then, as he did, the boy stood aiming, and as it went by he sent an arrow into it, and a fat buffalo fell rolling.

153. Four times they did this, and now four buffaloes (too many to be believed as real) lay dead, so the old grandfather sharpened his knives and outdid himself butchering.

154. Then, unbelievably, the sister of the child-beloved Cokaṗti was coming from the circle. She entered and sat down.

155. Iron Hawk in the guise of a boy was sitting there, and she sat so close to him as to almost kill him by pressure. So the grandmother said, "My grandson is covered with red paint, so he might get some on you, sit away from him." And instead she said, "What if he does!" and put the boy on her lap.

156. So she sat holding him, while the grandmother cooked the choicest meats and gave her food. In a wooden bowl she set it and let her take some home, so she really left, so definitely, and then later the old man stood looking into the distance and said:

157. "Well, that young girl who left here in good spirits, look out there, alone she stands, unhappy. What has displeased her? Perhaps you didn't give her the best piece and she is pouting."

158. Later she came back saying she was returning the bowl.

159. So the old woman said, "Daughter-in-law, when you left, you stood yonder in a bad manner, it seemed, what was it?"

160. "Yes, it was because of my sister that I stood unhappy,"

she said. "When she married, I tried to glimpse him who was my brother-in-law for just one time, but she forbade me, and now after that she wanted the food you gave me for her husband; but I withheld it so she slapped me in the face," she said.

161. "O dear, why didn't you give it right over and come again! Look at all this, who is going to eat it all, pray tell?" So she cut out the very best pieces and cooked it and placed it in two hollow dishes in equal quantities and said, "now take one of these to your sister, *takoś*!" So she took them home.

162. It was morning, and then a crier went around. "Get your bows ready and straighten your arrows. The red fox is running again; it used to be said who shoots it shall have Cokaṗti, but now that she is wed, who does shoot the red fox shall have the skin for his own trophy to hang at his tipi," he said.

163. All the people with clamours raised an uproar, and this time they tried to keep their wits as they stood aiming.

164. From time immemorial when this went by, they tried to shoot it, but somehow it always clouded their senses, as it were; now after it went by they censured one another, "Why didn't you shoot it?" they said.

165. Once more they were frozen on the spot, so the boy shot it and his grandfather ran and flayed it and brought the hide to him.

166. Again at exact noon they cried, "Now again it comes, the red eagle; this time stand ready, and at least one of you try to shoot it!" they cried, but it approached awesomely indeed.

167. It flew so low that as they stood looking up they could see its black and cruel eyes staring at them. So they were stricken with fear and nobody shot, so only the boy sent an arrow and brought it down.

168. Instantly his grandfather ran to pull out the feathers and brought them, not to be likened to anything for color; and they hung them up.

169. But of course this was out from the camp circle so the people did not know, and continued scolding each other.

170. "Grandmother, go and borrow a kettle," he said, so again she went to the one who had formerly lent her a large one, and

now many people were about so they all helped, and they gave a feast with the choicest parts of buffalo which all cooked. And the pseudo-Iron Hawk came first and spent much time posing.

171. In the morning a woman was coming from camp so the old woman watched and waited; and she arrived saying, "Sister-in-law, I was sent on an errand, but I came fast on it because you have fine meats and I thought I might get a piece to eat," she said jokingly.

172. "O yes, it is good you have come, Sister-in-law; food is so abundant who is able to consume it all! Go inside, I will cook for you." So now after a time she set out food for her, so she satisfied her hunger thoroughly and on finishing she said,

173. "Now, this is what I bring: I have come for the boy you have; Cokapti's sister wants to marry him," she said, and at once the old woman's face changed . . . long still she sat, and at last,

174. "O, surely not, Sister-in-law! To be sure my grandchild has supernatural power, but after all he is still a child, . . . more-over, he is quite homely, how would anyone want to marry him! Sister-in-law, perhaps they make sport of us?"

175. But the boy who sat hearing said, "Go and tell this: She is to come and turn about here before me, to start back, and as she turns she must say, 'I come to invite you.' After she returns, I will go there. If I arrive there but she fails to recognize and take hold of me, I will return home . . . four times she is to invite me, and I will go there four times . . . and if she fails all the time, well then, just hear this, I will never marry her!" he said.

176. So with that message the woman went away and told it, and at the chief's home there was great excitement. And already a beautiful white tipi was being erected so everywhere people were saying, "My, I wonder what that's for!" and some there are who always seem to have heard what is going on, and they said, "Haven't you heard? Why that sacred boy is going to be presented with a wife, that's what the activities are for; can it be you do not know?"

177. Meantime the boy asked his grandparents to go outside and wait beyond the hill, so now because he always has some wis-dom back of his requests, they went without questioning why.

178. "Sit there, when I come after you, or when I decide to remain at that place (the chief's), then you may return," he said.

179. Now, as it was going to be, the younger daughter of the chief made herself attractive and was coming, so indoors in the honor-place he sat in sight, and she entered without a word, and turned to go, and said, "I have come to invite you!" So he said, "very well," but still he sat, and she went home.

180. About the time she reached her home, he went there, with a holy body he went.

181. As he neared the place, while they all stood watching, he threw himself to the ground and rolled and stood up, a grey-horn, hollow-horn buffalo, passing extra fine, about a two-year-old.

182. Then directly pawing the ground he came, so he frightened the people and made them scatter to make way for him; and he went and in the very faces of the girl and her father where they stood, but instead (of catching hold of him) she hid her face and cried out, . . . afraid of him, so then he turned and came home, and becoming a man again he sat down.

183. Three times he did this, but each time she feared and did not touch him. The second time he was a slippery-horn buffalo, and the third time it was a great-buffalo but the kind called "*He-kaġipa.*"

184. When she failed the third time, the girl's father scolded her. "Daughter, I think highly of you, I raised you, lacking nothing, now you have the chance to benefit the entire tribe and you fail.

185. "This boy has *wakan*-power attached to him, so he is to be relied on, yet you are going to miss hold on him, the way you are acting.

186. "Remember this, Daughter, he comes for the last time. If you fail again to hold him, I shall consider it an easier thing to have you dead, and this failure I shall find harder to bear because you are going to bring evil on the people," so, holding onto her for emphasis, he warned her and now she stood ready.

187. And again the boy approached, and when he rolled close by he was an ancient-bull, with horns worn to the head (worn down to the base). Fearsomely he came running.

188. Almost knocking the girl down he came directly at her,

but she thought only of her father's stern warning, so she suddenly reached out with eyes tight shut, and took hold of him somewhere.

189. Immediately there was confusion, and then all recovered their senses, and lo, a helpless little boy had been knocked down and his nose was bleeding as he arose.

190. So now the holy boy and the woman given him lived in the white tipi.

191. Outside it there was a feast and it was a feast never surpassed in greatness; so everyone had part in it.

192. The boy's grandmother contributed good things too, and the newly married ones sat indoors and were eating when her sister, (why didn't she continue being proud?) now lured by the feast, came and stood looking into the doorway.

193. Now it was her turn, and the sister ordered her off, "No, Elder Sister, stay outdoors, we are yet soiled and full of lice, perhaps . . ." so she said, so the sister went off weeping.

194. Somewhere she must have allowed her tears to go back in, and now she sent for her father, "What is it, Daughter?" he asked, and she said, "Father, always you have said you have me for your favorite daughter, and that my sister being younger somehow grew up unnoticed, yet she, now she has taken a famous husband, is very vain from it, and makes sport of me.

195. "Tomorrow I want ten men to be sent by you to my tipi. There my husband has brought me some ceremonially red trophies, so I want them to be set up over my home that the people may see them." So the father said, "All right, I will send them, Daughter; do not be unhappy; your sister is still too young to have a settled heart, that is why she has done so," he said.

196. And soon after, the girl also sent for her father, so he went. "Father tomorrow will you send five men here?" she said. So the father said he would.

197. Now it was evening, and the holy boy sent for his grandmother too, and she came. "What is it, Grandson?"—"Grandmother, go to that yellow-legged one who lives within the camp circle and say to him, 'Iktomi, Iron Hawk sends for his clothes, you have been wearing them long enough!' Say so to him."

198. So the old woman, confused in her mind, went and stood in the doorway and inside many men who were visiting were seated with him and smoking.

199. "O, go along away! you can't come here!" once again Co-kaṗti said, but paying no heed, "Yellow-legged Spider, Iron Hawk sends for his clothes, you have worn them long enough!" she said.

200. "Well, of all the nerve!"—"She is just a foolish old thing!" so the men said, but Iktomi, smiling, called, "Pass them to her, pass them to her!" And he sent out the clothes he wore when he took a wife, so the old woman brought them home and went in, and there sat her grandson, apparently not the same as the little boy with sores in the nape of his neck whom she drew out of a pit; so he was Iron Hawk all the time! How handsomely he had righted himself, and he sat smoking.

201. He put on his clothes and called his wife: "Tell your sister to come," he said, so although they had recently hurt each other's feelings, she went and said, "Sister, he sends for you!" So she came.

202. When she was seated indoors, he said, "Now, Sister-in-law, you and your sister have used bad words to each other, you rated yourself as inaccessible, while your sister was more gener-ous, and now she is my wife.

203. "Perhaps you will think—now that my brother-in-law has elevated himself, he may be mean to me,—but do not think that; see that you do not," he said.

204. No doubt her heart had been heavy, for when he said that she was suddenly very relieved and happy; for it is especially hard when folk of one household turn against each other.

205. "Now go along, let us go to the wilds," he said, so his wife went with him. And there with no eyes to spy, he made her lie down and changed her into a cow. And he too rolled and stood up, a short-horn bull. And there he made her a young, and again in their human form they returned.

206. But while they still retained their buffalo form, he said, "Go meandering all over this plain, and drop buffalo hair as you go." So the beautiful cow did so, and then they rolled and became Dakotas again.

207. Now ten men came to Cokápti's home, so she gave them the packages her husband had brought her, and they revealed a common coyote skin, apparently the fur of a mangy coyote, and some crow feathers that were not perfect; so according to instructions they tied them to the tip of the lodge pole and went away.

208. And then five men went to Iron Hawk's home, and his wife gave them a bundle which they untied, and there was the scarlet hide of the sacred fox, which so many had tried and failed to shoot, and that eagle who seemed to live but to frighten the people—its feathers, as though dipped in blood, were brought to light.

209. So they tied them to the tipi top, and from all sides everyone came to see them, and crowds stood about the tipi.

210. Then again Iron Hawk said, "Now collect all the arrows you own, I want them," so they did so and brought them, and then he sent two scouts forth.

211. That was the first time what is commonly called "Being sent to the hills" was instituted.

212. First they feasted them, and when they were well satisfied, they sent them out to scout, so they went and climbed to a distant hill within sight of the tribe, while men watched from home.

213. Then all of a sudden they ran back and forth and threw their robes upward and then came rushing home.

214. Then Iron Hawk smoked with them, and said, "Now, young men, over the hills and vales always you roam about, at what special place it may have been that you saw something good, then tell it; and if you do not fool me, then point out the direction with your thumb!"

215. So they did and said that buffaloes have come beyond a certain hill and filled the place beyond, so it looked as if covered with black. "You make me grateful!" Iron Hawk said. (Thence the custom of buffalo scouts using the thumb to designate the presence of buffalo, if they are speaking true.)

216. "Now all stay quiet here," he said, so now because he so lived that it was not possible to overstep his commands, they obeyed and stayed.

217. So then he and his wife and the ten young men whom he

selected, and the collected arrows which he caused them to carry—
that many went out.

218. And out of sight he caused his wife to lie down in a hollow, and then threw a buffalo-hide over her, and commanded her to roll under it; and she stood up as a handsome buffalo-cow.

219. "Now, go among the buffalo, and then come and circle about me and go back out again; four times you are to do this, while these with arrows will stand ready behind me," he said.

220. So she went among the herd and walked about and the buffaloes grew restive and couldn't stand still, and they made advances towards her, and followed her part way when she left, but then they turned back.

221. Each of the four times they grew bolder and came closer, and the fourth time they simply accompanied her and crowded each other all around Iron Hawk.

222. So the ten young men, stationed ready behind him, now shot off arrows rapidly one after another and didn't miss aim one time; each and every arrow killed a buffalo. Of course long before it had been decreed for Iron Hawk that he should never miss a shot, and so he was able to cause the ten to do this.

223. Then he ordered them to collect all the arrows, and also all the tongues. "As for me, I will go on ahead," he said, and with his wife they came on home.

224. "Now you may all go to get meat!" So instantly the people—poor things, always so eager when food is available!—now went and amidst great activity they all went to the scene.

225. They walked, of course, so it was a great task to get that much meat home; but it was too good to be true that there was actually meat, so carrying it in blanket loads they brought it home, and for once in their lives they were satisfied and had a superabundance.

226. All day they hauled meat, and when nighttime darkened the scene, they had finished, and then they feasted and danced happily.

227. Soon after this the woman went out only with her husband to the wild places, and there in the form of a cow she kicked

and labored and brought forth her young, the most perfect little calf that ever was.

228. It being Iron Hawk's child, and a boy, he was overjoyed and proclaimed his name: After the manner of his little meadow-lark grandfather he announced it and did it in the same way.

229. A little calf, reddish tawny, very small yet already perky, ran about, so he caught it and holding it he stood, and though nobody was around, he called out and said:

230. "Now all, whatever lives all over this world; whatever has life and moves thereon, and the winged beings too, listen!

231. "This day a boy is born to me, so I am proud and happy and now he shall have a name, 'Red Calf' he shall be called! Wherever you see him, mine, if he appears to have trouble, take pity on him for me, my friends!" he said.

232. Having done so, they were again in Dakota form, and a beautiful baby, not yet with eyes opened, they brought him back, so all the people came to see him.

233. As he grew older, that grandfather who took Iron Hawk from the pit, often came to sit and hold his little grandson.

234. When it was very energetic and full of action, the old man said, "Grandson, your father-in-law already has four grand-children. They are the children of yellow-legged Iktomi so they are not what they might be, but they are his grandsons, so he continually has them about; so I would like to take this one and teach him," so Iron Hawk said, "All right, it is as you wish!"

235. So he taught him to walk, and talk, and play.

236. He made toy arrows for him and taught him to shoot, so the little boy always stayed close to his grandfather through fond-ness. "Now shall my grandchild be tall!" he decreed, and it was so.

237. Thus they lived on, and suddenly Iron Hawk returned from the center of the camp, and back of his lodge was his wife, fleshing a robe.

238. And the boy, now tall, ran around with his arrows, so he came to him and said, "now, Son, I have a grandfather at the edge of the world, there he raised me, and he gave these to me, this cap, and this knife and these bow-and-arrows.

239. "That grandfather heard when I announced your name, so he will always know you by these tokens, take a good look at them, and some day when something happens to me, take them and go to him," he said.

240. And that displeased his wife. "The idea! . . . it is sacred, to say that! (offence against taboo.) Why should anything happen to you?" she scolded.

241. But then he laughed, "Say, it is very warm, let's go swimming, you ought to have enough done by now," but she was unwilling. "O, this is all I have left to do, so little, I do want to finish before sundown," she said in objecting.

242. Thrice he asked her but she refused, so the fourth time he begged her with embraces to go with him.

243. But even that was useless, so then, for want of anything more to say, "Well then, I shall go alone," he said, and went.

244. The water flowed at a good rate, and it was not such a wide stream, but it was the kind of river bed wherein one can wade for a time, and then suddenly it is beyond one's depth— such it was.

245. The cooling water woke him up, and so he swam with vigorous strokes, and then he climbed to the bank and sat to rest, letting the sun warm him.

246. And suddenly somebody from somewhere shouted, calling him by name. "Iron Hawk!" she said, and it was a very beautiful woman-voice.

247. He sat up very straight and listened, and again she called, "Iron Hawk, from far away I have come to see you; do come over here! You who live in a way to demand fame, you being so, I have come to you!" and he saw that the call came from across the river.

248. "Why, it is deep, so I can't come over!" he called back, but again she asked, so impatiently he called, "It is deep, I can't come, I tell you!" but still she called him.

249. "Well! Isn't she unbearable! . . . if you are so anxious to see me, why don't you come over here?" he said, but she complained she could not cross.

250. So then, "Well, I have already made it plain! If it is impossible for you to come over here, it is just as much so for me to

cross to you!" Yet she asked a fourth time, so then, "All right then!" he called and rolled a few times in a wallow, and rose, a short-horned buffalo, solid and powerful.

251. Instantly he threw himself into the water, and the current was swift so even a bull had to struggle hard to get across.

252. And there among the tall grasses was a short, heavy-set but very pretty girl, who kept looking into his face, smiling.

253. "All right now, you invited me, and here I am. How are we going to cross back?" he said, and she said, "O, I shall sit on the small of your back and hold onto your hump." So he agreed to that.

254. Now again into the water with her on his back he threw himself and swam back, and when he was in midstream, suddenly she started to raise him up, and he was conscious of it.

255. With all his might he struggled, shook his whole frame, and tried to make himself heavy, but quite easily, as though fishing him out of water by a single grasp, she took him upward.

256. After a time, though they were not flying, they travelled toward the sky, and as they went the world grew smaller, and finally it disappeared, and way up there was a small hole through which they entered into the sky world.

257. It was now dark, but he had not returned, so the boy was fretful, so he asked for his father.

258. "Sit quiet son, your father went swimming; by and by when he is through, he will come home," she kept saying, but after a time she too became worried, so she told it, and then though it was the kind of night when the darkness is very black, they greased sticks and lighted them, and hunted for him all up and down the shores.

259. All the people made small, as it were, by their concentration on one thing, hunted all night, calling to him, but they did not find him by dawn.

260. At the very beginning she had first looked for him and called to him and he hadn't answered, so she had given the alarm, "Come here, all, do! My husband has gone somewhere . . . Mine has drowned, perhaps!" she had cried, so they had hunted for him, but now they had all gone home, and so again all alone,

"Iron Hawk, where have you gone?" weeping and calling, she roamed about.

261. "He has drowned," was the general verdict, so she was weeping over it but her son said, "Mother, just where was it father always went to swim? Take me there!" so she took him, and there were his moccasins and clothing that he had worn, all lying in the grass.

262. And the boy sat right down on the spot and said, "Mother, go home, here I will wait for my father." So the mother was alarmed, "No, Son, your father has drowned. If you sat here all alone, he would never return, and something might befall you too!" she said, in refusing to leave him.

263. Four times she forbade him, but when he would not obey her and was still determined, she finally said, "All right then. It was because I insisted on my own way that this happened in the first place," so she murmured, talking to herself as she stood.

264. "Well then Son, be on your guard as you sit here. By and by I will come to you," she said and left him. So when he was alone, he put on the magic cap, and with his magic knife and bow in his hand he said,

265. "Now then, Grandfather, wherever you sit in the east, hear me! You it was gave these to my father, and with them certain power and strength; and that power and strength I now beg of you. These my father left behind and went off, taking only his body, so I want to go out to seek him!"

266. Instantly he made himself into a great hawk, and very directly upward, so effortless as to seem as though he stood still, he soared upward, and through that small opening into the sky he entered the upper world.

267. Right near there in a circle were a people camped, and from them came a man with his head bound in a black fillet, and these were Śkibibila (Chickadee people). And he said:

268. "Well, young man, they brought your father here, so all the people saw him. Just about here he was exhibited, so the onlookers stood in a ring, and here are the tracks they left . . . But since then it is now nine days!"

269. So he went on from there and arrived at another camp.

From there a little man with his shirt-front well blackened with soot came to meet him and said,

270. "Well, they said a boy was coming to seek his father, can it be you? Well then, they stopped here with your father to exhibit him, and so the people in a great circle had their fill of seeing, and then they took him on . . . but since that time it is now eight days!" And these people were the birds known as the black-breasts.

271. Again he reached a camp, and a man came to him. That nation was made up of the birds called "Big—without eyes," those who return so promptly in the spring, and without so much as any fear like, "They might freeze for me," they promptly lay their eggs. That is the kind these were. They wear black around their heads and their collars, and otherwise they are grey.

272. "Well boy, your father was brought here and shown, and the people outdid themselves as spectators; right here you can see the tracks they left in a ring . . . but it is now seven days since then," he said.

273. Again he arrived at a camp, and the people were those birds called "Wings-of-eagles" (common snowbirds); they are the ones that stay on all through the winter. One came to him, saying, "Well boy, already it has been spread abroad that someone would seek his father; that boy must be you. They stopped here to exhibit your father, and because the people had never seen a man of the earth, they piled up on each other to see . . . but that was six days ago."

274. So at once he sat out from there and came to a camp. And that was made of those very little birds called bluebirds. They constitued this tribe.

275. From camp a man well painted in blue came to him. "Well, well, it was told that Iron Hawk's son is seeking his father! Well now, your father was brought here, so the people feasted their eyes . . . but it was five days ago."

276. So again he went and came to a tribal camp and rested nearby. And a man with red paint came out to him. These were the redbirds who formed this tribe.

277. In about the same way as the others he said, "Alas, now it is four days since your father was taken on from here."

278. Gradually they were indicating a place nearer and nearer in point of time, so he braced up at the thought, and again he went on, and he arrived at another camp.

279. And those were the robin tribe. Birds of a red-yellow coat with grey on the shoulders—such they were. And they said, "Since your father was taken on from here, three days have passed."

280. So he went on, and came to a tribe made up of very vociferous people. One could hardly distinguish what they were all saying, so universal was the chatter. You know those birds, blue-black, they insist on remaining in the corn-field and will not be driven away,—such they were, (Bluejays, I think.)

281. "Well well, friend, it is good you have come! Stay here with us! Please!" they said and clung to him, but he said he had to go on quickly, so then, "O, in that case, your father was exhibited here only two days ago!" they said. So from there he went on quickly.

282. He came to a tribe of big-nosed, blue-eyed people who wore black paint all over their bodies; and they came and surrounded him. "They brought your father here; but they took him on again, only one day ago. If you start and keep going, you will perhaps catch up with him," they said, so from there he went on and arrived at another tribal camp. And those were magpie people, and they came to meet him and escorted him home.

283. "My, my, he is such a young boy to be attempting such a stern duty as a trip like this!" they said, marvelling at him. "Now, friend, we know you seek your father. They brought him here but exhibited him only a short time, and they took him on . . . it was only this morning they did so; and the grasses which the spectators crushed down are only now righting themselves."

284. So having eaten, from there he went on and came to a great tribe in which all the men and women seemed especially roundish (squatty, with a big girth).

285. He would have gone to them, but they were so occupied with something at the center of the camp, and he for his part was tired enough to die it seemed, so he could not drag himself there; so out where there was a forked log of rotting wood he lay down, and cried from exhaustion.

286. A woman evidently was passing nearby, for she exclaimed, "Well, here is a boy crying! . . . But under no condition shall my grandson lie out here and weep!" and she picked him up.

287. She was an old woman, and she took him towards her home, saying on the way, "Grandchild, all the wise men are in council at the camp center. . . . they are the ones who recently sent a woman who is always desirable to men, and she returned almost at once.

288. "There was a holy man named Iron Hawk, at the east edge of the world, so they sent her to somehow trick and bring him home; and one would think it was already arranged and rehearsed the way she returned with him at once; that is what they are excited about.

289. "Long ago once he killed a woman from this tribe, so they wanted him also to hold as a captive. They are sitting there now, with him guarded there; and tomorrow when the sun is highest, they will kill him; so no matter how vast the multitude, don't you worry, you shall eat a bit of the liver! . . . of all the people in the tribe, in order that they all may have a share, they say they are going to cut him up into tiny bits," she said, so he started to cry, and she said, "Don't cry, child, you certainly *shall* eat of the liver!" This she said to comfort him!

290. It was dawn when the crier went around saying, "This is the last chance to view Iron Hawk before he is put to death! . . . Arrive on the scene with the rising sun, force yourselves awake, and with your children come narrowing the circle to this point!" he called.

291. "There, there, child, get up, it is exactly as I said. But you stay at home, I will certainly bring a bit of the liver to you!" she said, waking him up.

292. "No, Grandmother, I must go with you!" So again she explained: "No Grandchild, these are no ordinary folk, they are supernatural people. Even when they simply knock against each other in passing, they hurt each other, so they are dangerous; you better just stay at home!"

293. And they say these were the people who fall as "some-

thing moving" (supernaturally endowed pebbles), in the tying rites, wherein they go to work for the diviner.

294. Four times successively he said he would go, so then she took him with her to the center where the crowds were surging. And she worked herself through the mass of spectators with her grandson on her back, until she came to a place where she could see.

295. And there in the exact center of all a very beautiful but rather frivolous young woman sat smiling (defiantly).

296. She sat with legs spread wide, and in their midst sat the huge buffalo-bull on his haunches, filling tightly into the space. And the young woman had her arms fast about his waist in the small of the back so he could not get up.

297. But the boy knew that was his father. The bull, the instant he looked the boy's way, snorted as an angry beast, so the people backed up somewhat in fear, but Red Calf knew his father's language, so he understood what he had said, hidden in that buffalo's snorting:

298. "Alas, my son, why did you come? Even I, this day before it ends, I am to be killed!" he said.

299. "Grandmother, set me down!" he said, squirming frantically, but the old woman only tightened her blanket about her repeatedly, holding him more snugly in place, as she said, "No, Grandchild, even when these people bump into each other accidentally, they injure each other! I have already told you so!" but he insisted all the more, and now already he had demanded to be put down four times, so she said, "All right then, keep directly behind me!" and she set him down.

300. At once he placed one of his father's magic arrows at the bow and aimed at the woman who held Iron Hawk prisoner; from behind his grandmother's skirt he aimed.

301. And the young woman saw him and called out, "'O please hold him, or he will kill me!'—as if anyone would say!" And she hid back of the buffalo.

302. He tried four times but each time she would call out in those words and hide, so the people tried to think whom she referred to and they looked about. They never once suspected the

tiny boy that stood so small; so when this happened the fourth time, he sent the arrow anyway, and his father dodged very suddenly so the arrow pierced the woman and scattered her into grain-like bits.

303. She was a Rock woman, so of course everyone feared gravel in their eyes and ran in fear in all directions, for the small pieces flew about like hail stones.

304. At once the bull sprang up, and with snorts he rushed to his son and taking him on his back he fled, so all the people chased them.

305. But some old men were smoking, sitting off to one side, and as the pursuers ran past they told them to stop. "Let them go. That son of Iron Hawk, he who is named Red Calf is with his father, and never can you get them.

306. "Red Calf is little but he is magic, that is why he even shattered Rock-Has Horns-Woman herself; what show have you then, weak as you are!" So they turned about and went home.

307. So the two transformed themselves into humans, and with the boy carried on the man's back still, they came on running.

308. As they approached the first tribal camp on their way, which was the magpie nation, one ran out to meet them and then as they kept right on, he ran alongside, breathlessly saying, "Boy, stop, please—all the people are impatient to hear how you rescued your father, so they want you to relate it!" but the boy said, "Go right on, Father!" so he did, and they went on past and again they came on to the next camp.

309. These were the crow people with their huge noses and blue eyes. With pitiful entreaty they begged them to stop, but they kept on and came past, and the third camp was now near.

310. Again they begged them to stop, but they came on. That was the robin camp. Then they came on past the redbird camp.

311. Still they came on and passed the tribal circles of the bluebirds, the Wings-of-eagles, and the Big-lacking-eyes, and then the Black-breasts, and they also begged them to stop, but they disregarded them all and came on.

312. It was not the birds they feared, but they were afraid the Rock nation might catch up with them.

313. At last they came to that first camp where Red Calf went upon his arrival to the sky-world; they were the Chickadee people. They are the birds that always come first in spring before the snow melts, and they make it merry with their singing.

314. Then the late-spring blizzard comes and several freeze to death each year, but they do not profit by that; they still arrive too early.

315. It is later that the other birds return.

316. Now it seemed reasonably certain they would not catch up with them from the Rock nation, so they stopped there to rest, and they were shown every honor and feasted.

317. And the people said, "Rest here for some days, you are very weary. Meantime, your grandfathers will have a conference to decide how they may effect your return."

318. And so from each of the ten bird nations their best representative was picked and sent to this council as the best thinker, and those conferred.

319. Whatever their proposals, there they carried on in the council tent, and finally one was sent to call Iron Hawk and his son to their deliberations. And they told them:

320. "Now, this have your grandfathers decided as the best thing for you: A container shall be made for you in which you may ride down to your home. But one request only they beg: that as you step onto the earth again, you will touch your vehicle to the earth and then jerk on the suspension rope.

321. "Then we shall pull it back up. The Great Spirit made us as well as you, but because he had so many different activities he forgot and left us up here, and here we have stayed.

322. "But if that container is touched to the earth, then thereby we can go down there to live where we belong." At once all the birds went to work, and they built the one thing they can make better than anyone else, and it was a beautiful thing.

323. With fine willow they made the frame, and then they lined the interior with their own feathers of every kind and color woven into designs, and then it was nice and soft when they finished it.

324. Then they took very long willows and split and made braided ropes of them, and fastened them at four points to the rim of the nest, and then they twisted all four into one huge strand, and it was ready.

325. When the time was ripe, as they said, they caused Iron Hawk and his son to get in, but it was so large they were lost in it as they sat.

326. So, like letting a bucket into a well, they sent them downward and after a sufficient time, very gently they landed on the earth, so they stepped out.

327. Somebody saw them, so everybody ran to them across the prairie, but Iron Hawk bade them stand off. "My relatives, first, for a time, stay away. My friends have done me a great kindness; now I shall do them one!" he said, and with great reverence he touched it next to the earth, and then gave a few jerks on the rope, so they pulled it back into the sky. The next morning the ten entire bird nations came down to earth in the huge nest in which they sat, as though held in a cupped palm, and on landing, it is said they scattered over the earth.

328. Now then at last Iron Hawk returned to his people, and his father-in-law the chief, now an old man, came to him, and "Ha o, ha o, my son-in-law! Such unexpected good luck!" he kept repeating as he ran his hands over him tenderly. "Son-in-law, your wife, and mother-in-law, your grandparents, all have cried themselves out and are in mourning. It is well you have come home!" he said.

329. So Iron Hawk ran direct for his home, and his wife with eyes swollen from weeping came to meet him, and he embraced her, and when she saw her boy well, she cried for joy.

330. And behind the family came all the people in a great mass to welcome them.

331. Then it was that his old grandmother came half-crying to complain to him: "Grandson, you were lost so I went to Ikto and said, 'O Grandson, if there is any way your younger brother can be found, please think what it might be, and have it done,' and he said, 'that can't be helped, if he is lost, it is because he didn't have

good sense, what is that to me! Why all this fuss over one man, anyway!' he said, and Grandson, he sent me on by giving me a push," she said.

332. So Iron Hawk sent for "The yellow-legged one." So they brought him, but while he was yet far off, coming, he was talking gaily, "Well well, well, how nice you are back, my brother. Why all the people were poor because you left them, and they all but killed themselves weeping. If man died from weeping, I would have been lying a dismembered skeleton long ago!" he said as he came.

333. So Iron Hawk, who had planned to speak sharply to him, let it go. "What's the use! What is he, the wretch, is he worth anybody's making himself angry? Isn't he Iktomi!" he said.

334. But his grandmother stood with her cane ready and when Ikto passed, she dealt him such blows as left welts on his body, and thus she cooled off her anger.

335. Then a crier went by, "Come all, bring what choice foods you have on hand for Iron Hawk, so that he may eat!" So as if they were ready and waiting for this, they brought him everything, *wasna* among other things, and fine cured dried meat in great containers of parfleche. "Perhaps this is more than enough, but if so, his wife or his grandmother can lay it by for him," they said.

336. So he who was wont to feast the tribe now was feasted in turn, so that the entire encampment turned out for it.

337. So he was sitting within the child-beloved tent eating, when from back of the tipi someone came and called out through the tipi walls, "Iron Hawk, will you come outside?" So he went, and there was a man from away, and he stood there; so, "What is it?" he asked, and the man answered,

338. "Alas, friend, you have just returned, it is said, so I am reluctant to trouble you, yet over here towards the west a grandfather sends for you.

339. "'I pin my hopes only on my grandson, so call him,' he says. A terrible thing has happened to him, and he sits in great misery," he said.

340. "Very well, go and tell the grandfather I will arrive shortly," he said and came back in. So the messenger left for the west-land.

341. When he told this, his wife tried to restrain him with her tears; "You shall not go . . . no! Only now and with great difficulty have you returned . . ." she cried. But their son said, "No, Mother, do not say that, my father must go where men need him," and he returned the magic cap and knife and weapons, so he took them and left.

342. And it was a blackbird who had come for him.

343. So after he had left, Iron Hawk followed him, and at the western edge of the earth there was a tipi pitched towards the east, and inside sat an old man with his blanket over his head in spite of the warm day, he sat.

344. So Iron Hawk went in and said, "Now, Grandfather, you summoned me and now I am here. What is it?" And it was plain on the poor old man's face that his heart was sad.

345. "Alas, Grandson, across the water there is a tribal camp, and some men came from there to war on me, and they scalped me and took my scalp with them; so I suffer horribly.

346. "So I sat here thinking, 'Would that I might somehow or other get it back!' and so I sent for you."

347. So saying he opened out the blanket and exposed his scalped head, a red, wet spot that was ugly to see.

348. Iron Hawk gave some bear-cries of anger, and went out. "Just let me get at those wretches! . . . wait. Grandfather, I will be back," he said, and he caught such utterances from within as "ha-ye-ha-ye!" breathed out, but he went on (without stopping to acknowledge his thanks.)

349. He went a while, then he put on his cap with the little claws of the hawk on it, and he suddenly was himself a hawk, so he went flying and circled the tribal camp.

350. They were holding a war dance and dancing gaily, so he flew low and there on the center sacred pole, set upright, was the old man's scalp, tied to the top.

351. So he bided his time, and when they turned to the shinny

game, and used the pole for a starting point, and were now running away from it so that all eyes were turned that way, he flew swiftly and wrested the scalp from the pole and started back, so instant confusion reigned and everyone was up in arms, and they started to chase him.

352. And one wise old man said, "You'll never touch him, let him go. That is the one who calls himself Iron Hawk!"

353. So he came on with it and assumed his own form, and came to the home of the old man. He would have fitted the scalp back on, but it was dry by the wind striking against it out there, and it had hardened into a wrinkled knot, so he had to take time out to soak it in water, and when it was again wet and elastic, he glued it back on for the old man and healed him.

354. The old man was very grateful. "Ha-ho, ha-ho, (Thank you!) It was for that I chose you, Grandson, and sent for you! Now, Grandson, I am going to make you a present, for what you have done to win my favor is beyond measure.

355. "Yonder hang ten ropes, coiled. Choose and take one." So he took one that was not the best, hanging at the end. And then the old man said, "Now, Grandson, outside stand ten holy dogs (horses); catch one, and it is yours." So he went out and took a smallish one, buckskin colored, which he selected.

356. Never having done this, he threw the rope into a halter, and the horse came whinnying towards him and thrust his head through the loop, so he tied him fast.

357. Then he went back in, "Now, Grandfather, I have taken a horse," he said, and "Very good; you have done well, Grandson. For I am the one who makes holy dogs. I made them out of earth, and put wooden legs on them, and gave them a gentle push from the rear, and they started walking off and were living holy dogs. It is only comparatively recently that they have been making themselves, and that helps me.

358. "From these, my original handiwork, by and by all over the world there will be holy dogs.

359. "By some chance, you have picked the very first one I ever made. It is well, my grandson.

360. "Now, as you go homeward, do not look back. When you

reach the last ridge, then you may look. It may be that a herd
of them might be following you. If so, they will be for you." he
said.

361. So he started homeward, and brought only his buckskin,
and did not look once behind him, but when he reached the top
of the last ridge and could see the camp circle in the distance beyond, then he looked back and there all over the plain were horses
without number, all having followed him now come to a stop, because he had.

362. Some were with young, and the moment they stopped
the colts were at their mothers' teats.

363. Beautiful horses, so he was eager to get them home, but
as he neared the camp, it was deserted.

364. And then a boy came running from the wilds, away from
camp. "Father, it was you, but men said it was an attacking army,
so they all ran to the wilds for safety. I was with them, but I said,
'It is my father,' and I came running back."

365. So Iron Hawk was happy. "Certainly, you did well, my
son; now go and say, 'Grandfather, my father has returned, and
has brought something new with him, and you are all to return,'
—say that." So he ran back.

366. When he told this, all the people, eager to see something,
came back as fast as they could, and never having seen a holy dog
before, these being their first, they stood around admiring them,
and then Iron Hawk said,

367. "Now let the man on the end come forth." So he did, and
Iron Hawk had him catch any horse he wished, and it was his to
keep. Then the next, and so on, until all had one horse apiece.

368. Again he went the rounds, and again, and again. Thus
now all men owned four horses apiece. From that comes the custom of a man, however poor he was at the start of life, being considered as having tribal standing when he has succeeded in acquiring four horses.

369. Many horses still remained, and those Iron Hawk and his
son kept as their own.

370. Then Iron Hawk said, "Son, let us go to the hilltop. I am
thinking seriously about something and you shall hear it." So to-

gether they went there and sat down looking eastward, and he pointed ahead and said,

371. "Over in that direction, at the edge of the world, I was born. An old couple raised me and thought highly of me, but I did not stay with them, I came traveling.

372. "But I said that some day when I was tired of traveling, I would go back to them; all these years they have waited, but I have not kept my word to them.

373. "Alas, doubtless my grandfather sits facing this way, waiting, my son. So if you can, and have the courage to attempt it, I want you to go there. Tell them I am chief over a large tribe over here, and they all depend on me, so I cannot leave them.

374. "But ask your grandfather to come here instead. By and by, because this day I am scattering horses all over the world, when they arrive there, they shall serve as legs to bring him here . . . By these tokens he will know you, so take them along . . . go cautiously, for there is bad magic on the way." So the boy went.

375. [This too he is said to have said, but I forgot it.] "Son, in the west is a nation who understand my speech, and they are related to me. Whenever I confront a threatening enemy, they help me. So you too, if you face danger, say, 'I am Red Calf, son of Iron Hawk,' and certainly they will arrive and help you."

376. But being a boy, he didn't go in a direct path. "First I will angle towards the north, I want to see the world," he said, and so he was going.

377. And there was a tribal camp ahead, and he was making his way thither, when there in the road blocking him among the tall weeds, a very beautiful woman with eyes as yellow as melting suet, as it were, lay on the ground, entirely nude. He almost stepped on her.

378. "How does it happen you lie like this?" he asked, and she said, "I heard you conferring with your father, and when you said you were coming this way, I heard that too.

379. "And I knew I should never see you if you went directly into camp, so I lay here in your way. Stay here with me, later I will return first and later still, you can come too; the tipi on the end is my home," she said.

380. So he stayed there with her, and a good while later only the woman returned. After that he too went, and there in the tipi she had designated, a newborn babe, judging by its weak cry, was fretting. So he went in.

381. A little boy of a certain size was taking care of a tiny babe, but both were so hungry they were crying.

382. "What's the matter?" he asked, and "My elder sister returned from staying in the wood, and she had this in her belly and gave it birth and left it, and went on again, so I am guarding it. Last night she again returned here with a man," he said.

383. "In that case, this is my son, so take good care of him for me, my brother-in-law," he said. So saying he went outside, and called to the Thunders.

384. Instantly they came in a storm, and with crashing sounds they sent forth their shafts to earth, and they slew a deer, so he cut it up and boiled the deer-hooves till tender, and made a broth.

385. And he said, "Now, Brother-in-law, take the pericardium, and puncture a hole in it, fill it with the broth, and give it to your little nephew to suck. And take the liver uncooked, and cut it into tiny bits for him; he will swallow them after a while." So the boy took care of his nephew.

386. Then one day Red Calf heard the boy crying inside, so he looked in, and the boy said, "My sister returned and said, 'What pains you take to raise this one!' And she took us both and hit us against each other, and hurt us," he said.

387. So he soothed them, and he thought, "Well, what sort of woman was she that she tricked me!" and he marveled that he had been taken in so.

388. Again he asked the thunders to kill a deer, which they did, so he brought it, and the boy tied the deer-hooves together and hung them up to dry. And when the babe was now lively he tied the rattles to his little wrists.

389. Then, as his brother-in-law had instructed him, he took his little nephew to a hill and said, "All of you, hear us! According to what my brother-in-law has taught me to say, I shall speak: My nephew whom I raise with great difficulty, whom, lacking a mother, yet I made him grow, hear this for him:

390. "From now on he shall bear a name. He shall be called 'Rattling Deerhooves!' So among the peoples he shall live, spreading the fame of that name!" he said, and the little one heard and shook vigorously and rattled the deerhooves on his wrists.

391. Then the boy's harlot sister again came in from somewhere and said, "I am hungry! You are eating deer meat, why don't you share it with me? Instead you are so busy with this one, you even announce his name . . . as though he had a decent start!" she said.

392. Off she went again; so Red Calf was very angry, and said, "Take your nephew and go stand under that sacred tree . . . I am turning to my friends!" So he did as he was told.

393. And the Thunders returned in great fury, and they kept up a continuous opening of the eyes (lightning) that seemed to set fire across the sky from horizon to horizon.

394. So the boy and his nephew remained with eyes tightly shut, and when the storm cleared away, they looked, and his sister, the bad woman, was lying in the center of the tipi with legs spread, killed by lightning; and not far off was the man she had last come home with, and he also lay dead; and all the other people were gone.

395. And then it was clear this was a wildcat nation, and they fled and scattered all over the world, and from then they were never allowed to dwell in a tribal group, because they are congenitally bad-tempered.

396. To the little boy who saved his nephew, only, was supernatural power given, so he lived well, able to accomplish what he would. "Take care of your nephew. I will come back here and take you both home," he said.

397. From there he went on and was now heading directly towards the meadowlark grandfather's country.

398. As he neared it, there on a small hill a solitary figure sat, appearing grey; so with the intention of making some inquiries he approached him.

399. And it was an old man, looking westward, and wailing feebly.

400. When he stopped to catch the words, he heard, "Ah, my grandson,

> You said you would return!
> Where have you gone?
> A-hu-hu!
> A-hu-hu!

And it was evident he had been saying this from time to time for a long time now, for his sighs were real and came from 'away down.'

401. So he went to him. "Grandfather, stop. I came to see you, for my father sent me with a message for you.

402. "My father says, 'Tell my grandfather, "when I have had enough of travel, I will return," I said to him once; but over here I am taking care of a great people, and I cannot leave to come home.

403. 'But this day I am scattering horses all over the world, and when they arrive at my grandfather's, then he can use them as legs by which to come to me, with his people'—thus says my father, Grandfather!" he said.

404. And the poor little old man, who had now not smiled but wept only for a long time, at last was happy and smiled a wrinkled smile, and with great happiness he took Red Calf home.

405. "Wife, this is Grandson Red Calf who has come home to us. You remember, this is the son of our Iron Hawk whose birth and name he proclaimed—this is he! Also Grandson, I have heard recently that one named Rattling Deerhooves is your son," he said.

406. Hurriedly the grandmother prepared and gave him food, and having eaten he lay down to rest, and from all around visitors came to meet him.

407. They were greatly excited over his story of the horses that were coming, and they were eager to see them. And they all said they would go west to Iron Hawk's country and remain there.

408. When they left, just when he thought he would sleep— after the usual manner of the aged—the little old man filed his complaints.

409. "Grandson, I lived very well and had no enemies, until, recently, a terrible enemy is after me.

410. "After awhile, I could not stand it, and I said, 'Just you wait, when my grandson returns to me, he will have it out with you!' This threat I have been making, but your father doesn't appear, and now by this time, he makes sport of me!" he said.

411. So, "O, that's nothing, Grandfather. My father allows me to use his magic powers. So when it is day, I will go to this enemy; now go to sleep," he said.

412. When it was day he went there and found that the enemy was a snake; such a one as crawls into the nests on the ground where the meadowlarks have their eggs and chews up the eggs regularly. But Red Calf called to the thunders, so they came and quickly killed this rattlesnake.

413. And now the horses were heaving into sight over a ridge that lay across the west, so Red Calf brought them all in and distributed them.

414. Thus the people all struck camp, and now they migrated slowly westward, and meantime Red Calf sped on homeward ahead of them.

415. "Father, my grandfather and his people are coming," he said, so it was generally announced, and all the people sat ready to greet them.

416. Then one early-spring morning, a solitary one, first and ahead of the rest, came and stood on a little hill and sang out this little announcement: "Buffalo-calf liver, rich to taste!"

417. And Iron Hawk recognized it was his little grandfather, so he went and got him.

418. His voice was so pleasant to hear that the people were cheered by it, and happily they went to meet and welcome him.

419. And from then on it has been, that when spring comes, then at a certain time the meadowlarks return, with their very yellow breasts, and they sing out, "Buffalo-calf liver, rich to taste!" and once again men come back to renewed life.

Note: Rattling Deer Hooves' career comes along here somewhere in a copious version, but I can not recall it well enough to repeat it. I am also not sure about the order in which the bird-villages lay, but what I have is approximate. At least I am sure of the kinds of birds that God forgot in heaven.

Ella Deloria's Notes on Iron Hawk

(In the first place, let me say that I realize in recalling this that there are here all the usual incidents, but bound up and woven together around one hero. Some scenes I do not recall; but I re-member with extraordinary clearness the odd words which I do not usually use or hear, which go with some of these scenes and speeches. I have tried to indicate these as far as I can. I did not hear about Rattling Deer Hooves enough to repeat his adventures.

The Dakotas feel a very special thrill over the arrival of the meadowlark. It is considered cheering, and bracing, and life-renewing to hear him in the spring. "Well, to think I have lived the winter through and can hear the meadowlark again!" they exclaim, often in soliloquy. In some respects I think it is their specially loved and most closely related bird. He is everybody's love.)

unit 1. *wiyohinyanpata,* usual word for east. *wiyohinnape,* some-times in legends called *wohinnape, wi,* sun; *o,* in, *hinapa,* to emerge, come into sight.

unit 7. *tuwela kin,* the little body, the little somebody, a usual way of designating a person, and attributing some odd character-istic to him. *Tuwe kin iku hanska,* the somebody was one with a long chin, etc.

unit 9. Well, well, my grandson, my grandson. She is not ad-dressing him, she is exclaiming over him, quite apart. Explains the accent.

unit 13. *žahela s'e* describes a shrill sharp, ear-splitting cry. *yu-zaza,* to cut into long wide fringes, as a deerskin dress. *žahan* does not occur except in this simile.

unit 14. The Dakota custom and belief of saying it "audibly" for the spirits to hear, to give seriousness. Things happen, if you say them aloud, good or bad, (they think).

unit 15. *miciku!* an ungrammatical form, but used as in exclamation. mine-return here!

unit 16. *iśniś,* too good to be true, O, can it be! (what hadn't seemed possible.)

unit 18. *iyakitaninśni,* indistinct, no part showing up against another. *stusta* is not used now. cf. *śtuśia,* said of meat of animal that has been overheating by too much chasing. It spoils easily.

unit 25. *wokiciyaka,* to speak audibly in behalf of somebody. Make an audible wish for somebody (religious idea).

unit 27. This business of the importance of being related, being in harmony, is terribly important. It carries the same sort of significance as kinship in human relations.

unit 28. *yaececa,* to talk until you bring something about; to flatter someone; (to make himself more inclined to cry; here, until he does cry, after whining—*igla ececa*).

unit 30. Old people often say, *takoś,* (child-in-law) as a contraction for *takoźa,* grandchild.

unit 32. *pazica,* to push to stretch. As if somebody under the ground pushed the earth into peaks—hills. Heard only in this connection. *o*-in; *ca,* step; *icu,* to take; *ya,* used for. An unusually formed word.

unit 41. The north is the traditional earthly headquarters of the buffalo nation. *Oyate-luta,* red people, ceremonial people, aristocratic. like *Hunka,* the upper stratum of people. They are regarded as the chief of all animals.

unit 48. *Itehan,* long time after; *nake,* at last, all too late; contracts to this, in colloquial Dakota.

unit 52. "He with the weapons!" a form for pointing out the most salient point in a person's appearance. Just now, the most novel things about the boy are his new bow and arrows.

unit 55. In legendary material, *wicaśa,* man, is often used for any sort of creature, which is thought of as sentient, or personified in some way.

unit 71. There are several other standard phrases said to be the song of meadowlarks. But this is one of the most general and best known, perhaps the best. Often the bird's song is interpreted to say very pertinent and amusing things of local interest.

unit 78. This adverb has reference to the slimy feel of the babe, with fluid over him. *sloslo* describes such a thing as an overripe banana, but I can not think of the English for it.

unit 84. *śaśte,* the little finger. This would be the smallest nail or claw.

unit 87. *winyanpaya* adv. meaning, "with an interest in women." *yapa* may mean having women on the tongue, talking incessantly of them, women the preoccupation. This may be correct, because other preoccupations are expressed in the same way. "His every comment is about such and such," is expressed with *yapaya,* holding in the mouth.

unit 91. *wa,* thing; *o,* in *naġi,* ghost; *kunza,* to foredoom. uncanny; foreboding evil to one's spirit, etc.

unit 104. *awoglaka,* to tell one's own at somebody, is to turn to somebody more powerful than yourself and bespeak their help, patronage.

unit 107. *cinla,* to want, is used after adjectives to indicate a superlative. idiomatic.

unit 110. *kanpeska* I translate as abalone, but I am not sure whether that is just right. The white disk-shells used in ceremonial dress.

unit 111. *aoś'akelaka* is idiomatic and colloquial for, "It's a tough job, calling for more than ordinary ability—and then there is no definite hope of success."

unit 118. paying no attention.

unit 130. *kaskita yuza.* This is idiomatic. Usually we expect—and get—a contracted cvc in this kind of construction.

unit 131. A way of saying the child was uncared for. Neglected orphans are sometimes so described.

unit 133. *tokel,* how; *ecanunkta,* you will do? idiom for, what are you going to do with it? what do you want it for?

unit 138. *śakaṗ s'e* is a simile meaning everybody yelling at once. I do not know what *żaka* comes from, it does not fit the meaning of *żaka* to pull apart, as the eyelids, etc.

unit 139. *staka* is used idiomatically in *iyayustak* to mean closely together, inseparable. A closer adverb than *kici,* with.

unit 141. When anything is too good to be true, it is "like a wish."

unit 144. *k̇at'eyotak̇a* an adverb meaning "settling down, as if for keeps." *tanka*, big; *k̇at'a*, to strike dead. Always followed by verb of sitting down.

unit 146. *tiweṗa* is a variant of *tiyoṗa*, door.

unit 147. *ḣcihcik̇a*, ragged-edges, as it were. This is like saying "The pseudo—" something inferior, or false, taking the place of the real.

unit 149. *owohinsko* is a word showing disgust at somebody taking his time, keeping others waiting, though he is not worth it. Iktomi would do that.

unit 150. To not bother to open the eyes, to sit up unduly straight, are signs of "stuck-upness."

unit 151. To worry people to death, usually by making them wait, is expressed as "to veritably pluck them, hair by hair," or feather by feather. It hurts, and it is deliberate.

unit 152. I don't know what this is. I only remember the word. The calf-son of a certain kind of buffalo.

unit 153. As though not what it appears to be—i.e., too good to be real.

unit 155. *takoś*, the old woman addresses a strange girl as *takoś*. When kinship was unknown, but when a marriage looked like the only possible alliance, rather than be rude by not relating oneself to another, one said "*Takoś*—Daughter-in-law" (potential).

unit 157. *comniglakel* I don't know. I may not have it right. It means to feel bad.

unit 159. *śil-naźin*, to stand in a bad spirit. (unusual, except here).

unit 164. *ayuǵinmic'iya*, to doze a bit. This means to cloud their minds. *aoǵin* the red fox by magic makes them go off, a bit confused, as he goes by, so they can't shoot him.

unit 193. This is characteristic sarcasm among Dakota women.

unit 200. It is like Ikto to not finish his words.

unit 214. These are special words, heard only in these tales. *makoki-gnak̇e*??? *maka*, ground; *o*, in; *ki? gnak̇a* to place. *pazica*, to stretch (into peaks) by pushing.

unit 215. This is editorial comment by the narrator. Narrators often explain things this way for the small hearers.

unit 256. *taku wokitan* means "how little!" a measly amount.

unit 301. This quoted kind of remark is very characteristic when somebody wants to express defiance.

unit 328. *iśnikal eś* is the same as *iśniś*, q.v. unit 16.

unit 331. *śil-woglaka*, to file complaints.

unit 338. *wan, a* grandfather, because Iron Hawk accepts all relationships, but as yet he doesn't know this special one.

unit 340. he said *the* grandfather, but not yet *my* grandfather.

unit 346. *tokeśkekel*, by hook or crook, some way or other, I don't know how.

unit 348. *tkaś* is used here, because it means the hero disregarded the compliments. He might be excused for delaying to hear it, but so bent is he on his mission, he doesn't even stop for that.

unit 355. Indians are always taught to take *not* the best, when they are given their choice.

unit 375. This in brackets is mine. I forgot this part, so I commented on it before I included it. This incident belongs with Iron Hawk's speech to his son in unit 374.

unit 377. "like melting suet"—so yellow were her eyes. She was a wildcat woman.

unit 383. This is characteristic of legends and myths, that things happen with extraordinary swiftness without due allowance for time or space. This is one of the reasons why when anybody says anything that is unreasonble, people say, "*Hunkakapi s'e*" like telling a myth.

unit 391. *tantanyan*—verb—*ka ca!* is a sarcastic comment on the "how" of a thing.

tantanyan-manika ca! means "she has an awful gait."

tantanyan lowanka ca, lowan s'a lah! How she insists on singing,—as if she had a decent style of singing. (which she hasn't!)

Editor's Notes

units 12–13. Deloria combined the Lakota units into one sentence in the translation.

unit 152. Throwing or shooting arrows through a hoop was

both a game and a serious ritual, "played" to bring in buffalo. See Culin 504 and Deloria, *Dakota Texts* 100.

unit 271. Deloria uses "They might freeze for me," instead of "My eggs might freeze," because in Dakota and Lakota "the possessive pronoun is [usually] avoided, possession by the subject being expressed by a verbal element" (Deloria, *Dakota Grammar* 2).

unit 293. On the meaning and movement of flying stones in the *Yuwipi* (tying) ceremony, see Densmore 218; the stones are replaced by rattles in Mails, *Fools Crow* 94, and Powers *Yuwipi* 70.

unit 375. Deloria did not translate "Tohanl otehi wanži el nawažin canśna hena omakiyaṗe lo." The editor's translation is inserted: "Whenever I confront a threatening enemy, they help me."

Iron Hawk as Literature:
An Interpretation

The first section of *Iron Hawk* establishes the cultural priority of continuance and the certain recovery of every loss. The meadowlarks are "small" but just as the "sun emerges" each day, so the meadowlark nation renews itself in each generation. The two meadowlark people of this story are about to lose their individual lives, having already lost their active positions in the group. Their "little tent" is "at some distance" from the camp circle because older people, no longer able to participate fully in its usual work, "withdraw voluntarily . . . and live back of it" (Deloria, *Dakota Texts* 112n). But even though he is becoming less visible as an assertive individual, the aging meadowlark will live to transfer the sun that shines on his last days directly to Iron Hawk and indirectly to Red Calf, Rattling Deer Hooves, and the generations yet to come (cf. Black Elk's Dog Vision in *The Sixth Grandfather* 231).

Initially, however, the grandfather's mood is darkly sad. The tipi fire is completely out and his one spark of life is visible in the smoke coming from his pipe, the only indication that some inner vitality still remains. The detail that it was "windy outside," with the Lakota connotation of the winds as benevolent helping-spirits, suggests the potential fanning of the embers remaining in the old man into a ray from the sun itself.

Deloria's use of physical images to express the emergence of new cycles of life assuredly coming from the old ones imbues the whole introduction. "Floods" may destroy life or at least cause the temporary disappearance of firmly manifest being, but in this instance the floods have receded to reveal a healthy newborn baby lying in the midst of a patch of "red grass." The red of the grass represents the sun in another form, here sheltering the child until other protectors envelop and feed it with their fire. The baby represents the ever-present gifts of the benevolent powers that must be received respectfully and guarded from all harm. In camp circle days women gave birth unassisted away from the circle, and like the meadowlark grandmother here, cut the cord themselves (see *Waterlily* 5).

Just as the woman alone effects the baby's transition from the womb to her arms, so now she secures the baby as snugly as it had been sheltered before its birth. He had not "howled" when he was in the womb because he was protected by his mother's body. Now in his grandmother's arms, he stops "his howling instantly," and the howls are replaced by words of strength and love: "'Hinun takoża, tuwa wanakiĥme-wacin lel t'eniyinkta kecin iĥpeniyan he?'" "'Well Grandson, has somebody, to hide her shame, left you here thinking you would die?'" (unit 10).[1] Shame suggests loss of purpose, of culturally defined identity, a feeling of defenseless vulnerability. But the meadowlark grandmother wraps the child in a verbal blanket of confidence. She addresses him as "Grandson," his first lesson in the nature of the life he will come to live, surrounded by relatives he can depend on and for whom he as the culture hero will learn to be consistently dependable.

"How could you die?" the woman's initial words to the hero encapsulize the whole of *Iron Hawk*. The rhetorical question is ad-

---

1. Parenthetical numbers refer to units of meaning numbered by Deloria and preserved here. The numbers correspond in Lakota and English to facilitate bilingual reading.

dressed to the Lakota people of Deloria's time, the materially and spiritually depressed 1930s (see Mails, *Foods Crow* 145–50) as well as to readers who feel that life and purpose are about to burn out. Deloria mentions that the woman was "especially quick and alert" (unit 3), and that she has been "seriously intent on wood gathering" (unit 12). The power of renewal comes only through those strong enough to receive and shelter it when it arrives. A woman brings a healthy baby home to the camp circle because she is strong enough to have carried it before and after its birth, and because she has carefully followed instructions for its immediate care. Children require hopeful and disciplined adults, accustomed to long periods of deprivation. This is the lesson embodied in the preparative ritual crafts of vision questers and sun dancers, in the fasting and suffering of the ordeals themselves.

Bringing something home that has been "found" outside the camp circle also has a familiar but undiminished quality of celebration in a hunting culture. Men bring home food, horses, and honors and present them to the people in the circle, but women bring the gift of life itself. Perhaps the entrance of a woman carrying a bundle as the supreme gift of renewal is imaged in the most sacred spiritual event, the bringing of the pipe bundle by the White Buffalo Calf Woman (see Black Elk, *The Sixth Grandfather* 183–84, Densmore 64–68, and Walker, *Lakota Belief and Ritual* 110–112). Like a child the pipe is wrapped, reverenced, and used to create the people's future.

Deloria places particular emphasis on words as verbal wrapping: "eś he t'eye-wacin k'eyaś wanaś taninyan epe: 'T'inkteśni ye, mitakoźa!'" 'she thought to cause his death, but I have already spoken it out loud, "he shall not die, my grandson!"' (unit 14). Just as the arrival of any new child was a cause of enthusiastic celebration, so the old man, now suddenly brought back to life, uses ritualized words to claim and calm the child as soon as he sees him, "'Miciku! Miciku! Miciku!' eyaya ayuǧal yin nan icu ke'" "'Come mine, come mine!" In such words he went reaching out for him, and took him' (unit 15). The grandfather now possesses life for himself, because he has someone else he can call "mine." For the grandfather the return of the sun means the opportunity to act as the sun: "'an-ṗetu-ahanzi nan cante maśica can iśniś taku imakiblezinkta hunśe'" "'when days are overcast and I am gloomy, is it possible after all that I shall have something to cheer me up?'" (unit 16).

In the evening after the sun has set, he soothes the child's fears by massaging him with red paint, the color of the sun (see chapter 6), and calming words. The words themselves resemble what they describe, the influence of mild days, and the grandfather's power to comfort emerges like the sun from his initial depression: "'Wiyohinyanpatanhan iś wicaśa wan wicitowancaya wanyak hin-apa'" "'from the east, a man emerges who sees the whole world face to face at once'" (unit 18). The adult Iron Hawk, shaped by his grandfather, will also look upon his whole camp circle rather than only his immediate family, "and when he sees some pitiable one," he will care for his helplessness as a loving parent cares for an infant. In a Lakota circle, each person was assured that they would never fade into "the crowds of men" (unit 19), because the sun, concentrated in a relative, would bring them to life. And each strong person was distinctly alive only in the sense that they embodied and sent forth the rays of the sun. Individuals could see their own light only as their relatives, especially the children, reflect its rays.

The next morning after Iron Hawk's first night of sound sleep, the old woman is about to raise the embers into fire when she suddenly sees another fire she has kindled; in the accompanying metaphor at "dawn," the sun in Iron Hawk has suddenly climbed: "yunkan hokśilala k'un e ca iyotakehan yankin nan tima tiyokśank-śan wakil yanka" 'there was the grandson, sitting up and looking intently about' (unit 21). The direction of upward vision within the tipi toward the apex of the poles is the sunward direction of growth and of the story's first section.

The purpose of life may be first and foremost to produce more life, but surely the only way of doing so is to "get acquainted" with this place (unit 23). Later when Iron Hawk is bigger, the tipi expands to become the horizon—the hills are "step-taking places" and he is told that now "this place" is "the land." On each of the next three nights, representing the whole of boyhood, the grandfather warms the hero with manually transferred heat and vocally transformed light. And on each morning the boy awakens to a greater scope of awareness and mobility. Each revelation of growth is preceded by the old woman tending to her fire. On the last night the grandfather gives Iron Hawk his final child-lesson and impels his riskier journey to adult definition.

When Iron Hawk becomes accustomed to the sun, the grandfather advances his education to the four directions and from there to all the *wamakaśkan* (the animal spirits). Eventually a young man is favored by a particular direction and a particular spirit, usually through undergoing *Hanbleceya* (the Vision Quest). The nakedness of the vision seeker implies his willingness to accept help from any spirit who will pity him. He does not go up on the hill to pray to a specific spirit nor does he wear a particular spirit's color to attract its notice. After his vision he will agree to be "worn" by (be the body of) a specific helper in dangerous circumstances or in ceremonies (see chapter 7). Sun dancers, however, dress and paint themselves identically because each one seeks a vision from the sun (see Deloria, *Waterlily* 120).

As the sun makes Iron Hawk Lakota, supplementary powers define individual identity. Without telling him which particular direction will be his "stronghold" (see chapter 8), the grandfather explains their particular properties: the cleansing power of the west, the nourishing abundance of the north, the "fierce" generosity of the east, and the nurturing compassion of the south (units 39–43). When people understand the potential for protective alliance in their surroundings, they are "set free" and they can "go alone." From his first relatives Iron Hawk discovers his dependence on others for life and their enthusiasm for helping him live. Each lesson extends the child's sense of resourcefulness. Everything necessary for life attends on every hand. By the time he is ready to "go alone" the child has already learned how to handle weapons and summon helpers. He can also offer the products of these combined powers to those he loves.

At this point Iron Hawk turns from one who receives food and care to one who returns sustenance to its givers. In presenting his bow and arrows, the means of life, Meadowlark teaches the patience that hunting requires. The boy may be presumed to be excited about receiving his first bow, but the grandfather is gone for a long time. The bow is "sacred," made from the rib bone of the buffalo bull, the *akicita* (messenger) of the sun, and with the sun and the eagle, a primary symbol of the male ideal. In making the bow from the buffalo, the grandfather has presumably had to look for one, kill it, butcher it, and bring it home. The process of preparing the bow recapitulates the process of patiently nurturing the child (a good bow took up to a month to make. A child's bow took at least a week; see Belden 109–112 and Hassrick 229–31).

Iron Hawk is spiritually drawn from the wisdom of the grandfathers as the bow comes from the rib of the buffalo. The grandfather has produced a hunter as he now produces the bow, and in both cases he has provided the means of life for other people. Just as the boy was painted red, so the arrows are ornamented with red paint as if to impart life-bringing power to them as well. In supplementing the rib metaphor's statement that the child proceeds from the father, Deloria has the grandfather teach marksmanship by making the target a hair from his own head. And as he drew words from his memory to realize his parental dream, he now "decreed" that "he should never miss his aim" (unit 52). As before, the words realize and complete the shaped reality just as an herbal potency must be activated by its accompanying song (Densmore 254–67).

In the same way each animal that the boy brings home offers more than physical survival. The grandmother butchers the game, and the grandfather completes the discovery process of instruction and praise. The power to live in each animal satisfies the family's physical appetites, and the grandfather's words act as a medicine renewing the boy's appetite to hunt. To be a hunter also means to understand existence as continual discovery and to return spiritual sustenance to the circle.

The everyday existence of a hunting culture more nearly approximates the "creative process" than the routine activities of most work in agricultural or technological economies. Life is everywhere a process of discovery, but each discovery is specifically unpredictable. Hunters, visionaries, or pregnant women can regulate their actions as an exercise in capability, but the culminating discovery can happen at any time and the person must be ready to act in the proper way. In the same way, a good idea will not retain its goodness if it is received by someone who lacks the technical skill to contain it. Iron Hawk's hunting lessons require curiosity, persistence, technique, and finally, loving purpose—the desire to bring home not only the fruits of his labor but the story of the process itself. From the west he brings home the jackrabbit's endurance; from the north the skunk's resourcefulness and willingness to take what the world offers; from the east the badger's "special claim on the earth" as his home; and from the south the deer's ability to select only the most healthful of foods (units 54–63).

After each discovery, Iron Hawk learns that the completion of the process, the "butchering" and "cooking," is as important as its inception. A woman brings home a child, a hunter brings home life in the form of food. Vision seekers bring home physical remedies and spiritual strength, emulating the original bringer of the pipe. But development rather than origination is the real purpose of adult work. Tanning, sewing, cooking, wrapping, painting, singing, storytelling—all represent the creative use of physical, cultural, and spiritual gifts.

The sense of the body as a cover, wrapping mysteries of vitality and inspiration, is summed up in Iron Hawk's last find, the buffalo calf, the image of his own identity up to this point. Always the inventive guide, the grandfather falls upon the "twitching raw liver" Iron Hawk proudly gives him. By "tearing it to pieces" as if he is starved, as if Iron Hawk had not yet brought home anything so wonderful, he acts out the hunger for life that Iron Hawk's presence has renewed in him and that he gratefully instills in the boy. The liver, like the life of anyone fulfilled in a child, is "comparable to nothing for its goodness" (unit 65). Since the receiver of a sacred gift must always wrap it in some sign of thanksgiving, the grandfather chooses words to contain his joy, reinforcing this with his bodily posture, his clothing, and even the place of voice-sending: "'Ptehincala pi naṗin!'" "'Buffalo-calf liver, rich to taste!'" (unit 72).

It is only at this point that Deloria, following Riggs (*Dakota Grammar, Texts, and Ethnography* 84, 91), identifies the grandfather as a meadowlark. His idealized parental performance earns him this "name" (see chapter 5). The meadowlark's withheld identity reveals that people become themselves as a result of their actions (see Rice "How the Bird . . ." 434). They are not automatically endowed with identity-defining virtues at birth. As the generalized Lakota ideal, overt expression whether in hunting or in song "heralds" renewal. The meadowlark here is the mature person bringing the sun's warmth and wisdom in words that make life "rich to taste." Everyone, Deloria adds (chapter 2), has heard the meadowlarks singing these words in their springtime call and in the intuited voice of every past generation that makes the present live.

As Deloria makes clear elsewhere, older men were the camp criers, the admired storytellers, and in general the masters of words (*Waterlily* 49–52). Although their hunting contributions have lessened, their words have undiminished force. Prayer, like storytelling, creates a verbal reality that foreshadows and helps to bring about a physical one. Meadowlark anticipates his prayer that his son will have fine clothing by his careful wrapping of Iron Hawk's spirit. Though the old man cannot afford the societal ceremony of declaring his grandson a "child-beloved," clothing represents work and spiritual consciousness in Lakota culture (see chapter 7), infusing confidence into both wearers and beholders.

The dawn that breaks on Iron Hawk as he sets out to realize the dreams of his grandfather follows the dawns that have given generations of ancestors similar identities and values. Grandfather meadowlark's language brings results. Verbal prayer is automatically answered in the general sense that prayer creates inner integrity. When the clothes magically appear the next morning, the grandfather again ritually voices his thanks (unit 77). This represents the proper use of words, clothing, and everything else that life provides. As an esteemed gift, words are offered back to their givers in the form of prayer. The grandfather's action, helping his grandson to dress, complements his protective words (unit 76).

The symbolic acts of clothing and naming converge in the final act of the childhood episode. A hunting culture does not regard clothing carelessly or frivolously. Everyone participates in its manufacture and much of its decoration is meaningful rather than

merely aesthetic (see chapter 7). In *Iron Hawk* language and clothing are repeatedly associated with protective and generative power.
As the hero figure presenting the cultural ideal, Iron Hawk is
everyman, deprived of "natural food" at the beginning (as is any
child drawn from the "slimy water" of the womb) but adopted in
this world by loving parents who envelop him in language until he
emerges with a name.

Iron Hawk's name defines him as one whose responsibilities take
him far from the shelter of boyhood. Like the hawk he must cover
great distances for food and defense. Upon reaching his destination
he must strike the game and the enemy as the hawk takes its prey—
thus the talons rather than feathers on the hawk cap. Through all
of this he must have a protective shield of spiritual favor that in
effect makes his body like iron.

Like the prayer for clothing, the name not only expresses the
grandfather's wish for Iron Hawk, it indicates a probability strengthened painstakingly by the whole process of education culminating
in the name. The name would not be given if its meaning had not
already become manifest in the recipient. The naming ceremony
does not say, "I wish my child may live up to this name"; it says,
"Now that I know what my child has become, I can call the child
by a descriptive name." But while the name honors the emergence
of a particular incarnation of the sun, it may also be a glimmer of
recollection in situations of personal darkness. Later when Iron
Hawk loses his clothes on two occasions, he also loses his name.
Both clothing and name exist only in the minds of those who depend on their powers. As long as a named one forgets them, he
loses both clothes and name.

Such forgetfulness, however, is inevitable, and no Lakota culture-
hero is superhuman. Even the Creator forgets in section 3, strand-
ing the birds in the sky (unit 321). When Iron Hawk forgets himself he becomes a helpless child (unit 131) and a trapped animal
(unit 296). The grandfather foresees this danger when the adolescent Iron Hawk wishes to travel, but he knows that his reluctance
and Iron Hawk's persistence belong to a ritual that must and
should occur. When he forbids Iron Hawk to travel but accedes
on the fourth request (unit 83), he resembles the receivers of Sun

Dance pipes (see Deloria, "The Sun Dance" 404 and Mails, *Sundancing* 314). As a pipe is finally taken on the fourth request, so Iron Hawk's four requests show that he has reflectively considered his desires. No loving relative would insult him by refusing, whether or not he felt misgivings.

But even the anxiety is part of the ritual. The grandfather fears for Iron Hawk because he loves him, but he knows that a man's future is indefinite, that each man must discover the nature of strength and weakness by himself. He does not say, "go cautiously, there is evil in the way" but warns instead of mystery, "there is *wakan* in the way" (unit 82. Deloria freely translates *wakan* as "falseness" but literally it refers to the unknown). Each man will have to determine his own particular susceptibilities, the "evils" that threaten him as a particular person. Good as well as evil proceeds from mystery. A young hunter braves the unknown because the sources of renewal lie outside the predictable life of the circle. Armed with his upbringing, a name, and the hawk cap, he is ready to take his chance. Although Iron Hawk is not portrayed as having sought a vision, the hawk cap from the grandfather resembles the gift of a spirit who would also be addressed as grandfather. At the end of the first episode, Iron Hawk has been given an education in physical and spiritual provision. Now he must learn, sometimes the hard way, to find himself as the leader the people need.

Iron Hawk's miraculously rapid growth in the first four days of his life reflects a healthy childhood and skillful nurture, a flame protected until the individual is ready to manifest it in deeds. Nevertheless, the quenching of this potential in even the most advantaged adolescent was an accepted existential risk. Even supernatural guards, like the hawk cap, cannot make a person absolutely invulnerable to the tricky enemies who afflict heroes throughout the oral tradition. Iron Hawk's quick victory over the first Rock woman suggests an important challenge that every future leader must meet, but the ease of its accomplishment owes much to social lessons still freshly imprinted on his mind.

Iron Hawk presumably knows that an ideal courtship is lengthy and formalized. The Rock woman's behavior in pushing her daughters to stagger toward him and his four companions (unit 94) warns of danger in joining oneself to a family where respect for kinship and custom is lacking (on the complete avoidance between mother and son-in-law, see Bushotter 253:2 and Hassrick 116). The destructiveness of parents who neglect the rules arises from their will to personal domination in many stories (see Deloria, *Dakota Texts:* "The Feather Man" 142–45 and "A Woman Kills Her Daughter" 166–71). They cause others in their *tiyospayes* to stagger because they abuse the rules of respect to satisfy their will to manipulate as many lives as they can. The effect of such egotism destroys the balance of the kinship system. Iron Hawk is able to destroy the Rock woman because he knows what kind of marriage to make for his own good and that of the others around him.

He is also able to properly arrange marriages for his four friends (unit 98). Their identity as Thunder men suggests the societal and *kola* (fellowhood) bonds that are as important for a young man to achieve as marriage (on the *kola* relation, see *Waterlily* 98–99 and Bushotter 253:1–2; on warrior societies, see Walker, *Lakota Belief and Ritual* 260–70, Densmore 311–12, and Wissler, "Societies" 7–80). By playing an instrumental role in assisting their courtships, Iron Hawk can depend on them in times of physical danger. But the equivalent of warrior society membership and spirit helpers for war does not make Iron Hawk immune to Iktomi or the younger Rock woman in subsequent episodes. Having proven himself in war, and having demonstrated his knowledge of courtship and its value, Iron Hawk must learn the hard way to avoid dangers that cannot be transcended and that eventually fortify his mature strength once they have been suffered.

The clothing that Iktomi steals from Iron Hawk represents a man's achieved identity. At his departure from boyhood, Iron Hawk wears the clothing of a child-beloved, and in the young warrior stage of his development he lives up to his clothing's promise. When Iktomi persuades him to shed his clothes before gathering abalone shells (unit 114), Iron Hawk forgets the responsibilities that the clothes are meant to recall.

Abalone shells were a decorative rarity because they came all the way from the Pacific coast by trade. Unlike feathers and other parts of birds and animals they were not used to represent societal responsibility. Stripped of the clothing conferred on him as a lesson and a guard, Iron Hawk lowers himself into helpless immobility. While he had remembered to be wary of a marriage too easily bought, he fails to notice that the winning of a wife with wealth alone could only be offered by a foolish father-in-law to an equally foolish young man. The suitor who brings his wife's people status symbols may augment their prestige, but symbols of usefulness and dependability were understandably preferred—horses and meat, not shells or elk teeth (Deloria, *Waterlily* 149–54, Hassrick 125–26).

Ikto poses as a child-beloved in a story, because in reality men use symbols of manhood to childishly gratify themselves. The better self is then as invisible and ineffective as Iron Hawk in the pit. The trickster has free reign for a time: "Kaġi-mayan, tka! . . . Nakeś wana okablaya wicawoha-mninkte" 'He did cramp my movements . . . now at least I shall go forth to be a son-in-law, without being hampered' (unit 119). In the camp circle his influence is present before he arrives to the extent that he represents the worst qualities in human nature. He gets the wife he deserves, "so long pampered" that she is "vain and proud," and so harshly jealous of her younger sister that she orders her off whenever she comes near. As the *Hunka* ceremony represents ideal social harmony in a relationship of two, the behavior of Ikto and his wife epitomizes the threat to Lakota survival. If everyone emulated these socially favored individuals, the society would collapse.

The hero represents an adult identity that must endure if the people are to live. The person humiliated by the Iktomi in his immediate self does not have to go back to square one but does have to return to the values and activities of childhood (units 133–53). A boy is likely to be satisfied by the creative excitement of hunting, handling weapons, and seeking spiritual power. He receives much praise and recognition for socially beneficial action, but adolescence brings goals that require complex social interaction. A young man who has proven himself in hunting and war and who has had a vision may inevitably come to take these attainments for granted. He has already gained them, not entirely through independent effort, but with the feeling that his wishes will come true if he follows directions and works hard.

Social prestige on the other hand presents the temptation to win approval, no matter what it takes—marry a spoiled girl if her father is a leader, gratify a desire for tokens of individual superiority rather than provide for one's family and help decide for the tribe. The meadowlark grandfather had done everything possible to help Iron Hawk make the right alliances. Having been diverted by the pursuit of abalone shells, Iron Hawk is narratively sent back for a refresher course in family values. His lapse is perhaps meant to represent a natural process rather than a serious mistake.

Immediately before and after puberty boys are satisfied to hunt for their families. But the adolescent who imagines social importance in the future may think less or not at all of the extended family, except as an audience to applaud great deeds. Wise parents recognize a young man in the fantasy stage and withhold their daughters for someone more mature. The man who is ready for a wife will revive or maintain pre-adolescent concentration on hunting and family respect. The intermediate dreams of seduction or glory must be outgrown, so that the best adult returns to boyhood while the Iktomi adult is an adolescent forever.

Iron Hawk's alliance to the Thunder represents both his winning of supernatural power and his warrior status. Appropriately, it benefits primarily the relatives who depend on him, since the conclusion of the Thunder episode immediately precedes the entrapment by Ikto:

> Nitaoyate—niyate, nihun, nitunkaśila, nikunśi, niciye, nitanhanśi, nihakata, nicinca hena iyuha owicakiyaka yo, letanhan niho kin he ituya yeyayinkteśni ce.
> Now, tell all your people, your fathers and mothers, your grandfathers and your grandmothers, your brothers and cousins, your female respect relations and your children, tell them all, from henceforth you shall not send your voice in vain. (unit 101)

By voicing their readiness to respond to any relative's call for help, the Thunder men define the warrior responsibility of Iron Hawk himself. But the man who could fight valiantly with the power of the Thunder outside of the circle would not necessarily be ready to be the sun at home.

Alone and naked in the pit, Iron Hawk is as helpless as an infant. The recovery of a person temporarily lost in egotism recapitulates the first lesson learned by a baby. Once again a grandmother looking for firewood (unit 127) takes in a fragment of human kindling that will, given a second chance, become a fire like the sun. Iron Hawk reviews the basics with the additional depth that narrative repetition provides. The women's arts show that children, the next generation, are more important than anything else. Adolescents and adults who have regressed to childishness are also worthy of help: "Hina, hina! Taku sam tawacin-hinyans awicaye! Oyate kin le eca takupika ca!" 'O dear, O dear, how more and more heartless people are growing! What is the matter with these people indeed!' (unit 128). The matter with people is their neglect of nurture, education, and reeducation. Although Iron Hawk is no longer an infant and is very heavy for the woman to pull out with her pole, he appears as he really is within: "hokśilala wan nażute hlila ca unśi-yehcin ececala" 'a little boy with sores in the nape of his neck, pitiful and neglected' (unit 131), just as he had appeared with equal truth in the shape of a forceful hunter and warrior.

Iron Hawk now comes "home" to relearn his place as a boy, to unlearn adolescent ambition, and to make a direct jump from this second childhood to manhood. This time he uses his supernatural powers to feed a community rather than wastefully spending his power or seeking social approval. He snares multitudes of ducks, geese, and pheasants, an unashamed display of a boy's art for one who has already travelled as a hunter and warrior, but in the act of patient, unglorified provision he has unsnared his mind, and he is ready to teach the lessons of humility and freedom. As a hunter of food and wisdom, he tells the people to care properly for what he has brought—to cook the food and make an offering to its source. As a woman brings a baby, the hunter and the vision seeker initiate a process that others must complete. The giver is aided by spirits and everyone must tender thanks. The heads and feet of the birds are thrown into the water, and their miraculous multiplication shows that the nation will grow if the people feed the spirits of the animals that feed them (unit 139).

As a teacher of cosmic interdependence Iron Hawk moves directly against divisive feelings of pride and shame by urging his reluctant grandmother to borrow a kettle. When she returns with one freely given, the birds continue to multiply, underscoring the lesson that scrupulously observed kinship creates a society free from want. The posthunting ritual helps to maintain this reciprocity. The grandfather formally summons the people to a feast that symbolizes the common source of their life, and they sit in four concentric circles as if to emphasize their growth from the same center (unit 146).

The verbal invitation to partake together, supplemented by the concentric seating, sets up the humor of Ikto's performance at the scene. Childishness in an adult is not funny when it is socially disguised, but in the story Ikto is harmless because Deloria portrays the "successful" man as someone who lives to be fed rather than to feed. His social connection as son-in-law to the chief apparently allows him to live as passively as a baby, and he is not only immature but by Lakota standards inhuman. As he is fed one piece of meat at a time by several attendants, while the people wait hungrily, he resembles non-Indian dreams of transcendence, but Deloria portrays Ikto's "tricksterness" as well as any storyteller she transcribed:

> Unma toktok tohanl ceźi naslulkiya canśna talo hanke el egnakapi ke'. Hecetu canśna h'anhiyehcin yamahel icu nan owohinsko yatahan can kohan unma kin, ape naźinpi ke'. . . . canke oyate kin apepi kin kohan k'ok'oya tahnakipcapi ke'. Wana eyaś wicayuślahcin nan hehanl "Wana imapi ye lo!" eya canke hehanl nakeś wakpamni kin wicegna iyayapi nan woyute kin ecekce wicakikpamnipi ke'.

> One after another, when he stuck out his tongue, pieces of meat were placed on it. Then very slowly he took it in, and with complete deliberation he chewed on while the others stood waiting . . . so the people waited while they gulped down only saliva, so hungry they were. After he had worn

them out (practically plucked them, feather by feather), then "Now I am full!" he said, so at last they passed food out. (units 149–51)

By providing the bird feast Iron Hawk demonstrates that societal achievements serve only to enable more work. The hoop game that magically produces buffalo (units 152–53) is a common theme in the oral tradition (see Deloria, "The Boy with Buffalo Power" *Dakota Texts* 198–99). It is another way of saying that the lessons learned in boyhood have tangible results. When a boy repeats beneficial activities until he is expert enough to inspire trust in everyone he knows, then and only then is he ready for marriage.

After his new grandfather, like his meadowlark grandfather, praises him by energetically butchering the gifts he has brought, the younger sister of Ikto's wife "unbelievably" comes to the tipi (unit 154). The arrival is unbelievable because Iron Hawk and his grandparents are not part of the central hub of social activity, and the girl's father is a chief. And it seems improbable, as his grandmother later worries, that she could be seriously interested in a "homely" boy, but it is entirely believable as a thematic sequence in the oral tradition. Iron Hawk has proved himself a reliable hunter and is ready to marry because he has shown the will to care for a wife rather than the ambition to win one. As the grandmother says to the girl when she arrives, he is "covered with red paint"; symbolically, he has demonstrated generosity, though the humor here is that the grandmother intends to warn the girl off: "'Takoś takoża wase ececa ca iniyutatakte iheyapaya yankin ye!' eya yunkan 'Etanś tokaka,' eyin nan śiyute el egnaka ke'" "'My grandson is covered with red paint, so he might get some on you, sit away from him." And instead she said, "What if he does!" and put the boy on her lap' (unit 155).

The image of the great young hero sitting on the lap of his future wife invalidates stereotypes of female subservience in Lakota society. Women were leaders in the home and in many domestic matters (Hassrick 218–23, M. Powers, *Oglala Women* 78–103). At home a man was fed like a boy and his ideal attitude was one of quiet respect: "It is well to be good to women . . . because we must sit under their hands at both ends of our lives" (He Dog to Marie Sandoz, *These Were the Sioux* 103). Iron Hawk will become the adult ideal, but at home he resembles the boy his meadowlark parents raised. When he assumes the roles of ritual practice, social leadership, or warrior action, he embodies supernaturally assisted power, while at home he is only an unaided human being.

In the momentum of Iron Hawk's development several recognitions converge to prepare him for marriage. Iron Hawk learns to devote his special skills to recalling the people to their "red" virtues rather than to painting himself with glory. In the prevailing hunt metaphor, he arouses communal confidence by killing the red fox and the red eagle; his grandfather completes the process by bringing in the skin and feathers to confirm the presence of a protector. In the context of approaching marriage, the red trophies prove that Iron Hawk seeks to bring life to his family, not to be an Ikto-like recipient of their awe.

Since spiritual development is an inward process, his second grandmother does not realize that he is neither a child nor homely when the girl's messenger proposes marriage (unit 173). The mature Iron Hawk emerges in his performance as a buffalo man, a ceremonial role usually played by a distinguished elder. Presumably his future wife's parents would not have sponsored the Buffalo Woman (girl's puberty) rite, including the feast and give-away for a neglected daughter, and so Iron Hawk himself performs the ceremonial equivalent. Deloria uses ritual symbolism to develop the theme of adult definition. Iron Hawk's seeming ability to command his grandparents, regarding preparations for the hunt and other achievements, is not idiosyncratic but reflects the deference shown by parents and grandparents to young men. Children learn that they will not outgrow the obligation to honor others, and so their own wishes, even if not always wise, are usually honored.

The culture hero is wiser after surviving a few pitfalls, and Iron Hawk's instructions to the girl about ritually inviting him (unit 175) test patience and seriousness in the marriage relation. The buffalo charge ordeal (units 181–89) suggests the priority of trusting a husband, even one who may at first inspire fear, either because he must also be a warrior and hunter, or because sexuality itself may still be apprehensively unknown. For each of Iron Hawk's first three arrivals as a buffalo the girl fails the test of embracing him. On each charge the bull appears at a different stage of life to show the girl that she must commit herself to a man of many identities and duties throughout their life together.

Before her fourth and last attempt to overcome her fear, her father tells her that acceptance of Iron Hawk's reality is a matter of life and death. For a woman the recognition and love of relatives as-they-are is the only life her society allows, since the life of everyone depends on her growth into that role:

> "Kiksuya yo, cunkś, le ehanke-ukta ce, ake yuzinakinkte cin oyakihiśni hantanhanś iyeś nit'e cin he waśakala nan le e wotehiwalakte lo, oyate wacin-niyanṗe san wawicayakihtami kinhan" eya yusyus iwahoya canke wana wiyeya naźin ke'.

> "Remember this, Daughter, he comes for the last time. If you fail again to hold him, I shall consider it an easier thing to have you dead, and this failure I shall find harder to bear because you are going to bring evil on the people," so, holding onto her for emphasis, he warned her and now she stood ready. (unit 186)

By "holding her" in urging her to hold Iron Hawk, her father is teaching her that marriage is more than a relation of two. Extended families depend on individuals wholeheartedly accepting the relational roles they are privileged to play.

The ritual repetition of four charges suggests the girl's progression to marital readiness as a natural process, but she should not marry until she has had sufficient time to experience fear. The usual Lakota response to fear is to let it in by enacting it (see Rice, *Black Elk's Story* 75–87). If danger becomes familiar it is less fearsome, even when the danger is imaginary. When the girl's fear is finally overcome, it is because she has already survived several attacks of it, and because her father has caused her to remember him and the others who depend on her courage.

Women marry to serve families, not just a husband. With this preparation the girl "suddenly reached out, with eyes tight shut

and took hold of him somewhere." The magical result is again "unbelievable." Iron Hawk turns into a helpless little boy who along
with the girl has "been knocked down" and "his nose was bleeding
as he arose" (units 188–89). When she overcomes fear, the girl
discovers that her husband will take on fearsome identities away
from home but under her hands will always be a boy. In section 3
Iron Hawk slips back briefly into adolescence, but in the rest of
this episode he wraps the gifts of wife and family in a series of
exemplary acts.

By sending his grandmother to bring his clothes back from
Iktomi, Iron Hawk demonstrates that Iktomi is not an adversary
requiring a warrior's response. In fact Ikto only gains strength by
draining the righteous anger of his victims, and even if they gain
some temporary satisfaction by striking him, he is immortal and
will simply go on to a more vulnerable target. Iktomi's ascendance
here is based on a social deception that inevitably occurs, but in
resuming an identity that matches the clothing, Iron Hawk realizes
that people can be fooled and that a wise man's part is not to rail
or rebel against hypocrisy or even injustice. Instead he fulfills the
tribe's will to survive in the best possible way by transferring the
highest value symbolized by the clothes from the past (his grandfather) to the present (himself) and shortly after to the future
(his son).

When the grandmother calls out, "Iktomi, Iron Hawk sends for
his clothes, you have been wearing them long enough" (unit 199),
no one knows better than the trickster that though his theft is
always accomplished, its results are temporary. He can delay but
not block the return of the culture's best self here personified in
Iron Hawk. The ritual discipline that maintains Lakota culture is
suggested by the grandmother's formulaically repeated demand for
her grandson's clothes. Iktomi's humorously immediate surrender
and the familiarity of the scene as a conventional transition in the
genre enhances cultural confidence (see Deloria, *Dakota Texts:*
"White Plume" 106–13 and "Blood Clot Boy" 113–20).

As the culture hero Iron Hawk knows that tricksters do not
merit punishment and that he must devote his energies to healing
divisions in the circle. When his grandmother returns with the

clothes, she is amazed to see her little boy sitting as a man and smoking. The pipe is a symbol of harmony whether used socially or spiritually (Black Elk, The *Sacred Pipe* 4–8 and Densmore 65–68), and men, not boys, are fit to hold it. Accordingly Iron Hawk summons his sister-in-law. Though she has treated his wife badly, he assures her that she need not fear retribution. His speech exemplifies the feeling that should prevail throughout the camp circle as well as the ideal use of the voice: "Heceya cante-śica-un hunśe, heya yunkan lila nakeś nablayin nan wiyuśkin ke'; ecin tiwahe ena okiciyuśicapi can iyotan otehike cin he un" 'No doubt her heart had been heavy [but] when he said that, she was suddenly very relieved and happy: for it is especially hard when folk of one household turn against each other' (unit 204).

With everyone working together the people will always have what they need, and Lakota culture frequently taught this in the metaphor of buffalo transformation. When Iron Hawk turns his wife into the buffalo cow (unit 205) whose shed hair turns into large herds of buffalo, he expresses in still another way the priority of dedicating one's life to the group. "Buffalo" adults live for their children and give themselves to the people to provide the necessities of life. When he institutes the ritual of reporting the presence of buffalo using the upward pointing thumb to signify truth (see Deloria, "Camp Circle Society" 36, Black Elk, *The Sixth Grandfather* 145, and the Ben Marrowbone videotape, Oglala Lakota College archives), he helps the people to remember not to take the necessities for granted. Ritual disciplines instill the mindful wonder that makes life worth living. Then, when they depart for the actual hunt, he again puts his wife under a buffalo robe to turn her into a buffalo cow (unit 218).

The girl's puberty rite, or Buffalo Woman ceremony, also uses the clothing metaphor to teach the meaning of adulthood (see chapter 7). In the ideal scenario a human girl will grow into the maternal virtues of the buffalo cow. In Deloria's creative variation Iron Hawk's wife enacts the worst possibility. By enticing the bulls she draws the whole herd to the hunters (units 220–22). Just so a seductive or flirtatious woman can distract a tribe's protectors and render it defenseless. But as the bulls portray a nation weakened by its women, the Lakota hunters are shaped by Iron Hawk's suggestion, condensed again into unerring words. The ten young men, ritually positioned, each kill a buffalo with only one arrow, because Iron Hawk has "decreed" for them, as his meadowlark grandfather had decreed for him, that they "should never miss a shot."

After Iron Hawk has once again feasted the people, he is entitled to progress to parenthood, the gravest of human responsibilities. The next buffalo transformation suggests how the Lakota gained physical strength by identifying with the buffalo. His wife becomes a cow to give birth to a "perfect little calf" (unit 227) so that the ordeal of birth will be felt as a buffalo feels it. When mother and child return to human form they will have the buffalo's hardiness and resilience.

Iron Hawk's naming of his son extends the buffalo metaphor. Individual men may be like hawks or other animals outside the circle but at home all are like buffalo (Rice, *Black Elk's Story* 125–47). Grandfather Meadowlark's choice of the name "Iron Hawk" encourages the hunting virtues of courage and fortitude. Iron Hawk's name for his son, "Red Calf," represents the domestic virtues of generosity and wisdom (on the four virtues, see Hassrick 32–52). The names complement each other in defining the male ideal. The process of naming helps to make the virtues real. Iron Hawk "proclaims" his son's future "after the manner of his little meadowlark grandfather" (unit 228), and in both cases the future hero's shape is created by the name before it is filled.

Just as a man's clothing is meant to place a feeling of confidence in the minds of those he protects, so a man's name exists to make his virtues real in the minds of supernatural as well as natural others. A person is real only if that reality exists in other minds. Even if a man does what he thinks is right rather than what a majority of others may think, he is not acting for himself alone but as a person maintaining an identity for someone else. When Thunder dreamers violate social conventions, in the *Heyoka* ceremony, they are being the persons the western spirits require them to be (Deloria, "Camp Circle Society" 45–50, Walker, *Lakota Belief and Ritual* 156–57, Hassrick 272, Densmore 157–59, and Bushotter 4:420–25).

Iron Hawk makes it improbable for Red Calf to live badly, by securing an outline of his future in the minds of the cosmic powers. Deloria carefully mentions that he holds the baby up to show it to the spirits, to make it real in their eyes before speaking to make it real in their ears:

nan tuweni unśni k'eyaś eyapaha nan heya ke': "Ho po, taku maka sitomniyan hiyeye cin, maka akanal taku śkanśkanyan toni gluha un kin, wahupakoza kin koya, nah'unpi ye! Leanpetu kin hokśila wan micitunpi ca imatan nan ibluśkin nan lehanl wana caże yukinkta ca "Pethincala Luta" eciyape lo! Tuktel wanmiyecilakapi nan iyotiyekiya-iteka can unśimicilapi ye, kola!" eya ke'.

though nobody was around, he called out and said: "Now all, whatever lives all over this world; whatever has life and moves thereon, and the winged beings too, listen! This day a boy is born to me, so I am proud and happy and now he shall have a name, "Red Calf" he shall be called! Wherever you see him, mine, if he appears to have trouble, take pity on him for me, my friends!" he said. (units 229–31)

Then having first shown the baby to the spirits, Iron Hawk and his wife bring the baby, "not yet with eyes opened" to the eyes of "all the people," eager to realize the baby in their own minds.

This loving will to shape the future never assumes Pygmalion grandiosity. Adults direct children toward a "fame" that becomes a reassuring guarantee of provision and defense. Although some people will perpetuate Iktomi's legacy in every generation, the instinct to create heroes is cooperative rather than competitive. Heroes belong to the *tiyośpaye* and the tribe. Both of Iron Hawk's grandfathers, the meadowlark and the one of his adult *tiyośpaye*, have adopted him. The repetition suggests that all children are a mysterious gift and that only the adult who acts parentally is the true parent. The mother or father spiritually wraps and reinforcingly "paints" the child in respect and honor until the children are themselves ready to become protectors.

The doubling of Iron Hawk's adoptive grandfathers reflects the mutual agreement of everyone in a *tiyoŝpaye* to make the community's future more important than the competitive ranking of their own child's place in it. Iron Hawk grants his second grandfather's request to raise Red Calf, because a child who is not to become Iktomi needs the thorough grounding in Lakota values that only a grandfather has time to give (see Deloria, *Waterlily* 24–35). Iron Hawk's father-in-law has four grandchildren sired by Iktomi, and the probability of Red Calf following in Iron Hawk's footsteps is obviously lessened by association with such companions. It must also be remembered that the father-in-law was willing to sell his daughter for abalone shells. Because Iron Hawk and Red Calf are "grandfather raised" (see Deloria, "Camp Circle Society" 80), they learn by example that their future roles are to help rather than to win.

After Iktomi has been banished from the camp, the people "live on" in harmony with their societal values, within the protective clothing of observed custom. Red Calf is raised well by a grandfather, as his father had been, and Iron Hawk presumably carries on the uninterrupted work of a husband, father, and leader. The ongoing work of the people is also represented by the activity of his wife. At the beginning of the third episode she is fleshing a robe (unit 237). Her sense of domestic continuity is interrupted by Iron Hawk's recognition of the continuity of trouble.

In introducing his hawk cap, sacred knife, and arrows to Red Calf, he provides his son with the culture's ability to defend itself against both internal weakness and external threat: "tunkaśila wan maka-opȧpun kin ekta icah-maye c'un he lena mak'u we lo" 'I have a grandfather at the edge of the world, there he raised me, and he gave these to me' (unit 238). His wife does not like Iron Hawk to even speak of the need for such defense, since spoken words may come true. But the voice, especially in storytelling, was properly used to protect against dangers that could never absolutely be prevented. Although Iron Hawk himself is about to fall away, the heroic qualities of provision and protection symbolized by the hawk cap are transmitted in an unbroken cultural line. Great men may die or be corrupted, temporarily or permanently, but the quality of their greatness is transferable and immortal.

Instead of answering his wife directly, Iron Hawk's reply unconsciously validates his precautionary speech to Red Calf: "Wan, okata ca nunwe-unyinkte lo, wana eyaś henala ecun ye" 'Say, it is very warm, let's go swimming, you ought to have enough done by now' (unit 241). Swimming is probably a sexual euphemism (see Deloria, "Doubleface Tricks the Girl" *Dakota Texts* 49–50). Even for a hero the heat is sometimes stronger than duty. But his wife's refusal reveals another divergence from the ideal: "E, le wana niś-koyela ihewakiya ca wi mahel iyayeśnihanni wagluśtankta tka!" 'O, this is all I have left to do, so little, I do want to finish before sundown!' Although he makes the four ritual requests that a relative should always honor, his wife puts her material obligations first. Neither husband nor wife are guilty of anything, but subsequent events reveal the damage that sexual naiveté can cause.

Just as his youthful warrior experience had not prepared him for the complications of courtship and the social deceptions of a trickster, so his brief tenure as a husband and leader has not made him invulnerable to seduction by a determined woman. His lack of sexual sophistication is metaphorically evident when he arrives at the stream by himself: "Mni kin tanyan kaluzin nan otankayahceśni k'eyaś eyaś otohanyan copa yapi keś ungnahanla ohipiśni k'un hececa ke'" 'it was the kind of river bed wherein one can wade for a time, and then suddenly it is beyond one's depth' (244). As Iron Hawk has shed clothing to swim, so now the shield of his name is turned against him. The Rock woman defines Iron Hawk "ocaśtunpika cinla yaun" 'as one who lives in such a way as to demand fame' (unit 247).

This is far from the meaning his meadowlark grandfather intended the name to bear. "Iron Hawk" should not be a target for adulation or adultery. The call "from far away" turns Iron Hawk's perception topsy-turvy. By responding courteously to her four demands he begins to lose rather than reinforce his dignity. And while he easily stays afloat in the known current of the river, he drowns in the force that draws him to the sky. In a state of sexual intoxication, suggested by the woman's riding him into "midstream," Iron Hawk makes an impotent effort to resist, "but quite easily . . . she took him upward." Passing through "a small hole into the sky world," Iron Hawk not only diminishes himself, he lessens the community in which alone that self has life: "makoce kin sam ćisćila ayin nan hankeya otaninśni" 'the world grew smaller and finally disappeared' (unit 256).

Because he has been a male sun for the camp circle, Iron Hawk's departure leaves the people in an anxious darkness, suffered deeply but differently by his wife and son. The search for him diverts the community from their work and they are "made small" by narrowing the focus of their concerns. Eventually, believing that Iron Hawk has drowned, the mature men in camp return to their responsibilities. But Red Calf insists on being allowed to search further. After he makes the four binding requests, his mother realizes why she must agree: "Howe, eca, eyakeś miye wacin kin ogna yunkan lececa k'un" 'All right then. It was because I insisted on my own way that this happened in the first place' (unit 263). No one can be perfectly protected from inner feelings or external enemies. As much as she loves Red Calf she knows that she can only leave him with the admonition given to Iron Hawk when he set off in the world: "Ho, eca cinkś, waktaya lel yanka" 'Well then, Son, be on your guard' (unit 264).

The "guard" that preserves Red Calf and the tribe is both innate and acquired. The mutual love between parents and children overcomes the fear of physical harm and the desire for personal pleasure (see Makula's "The Buffalo Wife" in Walker, *Sun Dance* 183–90 and *Lakota Myth* 109–18). The instinctive emotion is then clothed in the cultural symbols that empower it, the cap, knife, and bow, as well as in the language that brings the virtue of the past to the present:

> Howo, tunkaśila, wiyohinyanpata toki nanka hecinhan, namah'un wo! Niye lena ate yak'u nan iyayustak wowaś'ake wookihi yak'u k'un hena lehanl iwacinciye lo! Lena ate ena ayuśtan nan tancan ecela tokiyaya ca owakilekte lo!

> Now then, Grandfather, wherever you sit, in the east, hear me! You it was gave these to my father, and with them certain

power and strength; and that power and strength I now beg
of you. These my father left behind, and went off, taking only
his body, so I want to go out to seek him!

(unit 265)

With only his "body," Iron Hawk neither wears his name nor is
he worn by the spirits that have protected him. But that same spirit
now wears Red Calf; "instantly" he became "a great hawk" soaring
upward with the "effortless" flight an uninspired mind or body
would never attain. On his first journey away from the camp circle
Red Calf meets the bird nations, and each displays a distinctive
costume or paint. The chickadee nation binds its head with a
"black fillet"; the "black breasts" blacken their shirts with soot; the
"big without eyes" wear black around their heads and their collars;
the red birds and blue birds naturally wear red and blue paint; the
robins wear "red-yellow coats with grey on the shoulders," and the
magpies have "black paint all over their bodies." Only the snow
birds and blue jays are not identified by their body covering (units
267–82).

Taken together the bird nations live in and by the clothing that
defines them. As Red Calf leaves the last bird nation before entering
the abductors' camp, the grasses trodden down by the enemy are
just beginning to "right themselves" (unit 283). The righting of
Iron Hawk will be complete when he is again contained within
the normative consciousness, the sanity as it were, of his own
people. His Rock nation captors personify the opposing dangers of
social fragmentation: "Ikce-ikicicaḣtak ya iyayapi keś ko ksuyekici-
yapi" 'they knock against each other in passing [and] hurt each
other' (unit 292). The liver promised Red Calf by his "grandmother" (unit 289) does not signify the perpetuation of life, as in
the meadowlark's song, but the meaning of spiritual death. It will
be pieced into appetizers for the Rock people unless Red Calf can
restore Iron Hawk to wholeness.

His father's loss of individual identity and social purpose is imaged in his humiliating captivity. The hero's buffalo body no longer
serves a buffalo function. Instead of protecting the group he is iso-
lated and trapped by one woman: "paġoḣ 'aṗe kin opta sutaya yus

yanka canke toka-inażinśni" 'her arms fast about his waist in the small of his back, so he could not get up' (unit 296). He cannot even speak, snorting "as an angry beast," as he uncharacteristically laments: "Miyeka yeś le anpetu tahena makte-pikte lo" 'Even I, this day, before it ends, I am to be killed' (unit 298). Using one of the sacred arrows properly, Red Calf kills the Rock woman and restores Iron Hawk's free will.

When a man becomes an animal ritually, as Red Calf became a hawk to reach the sky (unit 266), he offers his body for a spirit to wear. In acceding to the Rock woman's initial request Iron Hawk underwent an involuntary metamorphosis. Although he had taken buffalo form, he was not worn by the buffalo spirit and his body became a trap instead of an instrument. After they have returned to their human bodies, Iron Hawk and Red Calf race past any possible temptation to misuse these "garments" again. The magpies and other bird nations ask them to stop to vaunt their escape (units 308–12), but they resist this weakening waste of breath. After all, the Rock woman had diverted Iron Hawk by praising his fame. Self-praise outside of a ritual context exposes the boaster to "splintering." In some sense the Rock people are always in pursuit.

The hero and his son are safe only when they reach the circle of "śkibibila" 'the chickadee people.' Though these birds live a hazardous life, their courage never ebbs. Every spring they return early to cheer the people with their singing, and every spring some are killed in late spring blizzards (units 313–14; see also Deloria, *Waterlily* 57). Their songs are not stilled by the loss of individual birds. The chickadee nation lives as Iron Hawk's people have in his absence and would continue to do even if he had disappeared for good. Their camp circle is therefore closer to home in the travel metaphor that unifies this section.

The special nest commissioned by the bird council to lower Iron Hawk and Red Calf to earth epitomizes Lakota ritual. To place oneself within it is to be surrounded by appreciation for every living object of vision. The interior of a Lakota consciousness is "woven" from garments that reveal the diversity of Wakan Tanka. Inside the willow frame the birds lend their coverings, "feathers of every kind and color" (unit 323) to protect the occupants as if they are adopted children. Feathers cover participants and objects in various ceremonies as well. Within the sheltering nest of consciousness one is surrounded by the best of what one can spiritually see.

When the ropes attached to the four corners of the nest are twisted into one huge strand (unit 324), the story makes its most metaphysical statement: the various beings and spirits of the universe proceed from a single creator who has carefully equipped each species before lowering them them to earth. Once in a favorable environment, however, they must respond in ritual gestures of appreciation that will reintroduce the potential to create: "ognake kin he makicahtakapi nan hehanl ikan kin yutiktita po" 'touch your vehicle to the earth and then jerk on the suspension rope' (unit 320). The vehicle is a consciousness of reciprocal action and affection, human and spiritual.

The birds explain that the creator left his work incomplete (unit 321), so that his creatures could devise their own methods of completion. If the potential initiated by Wakan Tanka is to be realized, the people (of all animal nations) must continually cover and otherwise shelter their vitality. Shooter told Densmore of this universal responsibility: "Animals and plants are taught by Wakantanka what they are to do. Wakantanka teaches the birds to make nests, yet the nests of all birds are not alike. Wakantanka gives them merely the outline. Some make better nests than others" (*Teton Sioux Music* 172).

The bird nations in *Iron Hawk* also say that nothing can live upon the earth without continually building nests. Perhaps ceremonies like *Hunka,* Ghost Keeping, and the Sun Dance are spiritual nests. Without them the Lakota would die like babies without parents:

> "Taku Wakan kin nicagapi nan unkiś eya unkagapi k'eyaś otakiya śkinciya canke eunktunżapi nan leciyana unkayuś-tanpe lo. K'eyaś le ognake kin makicahtake cinhan hecel unglapikte lo," eyapi ke'. Hecena zitkala kin iyuha wowaśi ecunpi nan taku wan iśnala ihankeya kahwopikapi k'un heca wan lila tanka waśte ca kagapi ke';

"The Great Spirit made us as well as you, but because he had so many different activities he forgot and left us up here, and here we have stayed. But if that container is touched to the earth, then thereby we can go down there to live where we belong." At once all the birds went to work and they built the one thing they can make better than anyone else, and it was a beautiful thing. (units 321–22)

When the nest descends "as though held in a cupped palm" (unit 328), the simile suggests a healer's reception of empowerment (see Mails, *Fools Crow: Wisdom and Power* 53). The paradoxical "mistake" of the creator corresponds to Iron Hawk's defeats, and his recovery proceeds from Red Calf's remembering to employ a symbol. And while the hawk cap protects an individual young man, the ritual of the nest brings whole generations to the future.

To be at home in the world finally is to assume the responsibility that self-knowledge requires. Because Iron Hawk knows his weaknesses, he knows his strength and above all he knows his priorities. When his grandmother tells him how Iktomi insulted her in his absence, he passes over a vengeful impulse because experience has taught him how a warrior can misspend energy (units 331–33). Iktomi is fit to be punished only by those helpless enough for him to hurt, and so the grandmother "cooled off her anger" by beating him with a cane (unit 334). If Iron Hawk is to belong to the people as a leader should, he must respond only to dangers that threaten their lives (on self-restraint in leaders see Black Elk, *The Sixth Grandfather* 390).

Instead of breaking the skin of fools Iron Hawk reflexively defines the culture hero as one who heals and covers. The people bring vast amounts of food to feast his return in "great containers of parfleche" (unit 235). Everyone in the community lends their hands to preserve the common life, now personified in an honored individual. Feeding and clothing is not simply accepted as a necessity but celebrated as a privilege in continual, ritualized distribution. When the one who "was wont to feast" the people is feasted by the "entire encampment" (unit 336), Iron Hawk is reminded that leadership entails more responsibility than reward.

His warm reception occurs significantly in the "child-beloved tent" (unit 337). A "child beloved" receives abundant gifts after a special ceremony commits him or her to help those in need (see Deloria, *Dakota Texts* 110n). Iron Hawk had been mysteriously clothed as a child-beloved by his meadowlark grandfather's loving prayer (unit 74). In the last two sections two separate grandfathers are honored in return. Iron Hawk had established an alliance to the western spirits by arranging marriages for the Thunder men. They in turn had pledged assistance to any of Iron Hawk's relatives in time of danger (units 98–101). Now another western spirit, presumably a grandfather of the Thunder men, sends one of his *akicita* (messengers), a black bird, to summon Iron Hawk: "Tehiya waakipa ca iyotiyekiya yanke lo" 'A terrible thing has happened to him and he sits in great misery' (unit 339).

Iron Hawk's wife objects to his leaving since he has just returned. She had also tried to deny the very possibility of trouble when she overheard him telling Red Calf how to use his powers in case he himself could not (unit 238). Now, faced with the certainty of grave danger, it is Red Calf rather than Iron Hawk who answers: "'Hiya, ina, heyeśni yo, ate tokiyap wacinyapi ca ekta yinkte,' eyin na wapośtan nan mila, wan ko wakan k'un hena kicu" '"No Mother, do not say that, my father must go where men need him," and he returned the magic cap and knife and weapons' (unit 341). Red Calf and Iron Hawk both understand that power granted to an individual belongs to the tribe and must be used from then on by the original receiver or a designated substitute, if the whole tribe is not to have that power turned against them.

Awaiting Iron Hawk the western grandfather faces east (unit 343; see Black Elk's analogous placement of "Makes Horses" in *The Sixth Grandfather* 338–39), and accordingly Iron Hawk brings the generalized male sun power to comfort a despair as dark as that of meadowlark at the story's outset. After warming the grandfather with words of comfort he departs for the enemy camp to restore the lost scalp. Used correctly, cultural symbols can minimize individual limitations. By wearing the hawk cap Iron Hawk appropriates powers reserved exclusively for acts of courageous recovery whether physical or ceremonial: "Otohanyan yin nan hehanl wapośtan wan cetan-tanka śaśte ikoyake un he kic'un yunkan cetan-tanka-hingla canke kinyan yin nan wicoti kin aokawinga ke'" 'He went a while, then he put on his cap with the little claws of the hawk on it, and he suddenly was himself a hawk, so he went flying and circled the tribal enemy camp' (unit 349). After using the hawk power of the warrior and hunter to find, Iron Hawk resumes the domestic power to contain and cover when he returns the old man's scalp to his head and heals him.

Iron Hawk's sacrifice of comfort and security reflects the duty of every male adult. The bringing of power to generate life is equally expected. His introduction of horses facilitates mobility, spiritual as well as physical, since it is one of many gifts that free the people from fear. Deloria imaginatively reflects on how the Lakota regarded their first horses and why they named them "holy dogs." Makula told Deloria that historically the Lakota received horses from the Cheyenne in the early 1700s ("Camp Circle Society" 7; see also Black Elk, *The Sixth Grandfather* 314–16). Horses contained a mysteriously explosive power in their bodies while camp dogs were "willing slave animals," according to Black Elk (*The Sixth Grandfather* 230), and too ubiquitous and dependent to be "holy." Just as the Creator left the birds a sacred power to build nests and live upon the earth, so the Lakota integrated the horse into the relational vision they had long possessed. Like any other tool from a hide flesher to a sacred stone the horse existed to serve tribal continuity. With horses children had a better chance of reaching adulthood and making more children. The maker of horses reintroduces the nurturing motif when he says that he made the first horses himself, but that thereafter they learned to make themselves.

His instructions for Iron Hawk maintain tribal priorities unchanged by the new "vehicle." If Iron Hawk looks back to admire his possessions he will lose them (unit 360), but they will multiply infinitely if he keeps his eyes fixed steadily on "home," the place he had forgotten during his swim with the Rock woman. His arrival emphasizes nurturance in the image of the colts "at their mothers' teats" and the loyalty of Red Calf. Because his love for Iron Hawk is greater than the others' fear of "an attacking army," he alone steps forward to greet his father (units 362–65). Iron Hawk's distribution of horses is also consistent with pre-horse values. While wealth is measurable in any culture, tribal influence is determined only by maturity. The culture hero establishes the rule that a man need acquire only four horses to "have tribal standing," to marry and to speak in council (unit 368). The pattern number signals the completion of Iron Hawk's growth. Having generated sources of power, the latter part of his life will be spent in guarding and preserving. Now in the last section it is Red Calf's turn to recover the virtues of the past.

The last section of the story completes the cycle of the hero's life and reflects the fulfillment and meaning of individual existence. Iron Hawk's first departure from his parents had been a practical turning from home and family in adolescence. The hero narratives often express this as a journey to the West (see Jahner, "Cognitive Style" 44) for the purpose of gaining social recognition and winning a wife. After accomplishing these individual imperatives, Iron Hawk becomes responsible for the people's accumulated wisdom. In midlife he turns back toward the East to restore the most valuable lessons of his childhood (see chapter 8 for Lakota meanings of the East).

By sending Red Calf eastward instead of making the journey himself, Iron Hawk represents the group's need for both leadership and wisdom. Deloria suggests that one side of the adult male community must lead the society, while another side must direct the spiritual education of the young. In real life separate men often specialized in these duties, but as the culture hero Iron Hawk incarnates all facets of leadership. He faces both east and west, while as a young man Red Calf only faces west. Although Iron Hawk sends him east to renew the whole society, Red Calf's journey to the eastern edge of the world is individually and psychologically westward.

The narrative adaptation of the westward travel convention enhances the connotations of serenity associated with Lakota ritual and art. Although an adolescent initially contemplates a dream of personal strength, he traces a circumference that returns to childhood when he becomes the parent. Whether he travels west to begin the circle or east to complete it, the hero represents individual Lakota people learning to know and trace their collective life. In this section Red Calf travels west as a person of a certain age, and at the same time he travels east to bring back "grandfather" and renew Lakota culture.

Red Calf's acquisition of certain necessary qualities at each direction is suggested when Iron Hawk recalls his alliance with the western powers. His transferring them to Red Calf represents the orientation of a young person in the spiritual universe (unit 375). Both Iron Hawk and Red Calf acquire the warrior power represented by the Thunders before they encounter the greater obstacle of adjusting to sexuality. Telescoping the western journey, Deloria has Red Calf simply inherit the lightning before encountering his own version of the Rock woman (units 377–80). While the Rock woman episode portrayed the destructive effects of erotic obsession on a man, the Mountain Lion woman represents the damage done to children by a promiscuous mother. Oral narratives and *Iron Hawk* in particular often emphasize the nurturing process. Unnatural parents are seen as monsters in human form (see Rice, *Deer Women and Elk Men* 61–64).

When Red Calf discovers how the mother of his son seduces man after man, he is more outraged at the plight of the neglected children than jealous over his own betrayal (unit 392). He responds first by adopting his son's little half-brother as his brother-in-law, and then by departing briefly to hunt for food. On the journey toward his grandfather he is well on the way to personal maturity as he assumes the responsibility to feed and cover his son, just as the meadowlark had done in the beginning. By using his Thunder power to kill a deer, Red Calf employs a traditional tool of scourging evil against a traditional symbol of erotic distraction (unit 388; see Rice, *Deer Women and Elk Men* 33–46). Transforming the deer to food parallels his turning away from adolescent sexual pleasure to the lifelong work of hunting for children. As in Meadowlark's song the liver that Red Calf's brother-in-law cuts into tiny pieces for his nephew to swallow represents the essence of health, value, and purpose (unit 385).

In passing on the male priority of protection in the form of the liver, Red Calf shapes his brother-in-law long before he can consciously understand. Emulating the meadowlark grandfather he has not directly met, Red Calf introduces the children to the uses of speech: "hokśila kin taśaka kin hena iciyakaśkin nan pusya otḱeya ke'. Nan wana wakanheźala kin śkehanhanla yunkan taśaka kin hena napokaśkela kin el iyakaśka ke'" 'the boy tied the deer-hooves together and hung them up to dry. And when the babe was now lively he tied the rattles to his little wrists' (unit 388). Even before he can form words the baby can confirm his presence to himself and his relatives. The reference to the hooves implies the development occurring simultaneously in Red Calf, his brother-in-law, and the baby.

The same transfer of knowledge continually occurs through the generations and simultaneously at various levels of consciousness throughout the community. Instead of giving his son a name directly, as the meadowlark and Iron Hawk had done, Red Calf has the older child name the younger one (units 389–90). In each of the story's namings the ceremony is performed on a hill away from the circle, so that the child will exist in the minds of *all* his relatives including those that are usually invisible. The more beings who recognize and share their power to live with any individual in the camp circle and the universe, the more chance that person has of living creatively and well. The namer's prior abandonment and his small size, like that of the meadowlark, further suggest any individual's need for an extended family.

The unusual practice of naming by a boy also corresponds to the return to boyhood theme of section 2 (units 133–89). After being immobilized by Ikto, Iron Hawk returned to hunting for his family. Now after being seduced by the Mountain Lion woman Red Calf also concentrates on his dependent relatives. The diversions of adolescence interrupt but do not block the culture hero's boyhood momentum. Iron Hawk and Red Calf forget but then fulfill the promise of their names.

When the baby hears his name, "Rattling Deer Hooves," he shakes the deer hooves on his wrists, as if to say, now that I have a name I am here, and even at this stage I can offer a voice (unit 390).

The sound of the hooves represents the potentiality for speech. Speech enables life, from gaining the love of one's immediate relatives to eliciting the compassion of spirits who respond to prayers. Rattling the hooves transforms a cry for attention into confident participation. This is the proper use of the voice from the song of the meadowlark at the story's beginning to a reader's retrospective awareness of the written words themselves.

The improper use of speech is represented by the Mountain Lion mother's sneering comment on her older son's care of his younger brother: "caże ko laotanin ye. Tantanyan-icaġeca ca!" 'you even announce his name, as though he had a decent start' (unit 391). Only now does Red Calf feel fury at his unfaithful lover. Her effect on children rather than her betrayal of him as an individual makes purification a necessity. The *tiyośpaye* lives because the people consider observed relationships more important than bloodlines. The Mountain Lion mother's words only confirm the undermining influence of her behavior. Her contempt for bastard children (unit 391) reflects her own self-imposed isolation, suggesting that she is the bastard.

The beginning of the story emphasizes that a child's upbringing, rather than its biological or social origin, determines future standing. Every adult contributes to the shaping of every child, and all children belong to the community. The woman's words express a pride that threatens every man, woman, and child with social and spiritual disintegration. That is why Red Calf has no qualms about destroying her with lightning (on Lakota attitudes toward adultery and promiscuity, see Rice, *Deer Women and Elk Men* 33–35, 76–76, 76–83, 92–95).

After dispensing once and for all with youthful distractions and setting his mind on protecting the children, Red Calf promises to "take them home" when he passes west again with his grandfather (unit 396). Red Calf's enhanced stature is reflected on his arrival in the East. The old man who had so expertly formed his father is now pathetically sad and helpless, almost as he had been at the beginning of the story. While he looks westward, "wailing feebly," he sings of Iron Hawk's promise to return, as if he no longer believes it will be kept (units 399–400). But the story suggests that the only promise that matters reflects collective fulfillment. If Iron Hawk himself does not return to Meadowlark, Meadowlark's nurture is still fulfilled.

The Lakota ancestors rejoice when they are brought back in the honoring of their ways. Red Calf saves the eggs of the meadowlark future in his foray against the rattlesnake (units 411–12), returning the Thunder and nest metaphors to the reader in the process. The aesthetic refrain reflects the historical return of Lakota language and culture. Just as Red Calf tells Meadowlark that Iron Hawk is scattering horses all over the world, the story that bears his name simultaneously disseminates Lakota narrative potential. The news that Rattling Deer Hooves is the meadowlark's grandson carries through the idea that the people survive in and through language. As the baby drums the rhythm of physical survival with the hooves, the sound modulates and expands to become the totality of human experience: "Ptehincala Pi Napin!" 'Buffalo-calf liver, rich to taste' (unit 416).

The song is the hallmark of the finished narrative. Grandfather Meadowlark knew how to protect the gift of life when he raised Iron Hawk, and the bird nations resourcefully corrected the Creator's "mistake" through the boldness and delicacy of their art. Now the meadowlark completes the story's circle:

> Yunkan wetu hanl hinhannahcin wanzi tokeyalahcin hihunni nan pazolala wan akanl hinazin nan eyapahala . . . Onah'unwasteya hotaninla canke oyate kin ikiblezapi nan wiyuskinyan itkokipapila ke'.

> Then one early spring morning, a solitary one, first and ahead of the rest came and stood on a little hill, and sang out this little announcement . . . His voice was so pleasant to hear that the people were cheered by it, and happily they went to meet and welcome him.
>
> (units 416, 418)

Each descriptive word—"wetu" 'spring,' "hanl" 'early,' "tokeyalahcin" 'first and ahead of the rest'—speaks of renewal. The story's last paragraph associates meadowlarks with two predominant qualities—their "very yellow" breasts and their amazing voices. Deloria does not need to remind her listeners that the meadowlark's song is unusually long and clear. But she carefully revives the people's agreement on what the song "says." Much like that song her story of Iron Hawk is "rich to taste."

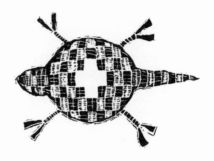

The Verbal Texture:
Tanin and *Icaġa*

Iron Hawk accentuates two major themes of the culture hero genre: growth and manifestation. Deloria portrays the growth of the individual Lakota man fully in Iron Hawk, partially in Red Calf, and potentially in Rattling Deer Hooves. Through them, and especially through their meadowlark grandfather, she reveals that words are no less important to survival than actions. In the Lakota language version, variations of the words *icaġa* (to grow) and *tanin* (to manifest) suggest that cultural consciousness must be spoken, sung, and acted into being, if the people are to live.

Tanin first appears when Grandmother Meadowlark uses it to solidify and guard her miraculous find. She speaks aloud as if to bolster the baby's visual presence with the resolute sound of her words: "'k'eyaś wanaś *taninyan* epe: T'inkteśni ye, mitakoźa' eya ke'" "'But I have already spoken it out loud, he shall not die, my grandson!' she said' (unit 14). Deloria's English translations of forms of *tanin* are accurate and appropriate to customary English variation, but the Lakota words preserve the thematic continuity associated with the concept of manifestation. "Taninyan" here does not literally mean "out loud" but rather "openly" or "manifestly" as applied to varying forms of visual, auditory, or conceptual showing. *Iron Hawk,* like other cultural expressions, proceeds from a consciousness of potential beneficence continually emerging into appropriate form. Such a world offers much joy but also requires firm preparation. A child must learn to filter the light to avoid being blinded by it.

The meadowlark grandfather tells the infant hero immediately of the creative power of the sun, and he also shields him from it (see chapter 6). Meadowlark allows for a child's need to be exposed gradually to experience. He alternates his description of the fierce man from the east that Iron Hawk is to resemble with the comforting shadow a man must also be: "Takoža, itokaġata anpetu wan *iyakitaninśni* ca hokśi-kigna ukte lo" 'Grandson, to the south is a day, indistinct, which shall come to soothe little children' (unit 18). Although Deloria translates "iyakitaninśni" as "indistinct," the literal meaning that manifestation does not "overwhelm" the eye maintains the thematic metaphor. *Tanin* has two initial uses: it establishes the baby's presence when the grandmother speaks his name out loud and it guards him from too much too soon.

The operation of the sun as a concept in the boy's development filters through varying forms of preparatory truth. As he grows, his world expands. Meadowlark prays that the sun will think of Iron Hawk, as he directs Iron Hawk's thoughts to the sun, so that he will "*wicoicaġe* sutaya luhakte" 'have a firm hold on life' (unit 19). Meadowlark's prayer appears to be answered when he applies the phrase, "*wicoicaġe* sutaya yuha yelo" to Iron Hawk's feat of standing for the first time (unit 27). The immediately preceding stage of sitting up had been praised by "letu ca itimahel *oinicaġinkta* ce" 'it is here [in the tipi] that you are to grow, so get acquainted with it' (unit 23). Throughout life the space for growth expands, but the purpose of growth is ultimately to guard and encourage the growth of others.

By stating his hopes for his son aloud, Meadowlark brings them closer to manifestation, just as his wife did in saying that her grandson would not die. He speaks of the sun's wrapping Iron Hawk in his light so that he may "*okitaninyan* icaġe" 'live a life of fame' (unit 35). The words for this hope combine the major verbal motifs. "oki" is a prefix meaning "through" the middle; to show through the middle is to emerge to distinction at the center. Iron Hawk is to "icaġe" 'grow' into this prominence. The phrase appears again when the narrator summarizes the meadowlark's actualizing "decree": "Heceś wocekiye un tohanni kin hehan *okitaninyan* unkta ca wakicunza ke'" 'Thus with this prayer he decreed for him a life of prominence' (unit 36).

To fulfill these words Iron Hawk must first proceed from being a thought in his grandfather's mind to becoming a name in the minds of the people. During an intensive period he must also learn to conceive of himself as an independent entity, for "tuwa maka akanl *icaġa* ca iśnala iyaya" 'all who grow upon this earth must go forth alone' (unit 46). People retain integral personalities throughout their lives but achieve maturity only when they serve the group. Thus the meadowlark's comment on how an individual "goes" alone precedes the general observation, "hecel *wicoicaġa* ai yelo" 'that is the way life comes' (unit 46). The individuality of each being is only part of the larger unity. Deloria's English words for the process of individual and general existence, "goes" and "comes," do not quite express the relationship between individual and general existence conveyed by "icaġa" and "wicoicaġa." And while both words are translated as life, they literally mean growth—life as a process rather than a state.

In detailing aspects of nurture the story also suggests the evolution of growth as spiritually impelled and humanly completed. From the moment his grandmother discovers him, Iron Hawk is a made-not-born hero. Even when he gains supernatural power later, his ability to keep it results from scrupulous teaching:

> Tannake gli yunkan tatanka tucuhu wan yuha gli nan tonacan yuwaśtehin nan yuśkopya eyuśtan yunkan itazipa ca kaġa ke'. Hokśila kin he itazipa wan wakanyan kicaġin nan hehanl canpa-hu kin etan wanhinkpe ko kiyuśtan nan wase un yu-hophopin nan k'u ke'.

> Then very much later he did return and he brought a rib-bone from the buffalo-bull; and for some days he was improving it and finished by bending it into a bow; and he had made

a bow for shooting. He had made a sacred bow for the boy, and then from chokecherry wood he fashioned arrows, and with red paint he ornamented them. (units 48–49)

The word "k̇aġa" 'make' applied to the magic bow is followed by "k̇icaġin" 'he made for' the boy (a sacred bow). The words *k̇aġa* and *k̇icaġin* here and in other contexts refer to conscious acts willed and carried out according to plan. *Icaġa,* on the other hand, refers to an action that occurs independently of human conception and effort.

In rituals and other creative actions *k̇aġa* and *icaġa* are different aspects of a unified energy. Life *icaġa* (grows) mysteriously, but human beings *k̇aġa* (make) varying objects to shelter growth. A ritual takes something that has mysteriously impelled life, *icaġa,* and acts, *k̇aġa,* upon it. *Icaġa* is begun supernaturally and maintained naturally by *k̇aġa*. *Icaġa* or nature brings the child while *k̇aġa* or nurture keeps its life. When Meadowlark teaches Iron Hawk the specific value and lesson to be learned from each animal he brings home, the word "woicaġe" 'things that grow' directly refers to the plant life that nourishes the deer (unit 64). The deer is said to be wise in choosing only food "that emerges from the earth." Like the animals, Meadowlark knows how to make the best use of every quality and ability he has to protect life. Wisdom is not hierarchically divided between varying species. Instead the story defines wisdom as the ability to *k̇aġa* (make) the best use of everything that *icaġa* (grows), from food to cultural traditions.

The first stages of the hero's growth culminate in his naming. To bear a name is to be responsible for one's actions in the full light of the sun after an education mutually accomplished by parents and children: "mitak̇oża tawoyute-cola *icah-waye* c'un" 'my grandson whom I raised without his natural food' (unit 78). The hyphenated word "icah-waye" translated only as "raised" combines the receptive attitude toward growth brought about by a supernatural subject, "icaġa," with the active contribution of "waye" 'I caused.' Thus "raised" literally becomes the growth, "icah," not caused by Meadowlark but fostered by him, "waye." Iron Hawk himself uses a variation of this compound in expressing his gratitude a few lines down; "icaȟmayayin" translated as 'you raised me' but literally "you caused me to grow."

The active contribution of human care through the use of *kaġa* next appears when Iron Hawk uses the bow his grandfather "kicaġin" 'made for him' to kill the first Rock woman. The act of making the bow is explicitly recalled to remind the reader that Iron Hawk's heroic actions arise from nurture. Iron Hawk himself nurtures when he revives the Thunder men in the sweat lodge, "inikaġin" (unit 98). The sweat lodge "kaġa" 'makes' "ni" 'life.' The active "kaġa" resumes but does not initiate growth.

Rituals correspond to the parental work of the meadowlarks. Later while he is still recovering from the Ikto setback, Iron Hawk "cangleśka wan kaġin" 'makes a sacred hoop' to materialize food (units 152–53). Each of the four arrows he shoots into its center magically produces a buffalo. A ritualist typically makes symbolic objects and words to realize a potential. A hunter makes arrows from branches that have already grown to feed people whose growth is mysteriously impelled at birth. The outer act transforms an invisible potential for life into full expression. Iron Hawk's ability to change in shape in section 2 implies the same ability to affect inner processes through external enactment. In the guise of a boy Iron Hawk himself "hokśila kaġin," literally "makes a boy" (unit 155). Conversely, ordinary human beings can assume the clothing or the ritual actions of the hero. But domestic and extraordinary situations require man's ability to *kaġa*.

Iron Hawk initiates his wife into womanhood by charging at her in the body of a buffalo bull (units 181–89) recalling the similar charge mimed by the man wearing a buffalo robe and buffalo horn cap in the girl's puberty ceremony (see chapter 7). They take buffalo bodies again in a food-making ritual where the word for transformation is "pte-ouncaġe" translated as 'buffalo form' (unit 206). The Lakota word, however, adds the sense of dynamic vitality in the shape. "Ouncaġe" refers to the assumption of a "growing" body. It suggests that ritual imitation exists for a particular purpose and result. Deloria uses the word with this association a few pages later when Iron Hawk's wife takes the form of a buffalo cow to give birth.

The words "pte winyela ouncaġe" 'in the form of a buffalo cow' (unit 227) connect the shape of health and strength with the inner vitality that shape protects.

The woman's body represents the power to live symbolized by the buffalo. By involving her in the making of food, Iron Hawk completes her buffalo transformation. She "ouncaġe" 'becomes' a buffalo to further growth. The theme of making the outer shape of an ability before that ability is realized cyclically returns when the grandfather who raised Red Calf "kicaġin" 'makes' [arrows] for him' (unit 236), the same dative form of *kaġa* used to describe Meadowlark's gift of the sacred bow to Iron Hawk (unit 49). Iron Hawk too passes on the sacred hawk cap to carry his son through adolescence. His words recall his own upbringing and make each individual raising represent tribal regeneration: "Ho, cinkś, tunkaśila wan maka-oṗaṗun kin ekta *icah-maye* c'un he lena mak'u welo, waṗośtan kin le, nan mila kin le, nan wahinkpe, tatucuhu-itaziṗa kin le" 'now, son, I have a grandfather at the edge of the world, there he raised me, and he gave these to me, this cap, and his knife and these bow-and-arrows' (unit 238). As he speaks Iron Hawk demonstrates the continuing presence of "icah" 'the power to grow,' protected not initiated by a human agent, "maye" 'he caused me.'

The stories also identify obstacles to growth. Iron Hawk's humiliation at the hands of Ikto and the Rock woman cushions the shock of such inevitable experience for the listeners. Everyone can expect a similar setback. Iron Hawk recovers because he is able to reintegrate the lessons of Meadowlark after his mistake. Had he not been "icah ye" 'raised' well, his reserves of Lakota identity would not have been deep enough to sustain him during individual dissolution.

Red Calf can rescue his father from the Rock people only because Iron Hawk recognizes his own plight. While *tanin* had been clustered to reveal benevolent potentialities earlier in the narrative, Deloria employs the word in the Rock woman episode to manifest the decidedly unheroic descent of Iron Hawk. In their initial encounter the Rock woman engages Iron Hawk in a childish debate over which of them should cross the river. She begins to undermine Iron Hawk's self-control immediately: "'Wan, śma ca toka-wauśni ye lo!' eye c'eyaś ake eya canke canzeze *hotanin* nan 'Śma ca toka-wauśni ce epe lo!' eya yunkan ake kico ke'" "'Why, it is deep, so I can't come over!" he called back but again she asked, so impatiently he called, "It is deep, I can't come, I tell you!" but still she called him' (unit 248). Deloria translates the words "canzeze hotanin" 'impatiently he called' to show a warrior becoming rattled. "Hotanin" means literally "voice coming out" but another Lakota word for "call" might have been used such as *pan*. The *tanin* word helps to make it apparent that Iron Hawk is out of his depth. His rising voice manifests his weakness in confronting this kind of enemy.

After "hotanin" reveals the onset of Iron Hawk's impairment, another *tanin* word indicates its full extent. He experiences his seduction as a progressive loss of self until even the earth that Meadowlark taught him to love is forgotten. The Rock woman draws him toward the sky until "makoce kin sam ćisćila ayin na hankeya *otaninśni*" 'the world grew smaller and finally it disappeared' (unit 256). The next use of *tanin,* however, manifests the potentiality for Iron Hawk's recovery and more importantly the recovery of the whole people from any historical setback. The bird nations have heard the message that comes through in stories and rituals. The people's will to live in accordance with their values always prevails: "Hunhi, hokśila wan atkuku okile keya *otanin* k'un" 'it has been spread abroad that someone would seek his father, that boy must be you' (unit 273). In this case "otanin" refers to a manifestation in words, literally "it is said openly."

As before when Iron Hawk's grandparents created reality in the flesh by preparing its pattern in words, Red Calf's verbal prefiguration is fulfilled in his physical presence. The next *tanin* word refers to language that is not raised into a patterned reality. The bluejay nation portrays the misuse of language and the voice. Their chatter is so undisciplined and unabated that "takeya *taninśni* wakinice s'e" 'one could hardly distinguish' what they were saying (unit 280). "Hardly distinguish" is an accurate translation, but *tanin* retains connotations created by its repetition. The Red Calf episode is meant to manifest the continual Lakota restoration of the best of themselves. Negative examples like tricksters and bluejays provide the shadows that highlight the ideal. In the first episode Meadowlark's words of the sun define the culture hero. Meadowlark himself enacts the ideal use of the voice from his soothing words to the baby to his concluding song of praise. Conversely, the babble of the bluejays cannot create; "takeya taninśni," literally "what they said did not come out."

After Red Calf's arrival in the Rock people camp, he briefly retreats into various forms of invisibility. First he disguises himself as a tree stump to rest. Then as his father had done before he was born, he becomes a little boy as if to reiterate that heroic deeds proceed from conferred powers, represented here by the sacred bow and arrows. Just before Red Calf manifests this power, his Rock woman grandmother carries him through the mob of Rock people gathered for Iron Hawk's execution. With Red Calf in her arms, she arrives at a place "*otanin* inaźin" 'where she could see' (unit 294). Deloria's English locates the grandmother accurately, but the words literally mean "she stood in view." "Otanin" means not only that Red Calf can see Iron Hawk but that he is emerging into adult distinction. Meadowlark had used the same phrase to define his hopes for Iron Hawk (unit 35). Prior to taking the heroic role Red Calf is only a little boy in his grandmother's arms. The rapid transition from boy to man that ensues telescopes the idea of growth as the ability to take on power. A man without a hawk cap or its equivalent has no more power than a boy.

A mysterious subject animates life. Living beings then maintain the momentum of their own growth. The most significant expression of this cooperation occurs in the chickadee nation where Iron Hawk and Red Calf rest before returning to earth. The chickadee leader tells them: "Taku Wakan kin *nicaġapi* nan unkiś eya *unkaġapi* k'eyaś otakiya śkinciya canke eunktunźapi nan leciyana unkayuśtanpe lo" 'the Great Spirit made us as well as you, but because he had so many different activities he forgot and left us up here, and here we have stayed' (unit 321). The Lakota version repeats the word for "make" twice, "nicaġapi" and "unkaġapi," literally "he made you" and "he made us" emphasizing the act of creation in the verb *kaġa*.

The most striking symbol of creative completion in *Iron Hawk* is the great nest that first lowers the heroes to earth and later all the bird nations. As a symbol of symbols the nest mediates between the Creator and beings that grow (see chapter 3). Beings emulate the Creator's making according to their own gifts. From clothing to ritual, human work is consistently directed to protecting the work of the Great Spirit. The birds "built the one thing they can make better than anyone else" and they "made" it out of willows and feathers (units 322–23). Both "built" and "made" translate the single Lakota verb "kaġapi." Deloria uses the word four times in a brief space to equalize the contributions of Creator and creature in making life: "nicaġapi," "unkaġapi," "kaġapi," and again "kaġapi." From the opening when the infant Iron Hawk is soothed and painted through to Red Calf's rescue of his father the creature finishes and even corrects what the creator begins.

In the next episode the horse-maker explains this sequence of creation to Iron Hawk:

> Miye le śunka-wakan *wakaġe* lo. Maka un *wicawakaġin* nanśna ca huye-wicawakiyin nan iwaśtela hektatanhan patan iyewicawaya can manipi nan śunka-wakan ca ni iyayape lo. Lecala s'e le iyecinka *icicaġahanpi* ca pilamayanpe lo. Minape un lena *wakaġe* c'un etanhan tokśa tukte ehan maka sitomniyan śunka-wakan yukanpikte lo. Tokeśke he tokeya *wakaġa* yunkan elahcin iyacu welo, hecetu we lo.

> For I am the one who makes holy dogs. I made them out of earth, and put wooden legs on them, and gave them a gentle push from the rear, and they started walking off, and were living holy dogs. It is only comparatively recently that they have been making themselves, and that helps me. From these, my original handiwork, by and by all over the world there will be holy dogs. By some chance you have picked the very first one I ever made. (units 357–59)

The first three variations on *kaġa* are "wakaġe" 'I made,' "wicawakaġin" 'I made them,' and "iciciġahanpi" 'they have been making themselves.' Another instance, "minape un lena wakaġe" is translated as 'my handiwork' but literally means "these that I made using my hand." *Ḱaġa* is used five times in close proximity to emphasize the horse-maker's ability to do what the hero cannot do. But Iron Hawk can keep this amazing gift only if, like a vision quester, he follows the giver's directions to the letter.

Horsemaker tells him not to look back at the buckskin horse he has chosen until he arrives at his home. Iron Hawk's dedication results in a multiplication of benefit to the people. When he finally looks back, the herd has become numberless, a manifestation to everyone that they have sacred protection. Deloria uses "otanin" in this context, applying it to Iron Hawk's long awaited first glimpse of home rather than directly to the horses:

Canḱe hetan glicu nan hinzila kin ecela gluha ku k'eyaś haḱiktaśni ku nan wana ehanḱe bloya wanḱa ce el iyahin nan akotanhan wicoti kin *otaninyan* glinaźin canḱe nakeś haḱikta yunkan śunḱakan eyapila kin blaye kin ataya ihakaṗ ahinaźin ke'.

So he started homeward, and brought only his buckskin, and did not look once behind him, but when he reached the top of the last ridge, and could see the camp circle in the distance beyond, then he looked back, and there all over the plain were horses without number, all having followed him, now come to a stop, because he had. (unit 361)

Where the translation speaks only of Iron Hawk's seeing the distant camp circle, the Lakota version refers to the camp circle "otaninyan" 'manifesting itself.' This places Iron Hawk's seeing in the context of sacred manifestation, a potentiality becoming physically real. As home is magnified in Iron Hawk's vision, the securing of growth in that home appears in the abundance of "holy dogs."

The thematic relation between active human making and spontaneous growth extends to Iron Hawk's distribution of the horses. The animal forever changed the tribe's material life but not their concept of wealth. They immediately decided that a man need own only four horses to have tribal standing: "uśiya *icaġe* keś" 'however poor he was at the start of life' (unit 368). The Lakota words mean literally "although he grew up in poverty." *Icaġa* (growth) is a con-

dition of birth, present in every living thing. The Lakota were relatively poor before they had horses, but they still had the involuntary presence of *icaġa* within them. Although they cannot create
horses any more than they can create themselves, they must *kaġa*
(make) use of their gifts to benefit rather than divide their society.

The cooperation of man and the spirits is as important as that
between men. Iron Hawk's speech to Red Calf before his journey
to Meadowlark introduces the theme of man's contribution to Creation in the last episode: "Ho, cinkś, kakiyotan maka-opapun kin
ekta *imacaġe* lo. Wicaȟcala wan winunȟcala wan kici *icaȟmayanpi*
nan lila temaȟilape san ihawicawaktaśni omani-wahiyu we lo"
'Now, Son, over in that direction, at the edge of the world I was
born. And an old couple raised me, and thought highly of me,
but I did not stay with them, I came traveling' (unit 371). While
the translation has Iron Hawk recalling where he was "born" and
the old couple who "raised" him, the Lakota words sound out the
unified momentum of events separated in English. In Lakota Iron
Hawk speaks of his youth as a single process manifested in separate
events. To be "born" is expressed in the passive "imacaġe", i.e. the
subject is the Creator, while to be raised is a conceptual compound
of both passive and active, "icaȟmayanpi," literally "they caused me
to grow" rather than simply "they raised me."

The willingness of the Lakota people to assume responsibility
for completing the Creator's work is underscored by the nearly
identical words of Meadowlark naming Iron Hawk (unit 78) and
Red Calf's brother-in-law naming Rattling Deer Hooves. Although
the infant is Red Calf's son, the brother-in-law like the meadowlark
is the actual parent. The story defines parentage as nurture rather
than sexual generation. The body is an instrument of the Creator
in conceiving life, but man is on his own in maintaining it. It is
therefore especially appropriate that the brother-in-law is only a
child. The diminutive meadowlark and brother-in-law represent
the loving determination to live on against the odds: "Mitunśkala
iyotiyekiya *icaȟwakiye* c'un, hunk-cola k'eyaś *bluicaġela* k'un, he
nakiciȟ'unpi ye" 'My nephew whom I raise with great difficulty,
whom lacking a mother, yet I made him grow, hear this for him'

(unit 389). The boy repeats Meadowlark's use of "icaḣwakiye" 'I raised' and intensifies it with "bluicaġela" 'I made him grow.' The repeated forms of *icaġa* maintain the renewal theme more effectively than the separate English words, "I raise" and "I made him grow." The parallel to the first naming also extends to the phrase "hunk-cola" 'lacking a mother.' Meadowlark had said "tawoyute-cola" 'without his natural food' (unit 78). Echoing Meadowlark again the brother-in-law prays that the future he imagines will be manifested in social reality: "ca wicacaże kin he oyate egna *otaninyan* unkte lo" 'so among the peoples he shall live, spreading the fame of that name' (unit 390). The phrase "spreading the fame" is simply "otaninyan" in Lakota; the repetition of a form of *tanin* makes the Lakota version more polished by carrying through the key word.

With Meadowlark's reappearance in the last two scenes, *tanin* reveals and affirms Lakota survival. From Meadowlark to Iron Hawk to Red Calf's brother-in-law the act of naming realizes a social reality. When Iron Hawk named Red Calf, he called "maka aḱanl taku śkanśkanyan toni gluha un kin" 'whatever lives all over the world' to protect the child (unit 230). The ceremony establishes Red Calf as a reality in the minds of a cosmic *tiyośpaye* by sounding his name (see chapter 3). Near the end Meadowlark recalls that the force of Iron Hawk's love caused him to hear the naming of Red Calf all the way over at the eastern edge of the world. He tells his wife: "Takoza Cetan Maza le cinca caś eyaś *glao-tanin* k'un, le e yelo" 'this is the son of our Iron Hawk, whose birth and name he proclaimed—this is he!' (unit 405). "Proclaim" is "glaotanin," literally "to manifest one's own," connoting in this case to realize one's hopes through words.

While a name confirms existence, it must be continually renewed by deeds. When the meadowlark warns an egg-eating rattlesnake of Iron Hawk's vengeance, the snake mocks him: "epahe c'eyaś niyate toki iyaya *taninśni* canḱe wana lehan-i iḣaḣa-makuwa ye lo" 'This threat I have been making, but your father doesn't appear, and now by this time, he makes sport of me!' (unit 410). The word "taninśni" refers to Iron Hawk's invisibility and sustains the thematic thread. At the moment Meadowlark speaks, Red Calf has appeared to save the remaining nests and the meadowlark nation will live on.

The final scene reveals how language gradually builds a reality strong enough to endure. Red Calf rides ahead of the main party to report to Iron Hawk that his grandfather's "people are coming." His message then expands to embrace the whole people: "'Ate, wana tunkašila taoyate op upe lo,' eya canke *yaotaninpi* ca wiyeya oyate kin yankapi ke" '"Father, my grandfather and his people are coming," he said, so it was generally announced, and all the people sat ready to greet them' (unit 415). "Canke yataninpi" is translated 'so it was generally announced,' but it literally means "to manifest with the voice." The specific announcement reflects generations of oral narratives that "decree" and exemplify renewal.

The meadowlark's song joyfully confirms the announcement, "Ptehincala Pi Napin" 'Buffalo-calf liver, rich to taste!' (unit 416). Every spring the meadowlarks use their invigorating gifts of song and "very yellow" color to bring "renewed life" to their Lakota relatives: "onah'un wašteya *hotaninla* canke oyate kin ikiblezapi" 'his voice was so pleasant to hear that the people were cheered by it' (unit 418). "Hotanin" 'to manifest with the voice' is less formal than "yaotanin," used just previously for the camp crier's announcement. The variations of *tanin* reintroduce the meadowlark as the story's primary symbol of revelation. He embodies the survival gifts conferred by the Creator, and he demonstrates the will to find their best use.

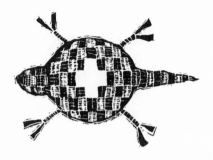

The Lakota Context: Meadowlarks

The beginning of *Iron Hawk* reflects traditions of child rearing. Lakota society assumed that a child's character would be derived from the adults closest to him. According to Black Elk the first woman to handle a baby after the mother brings it home, ritually wipes out its mouth with her finger in order to transfer her "good nature" and "character" to the child. Then, as the second woman washes the baby with a soft weed, she uses gentle speech to complement the action of her hands in the manner of Iron Hawk's grandfather: "So far I have tried to get along with my people and have raised a family" (*The Sixth Grandfather* 379). Finally, the anointment of oil and red paint completes the transmission of "all her good." The temperament of those who attended children shaped their willingness to be patient individuals and ultimately assured civil peace and political cooperation. Until adolescence most children learned the paramount lesson of treating each other gently under the tutelage of grandparents. This arrangement freed parents to pursue their unremitting work of providing food and shelter, fighting, governing, healing, and performing ceremonies. They wisely entrusted their children's education to the calmest, most mature members of the community (see Deloria, "Camp Circle Society" 80 and *Waterlily* 34–36).

While grandparents made ideal parenting a familiar reality of everyday life, meadowlarks often portrayed the same ideal in the oral tradition. They were associated with hope for the future as the first birds to return in the spring, and they are the appropriate "persons" to protect the emotional fire of the future in Iron Hawk. The meadowlark's resourcefulness despite its small size was widely celebrated (see Rice, "How the Bird . . ." 422–57). In one story a rattlesnake coils itself around a nest containing a mother meadowlark and her four sons. Although she had prudently placed the nest in tall grass, she must draw upon her innate courage and ingenuity to survive life's inevitable danger.

Controlling her pounding heart she offhandedly tells her oldest son to borrow a kettle so that she may cook a meal for their long lost relative. While she hospitably regales the "uncle" with chit-chat, the three other sons launch into their first "solos," ostensibly to seek their kettle-borrowing brother. When they are safely gone, the mother too takes off allowing herself a parting taunt: "Tuwe ca he wonicihinkta hecinhan!" 'There keep on waiting, whoever you are expecting to cook you a meal' (Deloria, *Dakota Texts* 81, 82). The portrayal of the enemy as a rattlesnake is echoed in the last episode of *Iron Hawk* (units 409–13) when Red Calf dispatches the intimidators of his aged (great) grandfather who cannot fight back like the mother bird in the short story.

The meadowlark is renowned for eloquence as well as courage. Transitional or revelatory events are often given songs in Lakota culture, and the meadowlark is the most accomplished singer, orator, storyteller, and even gossiper among the *wamakaśkan* (animal spirits). While other animals often spoke helpfully to human beings, only meadowlarks were known preeminently for intelligible, almost commonplace articulation as "the birds that spoke Lakota" and "the sun birds" (Vestal 21).

In 1971 an eighty-four year old Lakota woman, Mrs. Louise Hiett, described how meadowlarks repeated, sometimes helpfully, sometimes mischievously, anything the people might like to hear:

Sitting up on the tent pole at night, when people are awake you know, the poles are like this. Moonlight nights you can see them. And a meadowlark would be singing, and he would be talking about something they talked about. Somebody said, "We're going to move camp because," they said, "the buffalo are awful thick down so-and-so creek," the meadow-lark next was singing, so we listened to them and "we're gonna move down the creek where there's lots of buffalo," in Indian and then he laughs, the bird laughs, chatters like he were laughing. So they're a tattletale . . . they understand what the Indian people say. And one little lark was singing "grand-mother's lazy, grandmother's lazy." And then he says, "a calf's liver is rich, a calf's liver is good eating," "oyul waśte, oyul waśte," and bring it out twice. Things like that, they hear and they say. (Hiett 4).

Iron Hawk's later lapse suggests the social dangers of adultery, but the Lakota are not prudish. The meadowlark John Bruyier de-scribed for Dorsey even had license to invade the tipi. In the morn-ing from its perch at the apex of the poles a bird might repeat such phrases as "dance with little lefthand" or "ce sake i yelo" 'put the hard male member there' or "kola tawinye lo" 'friend, make love to your wife' (Bushotter 249:2–3).

From teasing humor to praising a boy's first kill, meadowlarks consistently affirmed existence in confidence and joy. Throughout the ethnography they are heard to say, "ptehincalapi naṗin" 'calf-liver tastes rich' (Bushotter 249:3). In Black Elk's "Falling Star" narrative the hero's meadowlark grandfather echoes Iron Hawk's: "My grandson brought me a good buffalo calf liver. The calf liver is rich" (*The Sixth Grandfather* 399). In the same passage Black Elk mentions that a young hunter's first opportunity to give-back was elaborately praised and feasted (see also Deloria, *Waterlily* 93). The liver of a deer or a buffalo was considered to be the animal's vital center, the equivalent of the "heart" in Western terms. In "Camp Circle Society" Deloria notes that all organ meats were considered especially healthful and delicious, but the liver was eaten raw and "still warm with life" at the butchering ("Camp Circle Society" 99, see also *Dakota Texts* 236). But while the liver is a focal point of song, the meadowlark's name, *tasiyagnunpa,* means "double guts" and refers to another delicacy, the intestines, thought to be a particular treat when eaten raw by birds or roasted into "crackles" by people ("Camp Circle Society" 99). Both in name and in the words of its song, meadowlarks represent the fat of the land, the gifts of health, and the skill to maintain it.

Their words also strengthen emotional relations. Meadowlarks are often heard to say, "Scepan, micakca" 'Sister-in-law, brush my hair,' or "Sice, micakca" 'brother-in-law, brush my hair' (Buechel, *Dictionary* 483). The request conventionally expresses deep affection between relatives, even those in a joking relationship (see Hassrick 118–19 and Deloria, *Waterlily* 164). Sometimes the affection may be expressed protectively as in "kola, wakinyan akiyelo, tiyo nape po" 'friend, the thunder is coming, run inside' (Buechel, *Dictionary* 483). Like the Lakota, meadowlarks often celebrate accomplishment: "Tasiyagnunpa, nitakoza wan gli yelo; iwakici yo" 'Meadowlark, your grandson has returned, dance in praise of him.' The one addressed then dances and sings conventional syllables of happiness, "Hahe, hihoho" (Buechel, *Dictionary* 483).

The meadowlark uses its voice and body as the Lakota were taught to use all their resources. Bruyier associates the birds with self-sacrifice in the Sun Dance:

> As for the meadowlarks, they follow a certain style of dancing, the Sun Dance style. They are black on the breast in a quarter-moon shape (*wi-kahaya,* made like a moon) . . . and in the very center of the breast they are marked with a yellow spot; and from that it is said they have painted a sunflower on their breast, as it were, and when they go into their dance, they do not do so in a group, but singly, they dance somewhere. Long ago a meadowlark cried, "Heya-a-he-ha-e!" and stood on a rock and straight up and down he sent himself, as though he had no wings, so closely held in they were.
>
> (Bushotter 249:2)

And more recently Frank Fools Crow attested to the place of the meadowlark in Sun Dance tradition:

> In 1972 when I was leading the Pine Ridge Sun Dance, a meadowlark came and sang and danced with us. The people saw it dancing around and singing, gracefully hopping on one foot and then the other, and stretching out its little wings like arms. Then it danced over toward the east entrance of the enclosure and flew off. The people were very happy about this. They knew it was a good sign, that the spirits were with us. (Mails, *Fools Crow* 184; see also Fools Crow's slightly different account in Mails, *Sundancing* 206)

Conversely, the absence of meadowlarks could leave the people bereft of joy. Louise Hiett associates the white man's intrusion into Lakota consciousness as having garbled the meadowlark's speech: "Lots of things I heard the meadowlark, I used to understand them, but I can't understand these meadowlarks, but I do know what they're talking about. I think they're talking Russian. Chatterboxes." Once it was a "big miracle" to "hear an animal talk, you know, that's a great thing, but instead they run from you" (Hiett 4).

Through the oral tradition, however, the meadowlark still dispels static. In a 1976 recording Vine Deloria, Sr., Ella's younger brother, tells how a tribe was cured of a mysterious epidemic when one of their leaders was given an herb and its accompanying song by "a little warrior" in buckskin clothes: "Nitunkaśila wanna hinapelo. Kikta hiyeya ye na kalya ye na lageya yo. Heconon kinhan mnayan wahe śni, tanyan yaunpi kte lo" 'Your grandfather the sun is about to rise. Sit right up, brew it up, drink it down, and you will live without diminishing' (*Stories of the Lakota;* my transcription of the Lakota song, Vine Deloria, Sr.'s translation as spoken on the record). As in *Iron Hawk* renewal is signified by the rising sun, and the meadowlark shows the way to health and joy: "And here that little warrior then sort-a-shook and it was a meadowlark, and as he flew away he broke a piece of that branch he was standing on, about six inches long, and it fell to the ground." The branch is the medicine and it produces a "red tea," the color of the sun.

The Lakota directions have different color sequences according to different holy men. The most commonly used are Black Elk's black-west, white-north, red-east, yellow-south, and Fools Crow's black-west, red-north, yellow-east, white-south. As a yellow being the meadowlark comes from the east or the south. It arrives literally from the south every spring. Whatever its origin *Tašiyagnunpa* never fails to herald warmth.

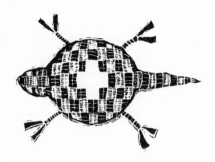

The Lakota Context:
Sun, Fire, the Color Red

Regardless of any particular association of color with direction,
the sun, fire, and the color red predominate in the Lakota symbolic
world, even though other entities and colors provide the harmony
that comprehensively prevails (on red as the favorite color of the
spirits, see Walker, *Lakota Belief and Ritual* 108). Deloria begins
Iron Hawk with the sun, the red grass, and the red paint. The sun
is the most striking visible sign of supernatural benevolence. Wakan Tanka (Great Mystery) is an abstract term, eternally beyond
representation. But to the extent human beings can know it, the
creative power of Wakan Tanka manifests itself in every dawn. Of
the four Lakota cardinal virtues—courage, fortitude, generosity,
and wisdom—the third, *wacantognaka* (generosity) is associated
with the east, the sun, and the buffalo.

The buffalo's generosity is a Lakota axiom. The animal gives every part of itself, body and spirit, to feed, clothe, and sacralize the
circle's collective life. The buffalo is also directly connected to the
engendering power of the sun (see Walker, *Sun Dance* 130 and
Lakota Belief and Ritual 231). The other physically felt emanation
of the sun's power—fire—was an especially immediate presence in
camp circle days. As Black Elk tells it, the human use of fire origi-

nated in a vision. A spirit taught Moves Walking to spin a soap weed stick on a piece of wood using the dried soapweed root as tinder (see also Makula's similar story, Beckwith 377). Through Moves Walking the people learned to cook with fire and to revere it as a sacred gift. They were to maintain an inextinguishable central fire, and whenever they moved, the chief of each band always carried its live coals in a hollow log (see *The Sixth Grandfather* 311). As a leader protected the life of the band, so a *wakicunze,* literally "holder" of the people, held the fire as an example of adult responsibility:

> A Teton man said, "In the very, very long ago, the magistrates carried a slow-burning log on migrations and when the camp circle was again in place, the people hurried to the center with tinder and faggots for a light from the eternal fire in the council tipi, for warming their lodges and cooking their food. Because the obtaining of fire was neither easy nor quick, nor sure, it must be carefully guarded and nursed at all times so that everyone might benefit from it . . . Thus, the *wakicunzas* were also the traditional keepers of the fire." (Deloria, "Camp Circle Society" 31)

At the beginning of *Iron Hawk* the grandfather sits at a dead fire in his own tipi outside the circle, but he lives in the place where the sun always emerges. When his wife goes to collect firewood, she brings home a source of fiery new life. On Lakota reservations today children are still cherished as the way "to keep it going," and most of the ceremonies honoring them as the fulfillment of all present endeavors are still practiced.

In addition to the ear piercing of very young children and naming of adolescents, the ethnography includes descriptions of the *Hunka* ceremony that honors children for virtues they will practice in adulthood. In descriptions by Densmore (68–77) and Bushotter (82:488) generous men carry children to the ceremony on their backs, as if to say that they too will one day carry the nation's life. The ceremony is intended to make the child "nothing but good in every way" (Densmore 76). Although *Hunka* customarily required large give-aways by only the most well provisioned parents, the ritual drama enacted a relational ideal for the whole tribe. As the children represent the purpose of adult effort, so they and other children not officially honored are powerfully imprinted with the meaning of their growth, the supreme value of spiritual endurance in the physical world (see Deloria, *Waterlily* 76–78).

Like the children's ceremonies, another form of *Hunka* enacted a societal model for adults. Walker describes the elaborate binding of two adults, usually a younger and an older man in absolute loyalty and support:

> What you have is his. What he has he will give you if you wish it. You must help him in time of need . . . His children will be as your children and your children will be as his . . .
> If he takes the sweatbath or seeks a vision, you should aid him and help to pay the Shaman. If he is sick, you should make presents to the Shamans and the medicine men. (Walker, *Sun Dance* 139)

In addition all men who have been made *hunka* are relatives to each other and will never let their fellow *hunka* "be in want." The dramatic form stimulates generosity in beholders as well as participants to manifest a practical, spiritual, and collective result.

The ceremony also foregrounds fire to transform participants and witnesses into suns, interchangeable sources of strength as each in turn goes to the center. Just as Black Elk had associated the origin of fire with a vision from the sun, so some of Walker's most respected informants, Sword, Bad Wound, and No Flesh, told him that the *ton* or power of the sun was immediately present only in fire and could not be directly imparted to a human being. Only an intermediary or *akicita* with a special connection to the sun like the buffalo or the eagle could transfer a safe but potent container of sun power called *tonwan* (see Walker, *Lakota Belief and Ritual* 95, 230). The *tonwan* of the sun was in the tail feathers of the eagle, prominently employed as a symbol of the highest virtue in *Hunka* and throughout Lakota culture, but the experience of an emanation so powerful it could not be possessed or worn was reserved for fire.

In Walker's account the door of the special *Hunka* tipi faces the morning sun. When the people have assembled inside, the conductor goes to the door and asks the meadowlark to impart fidelity: "The meadowlark my cousin / A voice in the air" (*Sun Dance* 129). The "voice" of the medicine man is then complemented by the smoke of the first pipe offering, lit by a coal carried on a forked "fire stick" painted red (Walker, *Sun Dance* 125 and *Lakota Belief and Ritual* 227). Burning through the tobacco in the pipe, the sun in the fire manifests the breath of the participants' shared being.

The sun is the "patron" of idealized relationships, epitomized by the *hunka* (*Sun Dance* 131). When the *walowan* (conductor) lights and offers the ceremony's second pipe, he again stands in the doorway facing east and addresses the sun as *tunkaśila* (grandfather), the term used to address all spirits in prayer. Referring to the younger man, he says, "Grandfather, we will bring you a grandson this day" (131). The opening section of *Iron Hawk* parallels the *walowan's* expressed hope. For each of the six pipe offerings in Walker's account a special keeper of the fire stick brings burning coals from the fire and places them on the altar. When the *walowan* lights the pipe from the first offering, he takes the *ton* of the sun into the pipe before passing it around the lodge for all to smoke. In subsequent offerings he shares the pipe with the four directions, passed by the sun on his "daily journey," and with the buffalo skull, blowing smoke through its nostrils. Then he smokes exclusively with the younger *hunka* candidate (*Sun Dance* 134).

Each lighting in Walker's version extends the *tiyośpaye* beyond the immediate audience and even the present generation. The burning coals carried on a ceremonial fire stick create "a spirit fire" that "attracts disembodied spirits of former friends" to "give good counsel" (*Lakota Belief and Ritual* 227). Similarly, fire is a principal metaphor of the energy that comes through the meadowlark grandfather to Iron Hawk. In its largest sense the *Hunka* ceremony brings the past to the present. The "good counsel" of the ancestors speaks through the ceremony, and they live again in the ceremony's participants who in turn will live in those still unborn. When Iron Hawk arrives as a gift, the grandfather's symbolic imagination has been developed highly enough to protect that gift. In the Lakota hunting culture everything necessary for life not only had to be spiritually sought, it had to be ritually protected once it arrived, from the drying of meat to the empowering of a *tunkan* (a sacred stone found by an individual and ceremonially wrapped by a holy man). The sense of extending the force of the sun through fire is also expressed by burning sage and sweetgrass, and it usually has the following intent: "The smoke from the contents of a ceremonial pipe lighted with a spirit fire is very potent for invoking the good and exorcising the evil powers" (*Lakota Belief and Ritual* 227).

Bushotter's explanation of the origin of the various honoring ceremonies offers a unique perspective on the meaning of fire, complementing the visionary origin described by Black Elk and Makula. When a young man for whom the *Hunka* ceremony had been performed in childhood grew up and took a wife, the couple was ceremonially honored in a special tipi. Outside, after and sometimes even during the ceremony, a large group of people gathered for a special give-away called *cetipi* (they build a fire). The ceremony inside the tipi, as in other forms of *Hunka,* celebrates the willingness of everyone in the *tiyospaye* to sacrifice for everyone else by concentrating fidelity in the husband and wife. The post-ceremonial give-away is a similar acting out by individuals of generally held values. This aspect of *cetipi* has a thoughtfully humorous dimension when generosity becomes competitive. Women boast of presenting their sons with "moccasins of solid quillwork," or of giving away horses upon his marriage, or of making cradleboards for this children. Each woman boasts one such deed as a separate accomplishment, standing before a kettle of the best food she can provide. If another woman wishes to "match her deeds," she steps forward, and after enumerating her own accomplishments in the same endeavor, takes the kettle of food. The food can be taken only by a woman who dedicates her daily existence to strengthening others (Bushotter 82:4).

By boasting in a legitimate, formalized manner, the women balance self-reliance with mutual reliance. They play a comic, almost *heyoka* role here (see Black Elk, *The Sixth Grandfather* 232–35). They pretend to boast of deeds every woman should lovingly do. To praise oneself for such acts on a non-ritual occasion would be humiliating. In the ritual, however, the multiple distributions of food remind everyone that no one can really outdo anyone else, and that passing feelings of rivalry are forgivably human. Once the second woman in each competition takes the kettle, those in attendance may partake of its contents:

> Those guests who have done none of these things enough to meet the challenge of that hostess, eat anyway, because somebody who has, has taken some food; and all who have taken food of various kinds share them together at the feast. But if there had been nobody who could personally match the hostess, then nobody might eat at all. For those who could not match her only get the food through some relative who can. (Bushotter 82:4)

There is no actual fire at a *cetipi,* the kettles being simply placed on the ground, but the shared food, according to Bushotter, replaces an ancient practice of sharing fire. The name *cetipi* comes from the days before the tipi had been developed and "fire meant something":

> a certain person would build a great fire, like giving a great feast. Much wood would be gathered, and the outdoor fire built to blaze large and casting pleasant warmth afar. To this warmth, others who had provided warmth in this manner to others in the past and could prove it, were to come there and partake of this fire's warmth . . . but now they use the food of a feast instead of a fire. (Bushotter 82:4)

Ritual boasting is more commonly known in the male expression of *waktoglaka,* the formal recounting of war deeds or in recent times of other significant accomplishments (Black Elk, *The Sixth Grandfather* 34–36, Bushotter 205:1–2, Walker, *Lakota Belief and Ritual* 265–66). However mature an individual's understanding may be, boasting is collectively performed on behalf of the people rather than over and above them. As such it has its place in the ceremony of cutting down the Sun Dance tree. In Bushotter's description four selected men relate their deeds and give horses away before receiving the axe. After they strike the tree another man steps forward to praise the deeds of four women who will strike next. The male raisers of the trimmed tree in the Sun Dance circle must also have distinguished themselves in acts that benefit the whole people. This aspect of the Sun Dance drama reveals that giving is its own reward. Men who have given much for the people have the opportunity to give more—their voices, their eloquence, the strength of their bodies, and their horses. Adults are entitled to wear red when they have given their bodies as garments to the sun.

As the color of the sun, red is the most frequently used color in painting, wrapping, or ornamenting ceremonial objects. Sword and the other men told Walker that red "belongs to the Sun," that it celebrates the beginning and the end of the sun's daily journeys, that the sun will recognize one who wears it, and that for any spiritual undertaking it is "the color that spirits like best" (*Lakota Belief and Ritual* 108). The red tipi in Short Bull's painting of the Sun Dance (*Lakota Belief and Ritual* 226) indicates that the Sun Dance intercessor has had a vision of fire and therefore receives guidance and guardianship from the sun. Red circles are painted on the Sun Dance tree, on the bundle of buffalo fat in the hole at its base, in the red of the dancers' skirts, and the bindings of their sage wreaths.

But the connection between red, the fire, and the sun is most directly expressed by body paint in a variety of applications. In the Sun Dance the dancers, the hole digger, and those who transport and raise the sacred tree after it is cut, all must have their hands painted red. The "scouts" who select and report on the tree's location have red circles painted around one eye while the singers have a red circle painted around their mouths. Each performs a particular function. The sun dancers give their bodies, a person's only permanent possession (Densmore 96, Mails, *Sundancing* 148, Lame Deer and Erdoes 187) to the sun, and the red circles that mark the points of piercing on their chests and backs channel power into the people. The heralds and *akicita* (guards) of the Sun Dance have double red stripes on their cheeks to represent their contribution to containing the group's sun power. Finally, the red circles on the tree reveal that it too contains the powers of sacrifice and creation (Walker, *Sun Dance* 66–78; see also Densmore 124–29). Like the dancers and everyone qualified to participate, the tree radiates power because it gives of itself. Again the reward of giving, confirmed in red, results in the opportunity to give more.

When the grandfather in *Iron Hawk* rubs the baby's body with red paint while talking of the sun (units 17–19), he uses sensory means to help create the best human being he can imagine. The mixture of red paint, oil, and grease used to paint babies was both protective spiritual medicine and a salve for skin disease (Bushotter 207:1). The woman selected for her "good character" in Black Elk's description of child care uses a similar salve to "transfer all her good to the child" (*The Sixth Grandfather* 379; see also Standing Bear 1).

As the ceremonial "symbol of all things sacred" (Walker, *Sun Dance* 135) red was "the tribal color" (Densmore 124). In *Waterlily* Gloku paints her grandchildren's hands red so that they will enjoy and give long life (41). *Hunka* children are also distinguished by vertical red stripes painted on their cheeks (*Waterlily* 76, Densmore 74, and Walker, *Sun Dance* 139), and in a similar less formalized demonstration of assurance and care a husband reddened his wife's hair parting and her cheeks (Standing Bear 94–95).

Even the faces of the dead received this honor (Hassrick 93). The Lakota believed in personal immortality and wherever they and their ancestors lived, the good life required giving; the grand cosmic giver was the sun, and the color of everything good was red. To redden parts of the body was more than abstract signing. The sensory process of application, the shared feelings of participants and witnesses deepened emotions and impelled action that fulfilled the individual and guaranteed the future.

The Lakota Context:
Clothing, Wrapping, Cover

Cultural concepts of clothing intensify two key scenes in *Iron Hawk*: Iktomi's theft of the outfit Meadowlark had "decreed" for the hero (unit 118), and Iron Hawk's transfer of his hawk cap, knife, and bow to Red Calf (unit 238). Prior to 1850 the Lakota derived both spiritual and physical cover from hides. As the first part of *Iron Hawk* shows, adult life constantly required the protective wrapping of children, food, and ceremonial objects (see chapter 5 and Deloria, *Waterlily,* 5, 10, 17, 40, 75, 144, 170–71). By hunting men initiated the tipi and clothing manufacture that women completed. The visible reminder of a *tiyóśpaye's* need for cooperation was always as close as one's own skin. No one could dress or paint singlehandedly. Everyone wore the evidence of someone else's concern, earned by their own reciprocal contribution.

The provision of clothing required continual work. While eight pairs of moccasins could be made from one deer hide, other garments required enough skins to make hunting a year-round necessity. It took one whole deer hide to make each leg of a man's leggings and a third to add fringes for ceremonial occasions. A single woman's dress required six deer, two each for the skirt, blouse, and sleeves, and a man's shirt needed four deer, one for the front, one for the back, and one for each sleeve (see Marriott 187–90). The deer and elk skins were tanned until they were as soft and smooth "as a delicate cotton fabric" (Lyford 33).

As long as the weather permitted, the softening of staked-out hides occupied most of the area surrounding the tipis. Women rubbed a mixture of "brains, eggs, ground-up liver, spleen, fat, and vegetable products" into the hides. Then they dried them, soaked them in warm water, and rolled them up (Lyford 37 see also Standing Bear, *My People the Sioux* 19–20). Their work also included the variable scraping of rawhide: thick for shields, thin for parfleche bags, moccasin soles, or drums. An outsider might think that women were forced into unshared drudgery, but the obtaining of skins was so pressing a necessity that hunters vacationed for only brief periods in the winter. Hunting was a major occupation, a practical chore that did not merit praise or produce trophies (see Pond, 48, 65).

Like food, clothing was not simply the product of fairly distributed work. As every garment protected the body, so every person was protected by the spirits that gave animals to the hunters. Plains peoples have made clothing as central to their spiritual identity as other tribal peoples have made masks. As a mask reveals a spiritual presence within its human wearer, so varying garments and ornaments manifest the spiritual allies of the Lakota man. When the man ritually summons them in a ceremony before encountering danger, he no longer simply wears his helper's token, his body becomes the garment of his helper. In a fight, in the proximity of dangerous game, or in a ceremony, a witness might see a hawk or wolf spirit acting in the body of a man. After the intensity of the circumstances had abated, the man had to carefully release his helper so that he could return to his family as a human being. Densmore includes a song that in each of its four renditions names powers that might "wear" the singer. The word "wind" changes verse by verse to "hail," "lightning," and "clouds":

he	it was
akicita ca	a guard
wamiconzelo	predicted for me

tate wan	a wind
komayakelo	wears me
wanyanka ye	behold it
wakan	sacred
yelo	it is

(Densmore 169; similar wearing metaphors
in *Teton Sioux Music* appear on pp. 121 and 296).

When a man wears signs of power it does not mean that he commands these powers like genies from a jar. It means that he can call his guards for help in fighting or healing but that once summoned they are in charge; he agrees to sacrifice his independent will in offering them his body. Through flesh offerings and piercing a sun dancer rends the garment of his body, as mourning women cut off their hair, to demonstrate sincerity to the helping spirits. A spirit cannot enter a healer's body if he does not first show that he knows his body's purpose. Ceremonial participants wear their own skins as they wear their clothes, to express the dedication of their lives to fulfilling the past and ensuring the future.

The present life embraces past and future when an ordinary person's body is temporarily worn by an immortal spirit. The concept of transferring power from body to body had many variations. A man healed by a bear medicine man often becomes a bear medicine man (Walker, *Lakota Belief and Ritual* 157–59). Lone Man told Densmore that he was guarded by the spirit of a swallow. Swallows display great agility while flying ahead of thunder storms, and Lone Man wore a swallow skin on his head to bring the swallow spirit into his horse during a battle. In his vision Thunder beings had taught him a song to accompany putting on the skin. As in *Iron Hawk,* something worn must be combined with something voiced to produce an effective shield. Once this had occurred an object and its empowering ritual could be passed from one person to another as Horn Chips gave Crazy Horse a sacred stone (W. Powers, *Yuwipi* 10, Ambrose 159), and as Iron Hawk receives the hawk cap, knife, and arrows from his meadowlark grandfather (unit 84).

In spiritual use wearing a particular object or garment must be

Sioux Dress. From *Vestiges of a Proud Nation: The Ogden B. Read Northern Plains Indian Collection*, ed. Glenn B. Markoe. *Courtesy of the Robert Hull Fleming Museum (1881.3.113).*

Sioux Hair-fringed Shirt. From *Vestiges of a Proud Nation: The Ogden B. Read Northern Plains Indian Collection,* ed. Glenn B. Markoe. *Courtesy of the Robert Hull Fleming Museum (1881.3.156LA).*

strictly limited to the appropriate occasion. Typically, particular symbols summon spirits who recognize their allies as being in need. Perhaps a spirit, like a man, does not want to be interrupted by trivial requests. The minimally clothed body in *Hanbleceya* (the Vision Quest) tells the spirits that the person praying is willing to give his body to the helper, while the helper protects the people, even if his body suffers in the process. *Hanbleceya* requires fasting and exposure to the elements as a sacrifice, but nakedness also indicates the seeker's willingness to wear the token of any spirit that agrees to wear him. A vision quester never attempts to receive a vision from a spirit of his own choosing by wearing the symbols of that spirit. Even if he goes on *Hanbleceya* repeatedly, he prays to all four directions, allowing spirits *maka sitomniyan* (all over the universe) to notice and pity him. As a result a man might be able to rely on several guards from several visions (see Black Elk, *The Sixth Grandfather* 227–232; Walker, *Lakota Belief and Ritual* 84–86, 129–31, 132–35, 150–53; Black Elk, *The Sacred Pipe* 44–66; Hassrick 266–95).

Densmore recorded Śiyaka's (Teal Duck's) description of a vision quest in which a buffalo robe was placed at each directional point of the prayer circle as an offering to any good spirit from any quarter. On his own body he wore only one undecorated robe, presenting himself as a tabula rasa. At the end of his second full day of prayer, Śiyaka heard a voice saying, "Young man, you are recognized by Wakan Tanka" (*Teton Sioux Music* 185). His vision begins just before daybreak the next morning. Nakedness and an undecorated buffalo robe are statements that are validated by twenty-four hours of fasting and prayer. The open robes at the directional points also say that Śiyaka offers his body as a container of power. Nakedness serves a similar purpose in the sweatlodge. Wakan Tanka has many aspects and many messengers so that nakedness maximizes the possibility of spiritual response. The dreamer is happy to augment his contribution to the life of his *tiyośpaye* by accepting the spirits that choose him. Correspondingly, Iron Hawk relies entirely on the Thunder man's promise of rescue (units 101–04) and later transmits it to Red Calf.

Symbolic visual and vocal expressions in their most important uses assure everyone of the group's collective security. Brave Buffalo told Densmore of dreams that allowed his body to be worn by several spirits in separate rituals. The buffalo spirit told Brave Buffalo to carry a special stick as a sign of that spirit's benevolence. To further demonstrate the connection Brave Buffalo wore an entire buffalo hide including the head and horns to make himself bullet and arrow proof in a ritual test. As Brave Buffalo wears the buffalo hide on the outside of his own body, the spirit wearing Brave Buffalo's body causes both skins to be impenetrable (*Teton Sioux Music* 174–75).

Brave Buffalo's additional dream of the elk allowed him to direct an atmosphere of beauty and wonder into the circle. Like the Elk man in his dream he wore a downy eagle plume on the right side of his cap at all times. For the Elk ceremony he wore a mask of elk skin made from an elk's head including the horns. He also painted himself yellow and carried a hoop worked with elk hide in each hand. By wearing the emblems of respect Brave Buffalo brought the spirit of the elk into his body. When he formally circled the camp, he left the footprints of an elk instead of a man (Densmore 178).

In an Elk song recorded by Densmore Śiyaka epitomizes the synthesis of wearing and singing in applying the herbs conferred in his vision:

taku	something
wakan	sacred
komanyake lo	wears me
sitomniyan	all
wanmayank	behold
au we	coming

(Teton Sioux Music 296)

Brave Buffalo also dreamed of sacred stones. The stones could fly through the air to find lost objects or people, summon game, and locate herbs for healing. Brave Buffalo painted his stone red and wrapped it in red cloth lined with eagle down to prevent it from flying away when not in use. The stone bore the natural outline of a small face. It may have been felt that stones, like men, would remain in their homes if they were honored with eagle feathers and red paint.

When the stones helped Brave Buffalo, they were stripped down for their mission like hunters and warriors. Beyond his loin cloth Crazy Horse wore only a single hawk feather, two sacred stones, and a dusting of mole dirt into battle. Observing these minimal and essential tokens, the people knew that his visions (or those of Horn Chips) had given him the swiftness and accuracy of the hawk, the durability and imperviousness of the stones, and the invisibility of the mole. The chief's clothing he wore in the camp circle spoke of different virtues. In 1865 Crazy Horse held the important position of shirt wearer (one of four tribal leaders; see Ambrose 135– 37 and Hassrick 26). The locks of hair on the honorary shirt were not from enemy scalps but from relatives, primarily women, who gave their hair and their lives into his care (see Markoe 94). Just as the protective spirits wore the body of Crazy Horse in battle, so the shirt wearer, as the embodiment of the band's security, wore the people whose individual vitalities were especially concentrated in hair (Hassrick 90). The people depended on their leader as their hair literally depended from his shirt.

As the account of Iron Hawk's infancy shows, the act of covering signifies the will to protect the person or object covered. The back of a young man's robe carried a vertical quilled stripe holding equally spaced medallions (Hassrick 241). The mature man often wore a buffalo robe bearing a large circular design for ceremonial purposes. Although it is now often called the "black war bonnet design" (Lyford 78), the sun-like rays extending from the center to the circumference strongly suggest the meaning of maleness. The robe's connection between the sun as spirit and the buffalo as body parallels the hair fringed shirt in which the people's inspiration is the shirt wearer. His virtues animate them all and every adult has similar responsibilities to their dependents.

Similarly the robe contains and channels its owner's protective love throughout the camp. Its material implicitly says that both buffalo and man sacrifice their bodies and that the sun can wear the people. Thus the honored individual enhances the people's power to live through the sunburst robe. In Walker's account of the *Hunka* ceremony the younger of the two candidates ritually gives his moccasins, shirt, and leggings to anyone in need, portrayed temporarily by the *Hunka* conductor: "My body is naked and I am cold" (*Sun Dance* 138). When the young giver is himself naked, having sacrificed all he has to give, he in turn is covered with the color of the sun, having earned the right to share its work:

> He gave me his moccasins, his shirt, and his leggings, and now he is naked and has nothing. I will put the red stripe on his face for he is *Hunka*. I put this stripe on his face so that the people may see it and know that he has given all his possessions away, and know that they should give to him. I will put the stripe on his face and on the face of his *Hunka* so that they will remember this day, and when they see one in want they will give to that one. (Walker, *Sun Dance* 138)

The buffalo robe then gives additional meaning to the *hunka* ideal. The two *hunka* candidates are covered by a single robe, binding their spirits in a single skin, just as the bodies of all the people should combine to form the body of the tribe. In supplementary symbols of wrapping the conductor passes two deerskin pouches, painted red like the skins of the men, in under the robe. After the ceremony the participants change into ordinary clothing, but the special *hunka* implements are wrapped in a bundle where their power will be guarded until they are needed. The *hunka* wands, like the sacred stones, pipes used for prayer, and other objects that can be animated with power are tenderly covered while they "sleep."

Implements of war were usually covered when not in use. The general male association with the sun was an important aspect of shield symbolism. While a shield often wore the sign of a major animal helper, every shield was hung on a tripod outside the tipi and turned throughout the day to face the sun (Lyford 77). Wissler mentions that the oldest shields he saw were painted only in concentric circles, as if to represent the sun ("Protective Designs" 30). But designs representing other visionary helpers were painted on the rawhide surface of most nineteenth century shields. The designs helped to summon the helpers in special activating rites im-

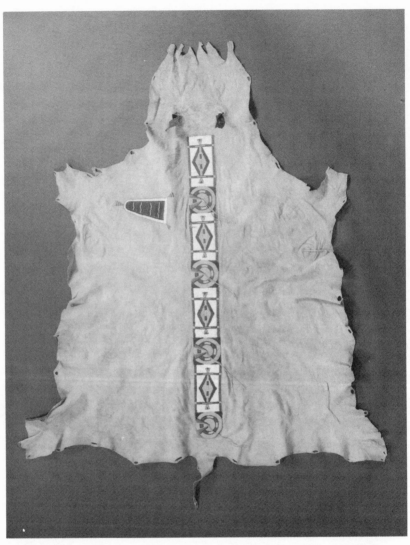

Crow Buffalo Robe. From *Vestiges of a Proud Nation: The Ogden B. Read Northern Plains Indian Collection*, ed. Glenn B. Markoe. *Courtesy of the Robert Hull Fleming Museum (1881.3.18).*

Buffalo Hide. *Courtesy of the Denver Art Museum (1959.188).*

mediately before combat. Although a war helper would preserve a warrior's life, certain spirits like that of the hawk might be dangerous to bring home. The warrior would therefore ritually deactivate and cover the shield when not in use, dedicating it instead to the sun and the domestic warmth that the shield would then express (Wissler, "Some Protective Designs" 21–31).

Symbolic designs in clothing, shields, pipe bags, and other male possessions depicted both past and future experience. If the designs represented power "found" in a vision, they assured the finding of defense, food, or additional visions in the future. If the designs represented a war or horse-stealing record already accomplished, they also promised more vigorous action on the people's behalf. So called "protective" designs signified individual invulnerability, if literally read, but also spoke of group safety whether or not everyone understood them that way. The missile-proof medicine of an individual might fail on any given day, but the message spoken while the person lived would always be renewed by someone else.

Living and dying for the people meant that while one's body would wear out, the self that lived for the people would find new bodies. As a meadowlark Iron Hawk's grandfather is the ultimate parent, but since he is poor, Iron Hawk's *hunka* clothing must be magically supplied. Although it is not narratively conferred in the ritual, the clothing of a "child beloved" represents Iron Hawk's potential to fulfill ideal expectations (see Wissler, "Decorative Arts" 271). Wealthy parents who could afford the feasting and giveaways formally honored their children to teach them and all other children that they must reciprocate the protective love they have received.

The honoring ceremony in *Waterlily* makes a group of children *hunka* to each other and to the tribe with the same solemn responsibilities conferred upon the older pair of *hunka* in Walker's rite. Waterlily's dress is described not simply as a temporary costume for a big day, but as a demonstration of loving effort in her behalf. Only two of the teeth in an elk's mouth were suitable for decoration, and although she is only six and may not realize the ornament's rarity, Waterlily knows that many adults are exerting themselves on her behalf. A special design to be worked into the dress is dreamed by a woman gifted with this power. For two years before the actual ceremony, while the elk teeth are obtained and the embroidery is finished, Waterlily absorbs the meaning of *Hunka*. When she wears the dress and the red *hunka* paint in the ceremony, she realizes to the limit of her eight year old capacity that "she had been set apart as one of those who must make hospitality their first concern" (Deloria, *Waterlily* 78).

The child who is specially fed and clothed will grow to know that these acts were not intended to elevate an individual but to teach a lesson in the ritual drama of *Hunka*. The child's part is to wear the symbols of hospitality and the other virtues. Even if she betrays this obligation like Iktomi or Iron Hawk's sister-in-law, she will still teach by negative example. Like a false report of a vision (Black Elk, *The Sacred Pipe* 61) signs of honor unworthily worn would eventually destroy the deceiver. If a man falsely painted a red cross on his horse to pretend that he had rescued someone in battle while riding that horse, the horse would get sick or break its leg (Bushotter 56:2). Perhaps the punishment shows that someone who needed to invent their courage would not be able to protect anyone in their care.

While *Iron Hawk* primarily portrays the protective responsibilities of the male culture hero, the story includes examples of the feminine ideal and its antithesis. The clothing metaphor in the Buffalo Woman ceremony is analagous to the buffalo transformation undergone by Iron Hawk and his wife before and after their marriage. By charging at her in the form of a buffalo bull, Iron Hawk teaches his wife not to fear him. He further prepares her for her role as a "buffalo woman" dedicated to providing for the people when she draws in real buffalo from the hunters. Lastly, he fortifies her with the self-reliant confidence of the buffalo cow in childbirth.

The buffalo ceremony enacts the woman's virtues of chastity, fecundity, industry, and hospitality (Walker, *Sun Dance* 141). As might be expected, all domestic virtues proceeded from the sun and the buffalo, the ultimate symbols of healthy growth and adult sacrifice. The door of the ceremonial tipi faces east and, as in *Hunka* and the Sun Dance, a buffalo skull is placed on the altar.

The conductor wears a cap of buffalo skin with the hair still on it and the horns attached to each side. His first song identifies him with the buffalo spirit, who then wears him during the rite (Walker, *Sun Dance* 144).

Through the spirit of the buffalo within him the conductor will take the young woman into relationship with the buffalo nation and the sun. The connection between the people and these powers is symbolized by the red paint applied to the forehead of both the woman and the buffalo skull. As the paint reveals inward qualities covering the body, the conductor places a piece of red cloth on the buffalo skull: "My oldest sister, I make an offering of this robe to you" (*Sun Dance* 146). The woman should always remember that she is the "woman" of the buffalo, that she belongs to a *tiyoŝpaye* of spirits that reciprocally fill her people's needs:

> The buffalo horns are on my head and I speak for the Buffalo God. The buffalo tail is behind me and this makes my word sacred. I am now the buffalo bull and you are a young buffalo cow. I will show you what the bad influences would have you do. I will show you what the good influence would have you do. (Walker, *Sun Dance* 147)

When Iron Hawk has his wife seduce the bulls away from the herd, she enacts the divisive power of the bad influence. In the ceremony described by Walker, the socially divisive danger is directed against the woman rather than by her. This is appropriate since the girl in the ceremony is entering adolescence rather than beginning marriage like Iron Hawk's wife. The conductor imitates a male buffalo in rutting time, bellowing and pawing the ground. When he advances on hands and knees to rub against the girl, her mother puts a sprig of sage under her arm and on her lap to show that the girl knows how to recognize male power when it is "crazy" (on Makula's use of Crazy Buffalo in his stories see Walker, *Sun Dance* 148 and *Lakota Myth* 105–06).

The Buffalo Woman ceremony teaches girls that sexuality exists for the benefit of the tribe:

Then the Conductor painted red the right side of the young woman's forehead and a red stripe at the parting of her hair, and while doing so he said, "you see your oldest sister [the buffalo skull] on the altar. Her forehead is painted red. This is to show that she is sacred. Red is a sacred color. Your first menstrual flow was red. Then you were sacred." (Walker, *Sun Dance* 149)

A bowl of chokecherry juice is sipped by the conductor (the Buffalo spirit) and the girl before it is passed around to share with everyone in attendance. Its red color represents the personal qualities renewed in witnesses as well as participants. The paint, the buffalo parts, the red liquid, and all the other sun and buffalo symbols combine to bring an intangible presence and a common consciousness into the ceremonial tipi. The transition from girl to woman is celebrated no less than the gift of the ceremony itself, the ability to see, hear, and taste sacred mysteries.

The clothing metaphor is reserved for the consummate expression of transition. Clothing, paint, all forms of "cover" are acts of care. As undifferentiated receivers of this care girls and boys wore almost identical clothing. At the beginning of the ceremony the girl wears a breachclout like a boy. At the end her mother removes it "without exposing her person," immediately after the girl has taken off her child-dress and the conductor has applied the red paint (Walker, *Lakota Belief and Ritual* 252). In the camp circle girls and boys played separately except when they were very young, but adulthood required a distinct division of labor based on gender (Hassrick 209–42). At the ceremony's conclusion the father takes up the girl's breechclout and leaves it outside the camp. Her new previously unworn woman's dress (Walker, *Lakota Belief and Ritual* 243) represents adult responsibilities for child bearing and the making of shelter.

Although adults were not permitted to express childish desires for gratification or attention, they wore a reminder of the parental care bestowed upon them throughout their lives. Shortly after birth, a piece of umbilical cord was placed in a small beaded pouch

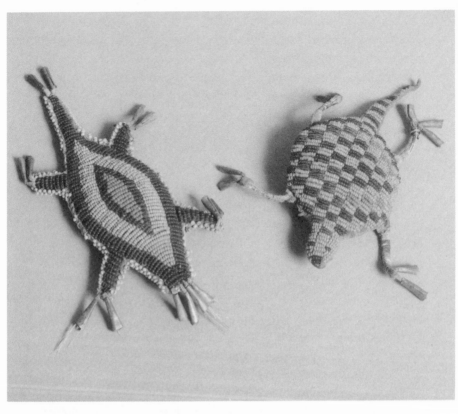

Sioux Umbilical Cord Amulets. From *Vestiges of a Proud Nation: The Ogden B. Read Northern Plains Indian Collection*, ed. Glenn B. Markoe. *Courtesy of the Robert Hull Fleming Museum (1881.3.138 B and A)*.

that was shaped and decorated like a turtle or lizard. These animals were hard to kill and symbolized inherent survival instincts (Mails, *Mystic Warriors* 510). The amulets served as teddy bears for small children (Deloria, *Waterlily* 23) and were put away for safe keeping from about age six to puberty. Thereafter men wore their turtles attached to the left corner of their shirt or from one horn of a buffalo horn cap if they had earned that honor (Mails, *Mystic Warriors* 510–12). Women wore their turtles in their belts at the center of their backs as "a talisman ensuring long life" (Deloria, *Waterlily* 23).

As a sacred mystery like birth and puberty, death too was contemplated through ritual. The ghost-keeping ceremony includes extremely complex variations on the wrapping and wearing metaphors. After the body has been placed on a scaffold, a lock of hair from the dead relative was wrapped in a small piece of red cloth and carried on horseback by the keeper. In Densmore's account a father keeps the soul of his fifteen year old son. The hair wrapped in red cloth is placed in a specially decorated case that is then also wrapped in red cloth. Then the hair-in-the-first-cloth-in-the-case-in-the-second-cloth is wrapped inside another piece of soft tanned hide (*Teton Sioux Music* 78). As in the tribal executive's "shirt," hair often symbolized the life-force. The dead one's hair is protected by a four-layered "ghost bundle" hung on a tripod throughout the ceremony to represent embodied life (79). The outer wrapping must show no sign of sewing, perhaps because it speaks of the body as a gift that must be returned, not something that can be designed and possessed by the wearer. When the ceremony includes the placing of the bundle on a white buffalo robe, only children who have undergone the *Hunka* ceremony can touch the robe (80). The robe like the body is treated with reverence by children who have just learned the purpose of having a body through *Hunka*. Though forgetfulness inevitably occurs in adults, ceremonial attendance helps everyone to resume their bodies' proper use.

The return of individuals to the spirit world is a natural extension of the principle of giving practiced by every adult. Before the spirit bundle is unwrapped, an additional image of embodied life appears in the "spirit post" standing about three feet tall with a beaded face and dressed in clothing appropriate to the age and sex of the deceased. When the post is ritually fed, food is simultaneously offered to those in attendance to show that life enters the body to give life to others. At the end life is symbolically returned to its original giver. The four-stage unwrapping of the bundle suggests that death, even for a young person, is not an abrupt shock but the last stage of a process begun at conception. The wholeness represented by "four" cannot be measured in years.

Finally the parents and other relatives remind themselves and the whole community that the last unwrapping of the body is the natural resolution of lifelong giving. Weasel Bear told Densmore that after the give-away following the ceremony, he and his wife were left without a single material possession:

> That evening one of our relatives came and put up a tipi, led us to it and said, "This is your home." Others brought kettles, blankets, provisions, and clothing for us. Our relatives did all this for us, in order that we might begin our lives again. (*Teton Sioux Music* 84)

The ghost keeping represents transition through the ghost bundle and the spirit post, but the attending players embody a vital present. At the ghost keeping in *Waterlily* the girls enact the continuity of the group in "slender white doeskin gowns long enough to brush the grass . . . the waists of their gowns were heavy with solid work extending to the ends of the loose open sleeves bordered with fringe" (Deloria, *Waterlily* 156). The girls' dresses also display parental care and outline their own future as artisans of health and respect. By the time it is opened the ghost bundle in *Waterlily* has become heavy with the many gifts added during the keeping, representing reciprocal love. Its unwrapping suggests that a person's innermost life is a composite of the relationships the person has known. A person is all the other people with whom he or she shares cover.

The idea that covering the body reveals dedication to the group may also be observed in a *wacipi* (dance or powwow). Ben Black Bear, Sr., explains how failure to dress for a *wacipi* with or without a good excuse becomes a playlet of social responsibility: "In his street clothes, he is made to dance in the center (of the dancing area) and he is made to tell the reason why he is not dancing" (Black Bear, Sr. and Theisz 43). In another instance, the "Dropped Article" dance and song, a man intentionally drops a piece of his outfit and then, after recounting his accomplishments, distributes gifts (43). The dropped "cover," the recital of his efforts on behalf of the people, and the donations of his material substance confirm the message that everything the dancer has, including his body and mental abilities, are brought home and set down. A case of apples symbolically replaces the deer or buffalo the dancer's great-grandfather brought, but the basic symbol remains the same.

Although dance outfits are worn in a non-sacred circle, they still speak for an individual's dedication to the community. Their elaborate decoration requires patient workmanship either by the dancer or by caring relatives. Even if the *wacipi* includes age and gender graded competition for prize money, many more people participate than can possibly win and most participants never win. People of all ages wear the outfits appropriate to their age and sex and do the corresponding dance step. Much powwow dancing is "intertribal," i.e., the whole group dances non-competitively to the same songs, though the men move counterclockwise and the woman clockwise. The age groups are clustered together so that onlookers can see a microcosm of the present Lakota generation from the girl shawl dancers and boy fancy dancers to the mature male and female "traditional" dancers.

The word *epazo* (to show) is used over and over again in *wacipi* songs. "Ikpazopi Olowan" is translated as "Parade Song" in *Songs and Dances of the Lakota,* but it literally means "showing oneself song." A powwow brings together so much color and intricate design in the outfits of so many dancers that no single outfit can stand out. To show oneself means to help show the spirit of the nation to its members. The onlookers too contribute assurance of the continuing joy of expression by their appreciative presence. Doing anything well for a sustained period requires the presence of someone who needs and values the action. The powwow audience plays this part, while those in the center enact for the time being the endurance and exertion of the givers.

As in a sacred ceremony the people sing and dance beautifully to make relatives feel alive. The "showing oneself song" accompanies a special procession to the dance circle in order to honor an individual:

Oyate kin ikṗazo au welo, heya pelo.
[Name] tokeya au pelo, heyapelo.
Blihic'iya yo, oyate kin wacininyan au we.

People are parading this way, it is said.
[Name] is being brought along first, it is said.
Take courage, the people needing you are coming.
                    (Black Bear, Sr. and Theisz 40–41)

Through the song each individual understands that their personal courage will not fall short if they remember those who await cover.

In preceding centuries the cover was literally supplied by the skins hunters brought home. At present the cover is a spiritual shield against selfishness and despair. Dancers, sacred or secular have always kindled the nation's life. A *wacipi* dancer's sacrifice is not as profound as a sun dancer's, but each dancer makes Lakota consciousness the focus of their time and effort. A powwow outfit visibly confirms Lakota continuity. By wearing their culture on their bodies, the dancers are worn by the spirits of previous generations.

While clothing often symbolizes disguise, hypocrisy, or illusion in Western literature, it is usually a true indicator of value and identity in Lakota stories. The loss of Iron Hawk's fine outfit suggests forgetfulness of the meanings it projects. Most clothing revealed that the wearer had been gifted by others who did the hunting and the manufacture that he or she did not do. Stories often depict the unnatural (from a Lakota point of view) individualism of Iktomi in his comically improvised costumes. Since Iktomi works on no one's behalf, he must clothe himself. The beginning of "Iktomi and the Raccoon-skin" (Deloria, *Dakota Texts* 36) centers on the trickster's outfit as a parody of adult ability and effort. His covering requires neither hunting skill nor the sewing of women he should hunt for:

Ikto kakena icimani-yahan yunkan lecel hakitun śke'. Wizi wan kazazapi ca otun nan ptehinpahpa wan pegnakin nan wica ha wan sinte-aopeya in śke'. Tasinta-mila wan yuha nan itazipa wan nunpko hecel yuha śke'.

Ikto was starting off on a journey and this is how he was dressed. He wore leggings made of tanned tipi-hide and slashed down at the outer seams, and a headdress of buffalo hair; and he wore about him a robe of raccoon skin with the tail left attached. He carried a ruminant's tail knife, and bow with two arrows. (*Dakota Texts* 41)

The last item takes on comical connotations because Ikto so obviously carries it as a stage prop. He is unable to kill anything usefully.

Other stories in *Dakota Texts* emphasize the clothing metaphor, especially "Doubleface Steals the Virgin" (51–64), "Boy-Beloved's Blanket" (82–86), and "White Plume Boy" (106–113). In "Blood Clot Boy" (113–20) as in *Iron Hawk,* the hero loses his clothes to the trickster. Iktomi is "well dressed" when he first meets Iron Hawk, but Deloria allows the reader of Lakota to note that he has "igluzin" 'dressed himself' and "aiglupi" 'gotten himself up by his own efforts' (units 105–06). A neutral verb like *kic'un* (he wore) would not have conveyed the message that Ikto only impersonates a human being.

When Iktomi is being hand-fed like a king at Iron Hawk's bird distribution, Deloria uses a clothing metaphor to accentuate the form of his exposure: "Yunkan Cetan-maza hcihcika tokeya hihunni" 'And lo, the Ragged Iron Hawk . . . arrived first' (unit 147). The implications of "hcihcika" 'ragged' in Lakota culture went beyond the surface meaning of carelessly groomed. From the killing of an animal to the ornamenting of the tanned skin, beautifully finished clothing revealed cooperation rather than vanity. Excessive display was always "ragged," while everyday good taste made mutual care a tangible, visible, and constant presence.

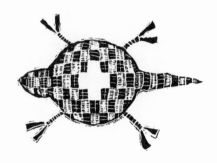

The Lakota Context:
East and West

Black Elk's Great Vision represents the whole range of Lakota religious symbolism. Similarly, *Iron Hawk* is Deloria's ideal hero narrative, consummately remembered and imagined after many years of listening and study. Both Black Elk and Deloria achieve holistic expression but emphasize the symbols of one particular direction, the West for Black Elk, the East for Deloria. Black Elk's Great Vision like his later Dog vision is a gift from the western powers and is conveyed predominantly by their messengers: horses, swallows, water, thunder, and lightning. Deloria's *Iron Hawk,* on the other hand, makes symbols of the East preeminent: the sun, the color red, the buffalo, the hawk, and the meadowlark.

The Great Vision and *Iron Hawk* clearly emphasize one direction while embracing the values and metaphors of the others. One of Densmore's most articulate informants, Śiyaka (Teal Duck), explained how receptiveness to every power continued even after a man discovered a special affinity for one. After receiving a vision Śiyaka realizes that his "stronghold is in the east but the west was also a source from which I could get help." He adds that all the birds and insects in his dream—a crow, an owl, and an elk from the East as well as dragonflies and butterflies from the West—were "things on which . . . I should keep my mind and learn their ways" (*Teton Sioux Music* 188). Conversely, Black Elk's "stronghold" is the West, but the imagery of the other directions and their *akicita* balance and complete his *hanbloglaka* (visionary descriptions) (see *The Sixth Grandfather* 114–42, 227–32).

Iron Hawk begins and ends with the sun and the meadowlark while incorporating the conventional adolescent journey to the West. The hero's childhood "emerges" with the sun in the story's first line. His upbringing immediately associates the sun with the Lakota male ideal. The meadowlark embodies the generosity of the sun impressed on children from their infancy through touch, color, and language. The child begins his education in two of the four Lakota virtues, generosity and wisdom (east and south) long before he is seriously tested in courage and fortitude (west and north).

The culture hero narratives in *Dakota Texts* are far more abbreviated than *Iron Hawk* in their accounts of the hero's childhood. Some describe the acquiring of warrior power and the ability to destroy a threat with the power of the thunder (see "White Plume" 107–09 and "Blood Clot Boy" 115–16). Iron Hawk receives Thunder power explicitly as a reward for destroying the Rock woman mother and helping the Thunder men to marry (unit 98). These achievements demonstrate warrior prowess and social development. The lessons of the West, the knowledge of one's own courage in the face of danger, come after the preparatory lessons of the East, and they are usually accomplished in the first stages of independence.

Both Black Elk and Deloria emphasize the persistence of human weaknesses after warrior and healing powers have been gained. The fear of Thunder paralyzes Black Elk before his Dog Vision and Ikto humiliates Iron Hawk as he continues west. But near the end of the Dog vision and after Iron Hawk arrives in the camp he will eventually lead, the westward journey halts. Turning to the East the visionary and the hero look more to their people's future than their own individual growth.

Only a few advanced *wicaśa wakan* (sacred men) are privileged to apply the Thunder power to healing. In Black Elk's Horse Dance a storm arrives to encourage rather than hinder the ceremony, and it accordingly rages nearby without "approaching any closer" (*The Sixth Grandfather* 220). At the end of the ceremony people and even horses were cured of their sicknesses (*The Sixth Grandfather* 225). In addition to its combative and curative uses Thunder power purifies (see Walker, *Lakota Myth* 213–14). Red Calf summons the lightning to kill the Mountain Lion woman and to free children from neglectful and abusive parents (unit 394).

Sexual obsession is also a formidable enemy and Deloria suggests that a mature man must recognize its dangers (see Rice, *Deer Women and Elk Men* 33–46). Midway on his western journey Iron Hawk had naively thought to buy himself a wife with the white shells (units 109–17). Later Red Calf interrupts his quest to recover the Lakota past for an affair with the Mountain Lion woman. When these diversions end, father and son can approach the center and adult responsibility. Iron Hawk stops thinking about fame. He returns to providing an abundance of food and to establishing the right kind of relationship between a man and a woman as the basis of marriage (units 175–227). Red Calf continues the journey that symbolizes cultural continuity, bringing the Lakota past to life in each present generation (units 397–419).

Iron Hawk follows the same directional circuit as Black Elk's Dog vision. A prayer or a story begins facing west, not in the West. Initially Black Elk is as immobilized by historical events as Iron Hawk had been in the pit where Iktomi abandoned him: "I recalled the days when all my close relatives had been living and now they were gone. I just cried myself to death nearly" (*The Sixth Grandfather* 228). His despair is dynamically lifted midway in the vision when the two initiating guides of his first vision swoop down and kill a dog. In the same way that lightning destroys regressive lechery for Red Calf, sprightly butterflies, dragonflies, and swallows surrounding the two men help to transform the "slave animal" of self-pity into mature responsibility. The Dog vision ends serenely with the sunrise and the morning star:

> The east was just getting light . . . It seemed there were many little faces all around the [morning] star. These faces were all

smiling at me. These were the faces of children yet to be born and I thought perhaps they would be my grandchildren (*The Sixth Grandfather* 231)

The voice that speaks to Black Elk tells him what the oral narrative heroes learn more than once in each story and on and on in different stories: the "people are in difficulty" and "they need you." The repeated reminders of his life's purpose are accompanied by the tools to effect it.

Just as Black Elk acquires spirit helpers and herbs, Iron Hawk and Red Calf receive and share the hawk cap and the sacred bow and arrows (units 84, 238–39). Lakota existence depends upon concentrating spirit power in symbolic forms including verbal ones, such as vision-talks and oral narratives. In Black Elk's Dog vision the many-colored stars and the faces of the unborn children form a stationary image of love. The vision culminates when everything begins to move, reflecting the mystery of *takuśkanśkan* (what-moves-moves) or animation itself (see Walker, *Lakota Belief and Ritual* 35–37). At the end this life-force becomes audible, transforming itself to Black Elk's own words and voice: "Right underneath the stars I could see the heads of men and women moving around and even the birds singing and the mooing of buffalo and the whistling of the deer and the neighing and snorting of the horses. I could hear what I did not see" (*The Sixth Grandfather* 231).

Eyes and ears are used as hunting tools. Upon Black Elk's return neither food nor vision can be of immediate use. For the vision to feed the people it must be transformed into the songs, words, and ritual drama of the *Heyoka* (sacred clown) ceremony (*The Sixth Grandfather* 232–35). Food and vision are symbolically taken in the West, the direction faced at the beginning of each circuit of prayer. Bringing a vision home means returning to the East, the dreamer's home before the vision. In a sense the dreamer brings the West to the East and with it new life for the people. In the place where he began he brings strength for new beginnings.

After Red Calf witnesses the supernatural killing of a deer by lightning, he tells his brother-in-law to cut the liver into tiny bits for his son. If individually received wisdom were not similarly converted into structured ritual or traditional narrative, its relation would be mere self-praise. The teller could only boast crudely like Iktomi of personal accomplishment. Many trickster tales begin with the conventional "Iktomi was walking along at random" (see Deloria, *Dakota Texts* 5, 23, 30, 41, 45) because he lives only to glorify and gratify himself. When Iron Hawk meets him, both are traveling north and west. In the directional structure of *Iron Hawk* and in the oral tradition (see Jahner "Cognitive Style" 48) these are Iktomi's primary locations. He never turns psychologically eastward toward childhood and parental priorities. In some stories he even kills or abuses children (see Deloria, *Dakota Texts* 8–11, 11–19, 30). When Iron Hawk and Red Calf turn east in the story's symbolic pattern, they attend fully to childhood matters, although they are no longer children (units 133–89, 381–96).

In Black Elk's Great Vision the pipe and the morning star fly from the East to the sacred tree at the center of the nation's hoop (*The Sixth Grandfather* 129). While the pipe is a general conduit to the virtues of each direction, it arrives in Black Elk's vision from the place of all origin. The morning star more specifically represents the linkage of generosity and wisdom; one is impossible without the other. Generosity can be wasted if the giver does not know how or where to apply it. The morning star defines wisdom as knowing life's essential purpose when it illuminates the faces of Black Elk's unborn children, for it is only for them that the spirits have taken him on these extraordinary hunts. In his Great Vision Black Elk is introduced to the spirit world by the "two men flying" who bring him to the six grandfathers (*The Sixth Grandfather* 114). The men symbolically foreshadow all the potential messengers Black Elk will meet. Because they initiate a process that leads Black Elk to comprehend the universe from every direction, they themselves are associated with the morning star. The morning star and the two men, like the meadowlark in *Iron Hawk*, begin and end enlightenment. Pointing to the star the third grandfather says: "All the fowls of the universe, those he has wakened, and also he has wakened the beings on the earth" (*The Sixth Grandfather* 117). Later Black Elk receives his most potent healing herb where "the daybreak star stood between the two men from the east" (134).

The herb's four colored flowers—black, white, red, yellow—define wisdom as comprehensive knowledge directed toward the continuance of life. Light flows upward from the flower. The colors also suggest the function of the human body as an illuminating medium of *takuśkanśkan* or creative force. A person does not soak up light to become individually greater but receives light to manifest the nature of creation. The daybreak-star herb represents a holistic knowledge that heals individuals and communities, restoring the best of what they have always been: "I was to see the bad and the good. I was to see what is good for humans and what is not good for humans" (*The Sixth Grandfather* 135).

Such wisdom belongs to the whole people. Black Elk receives the Great Vision when he is only nine years old. Perhaps he means to tell us that the wisdom of Lakota culture begins as an intuition long before understanding dawns (see Rice, *Black Elk's Story* 12). Black Elk's reflection on reexperiencing his vision after acting it out in the Horse Dance suggests a long, gradual brightening. Over the years the Great Vision "wore" more and more of him until he became a daybreak star himself: "my people were to have knowledge from this star and . . . they were eager to see it come out and by the time the daybreak star came out the people would be saying, 'Behold the star of wisdom'" (*The Sixth Grandfather* 225–26).

For the Lakota wisdom has always required rigorous discipline. In the 1944 Neihardt interviews Black Elk recalls how he reconciled mourners to mortality by directing their gaze to the future. Grief must never cloud a person's love for life and living. During the formal four day grieving period in particular, but thereafter as much as possible, a bereaved person should try to get along with everyone, provide food, and "try to see the morning star every morning" (*The Sixth Grandfather* 382). As usual four days represents a complete cycle. Each individual life is seen as part of a generation, and the generations renew themselves. A mourning period of four days helps each person to remember that whole generations die. But while individuals have varying life spans and people of different generations are alive at the same time, no one ever ceases to give. People are dying all the time, but the mourner is told to live as he has always lived, on and through the dying that enables life. The morning star, appearing and disappearing quickly during its brief visibility, idealizes individual identity. It unites the night and the day, serving as a marker of transition and renewal.

Like the morning star in *The Sixth Grandfather* the meadowlark in *Iron Hawk* is both transient and eternal. As an old man he will surely disappear, but as the spirit of nurture and joy he not only reappears in the story, he embodies the story. When Red Calf brings him west to Iron Hawk at the end, Deloria plays an interesting variation on the hero tradition recorded in *Dakota Texts*. The narrator of "White Plume Boy" leaves the hero at the apex of his power in his wife's camp in the West (Deloria, *Dakota Texts* 113). In "Blood Clot Boy," on the other hand, the hero brings his wife to his rabbit grandfather in the East (*Dakota Texts* 120). Iron Hawk sends his thoughts east, but he instructs Red Calf to bring the meadowlark west. Perhaps Deloria is underscoring the situation of her own writing and time, in which it was not enough for her to simply praise the culture of her ancestors. By carefully wrapping their oral tradition in written Lakota she too brought the East to the West, the past to the present.

Appendix I

Martha Warren Beckwith's "Iron Hawk"

Makula, under his other name of Left Heron, told the following version of "Iron Hawk" to Martha Warren Beckwith at Pine Ridge, South Dakota on July 17, 1926. The interpreter was William Garnett. The story was printed in Beckwith's "Mythology of the Oglala Dakota," *Journal of American Folklore* 43 (1930): 339–439 ["Iron Hawk" 379–91].

The Story of Iron Hawk

A little tribe lived near the ocean. An old man and his wife lived near. One morning the wife went out for wood to start a fire and she heard a cry. She looked in a stump and found a child, a boy. The cord was still there as if he had not been born. She picked up a piece of wood and cut off the cord and brought the child into the house. He cried and cried and the old man painted the boy with red paint and grease. They made a smoke out of a weed and smoked him and he stopped crying and went to sleep. The old man said, "This is night-time. That means everybody goes to sleep. In the morning the sun will rise and everything will shine; then we shall arise. The sun sees everyone. He may pick persons out for old age even though they are poor. Perhaps you will be one of those."

The next morning when the parents awoke the child was sitting up and looking all around. The old man saw that he was looking about at everything in the lodge. He said, "That is right: you should notice all you see. Now there is a man coming from the East. He notices everything. When he sees you he will pick out certain things to help you. Although you are poor these may help you to reach old age." When the sun went down at night the child began to cry again, so the old man painted him again and smoked him with the weed and rubbed him with it all over his body.

The next morning the child was standing up before the old people awoke. The old man said, "That is right, boy: this is holy earth and you are going to walk on the earth. It is on the earth that you are going to be brought up. When the day comes there is a man coming from the East. He notices everything. When he thinks that a man who is on the earth should live, he will live to old age, even until he leans upon a cane. It is the man called 'Giver-of-all-life'." At night the boy cried, again. Again he was painted and smoked. The old man said, "There is a man who puts all the animals and birds to sleep during the night. When the yellow day comes that is another man; then all awake."

The next morning the child was the first one outside the lodge. The old people went out and found him looking all about. "That is right! you are going to walk all about, travel all over the earth," said the old man. At night the child began to cry and again he was painted and smoked and the old man said, "There is a man at night who puts all creatures to sleep even though they have wings or walk over the earth. And in the morning another man comes who seeks those who wish to live to old age, even those who will lean upon a cane." Then he told him that this was the last night he was going to paint him; after this he must go to sleep by himself. He said, "I wish that this grandson of mine may grow at once as large as he is to be; I wish for him clothing, leggings, quiver; I wish him to be a good-looking man."

The next morning the child was grown a fine-looking man and the clothing and quiver were there. The old man took the boy to a high knoll above the village and showed him to the people of the village. He told them how he had brought up this abandoned child. He gave him a name—C'eṭą'-Maza, that is, Iron Hawk. After they came home the old man took an animal rib and straightened it up and made a bow and cut off four cherry-stick arrows, two with blunt ends (for shooting small birds), two with sharp points. He held up a hair from his own head. The child shot with a sharp-pointed arrow and cut the hair in two. "You will be one of the best of shooters," said the old man.

The next morning the boy went out with his arrows and brought back a big jack-rabbit. So they cleaned and cooked the rabbit. The old man said, "The rabbit goes about almost all night, he is industrious. This is a good meat for you to eat as your first meal; you will be industrious and able to travel at night." The next day he brought a skunk. The old man said, "This animal eats all kinds of small creatures—anything he can pick up. He is a good medicine: he will make you fat." The next day he brought back a badger. "Grandfather, come out and look!" he shouted. The old man said, "The badger eats nothing but flesh. He is an earth animal—he lives and digs in the earth. This food means that you also must live on the earth. It is good food for you." The next day the boy was gone (all day) and when he came back (at night) he threw down something heavy. It was a white-tailed deer. The old man said, "Early in the morning and late in the morning the deer picks out good things to eat. He goes among the young trees and eats the cherries and the young leaves. He tastes all that is good. So the deer-flesh will strengthen you well." The fifth morning the boy brought a buffalo calf. The inside gut (called the "marrow gut") he washed out clean and filled with marrow for the old man, and told him the liver was to be eaten raw and the fat was to be cooked in the pot. After this meal the old man went to the knoll overlooking the village and announced to the people what his grandson had done for him. Now the old man and woman were the Meadowlark and his wife. The lodge spoken of is the nest in which they live. From that day the meadowlark has the name "Marrow Gut;" "*Taśiyaknunpa*", an old Indian when he listens hears the meadowlark says. Many a word the lark utters an Indian can understand. The larks are clever birds.

Their nest is made on the ground out of grass, oval like a wigwam, with a hole where they can go inside out of the rain. The magpie is a clever bird also. He builds a roof, only it is in the tree and he stays in there all winter.

The young man now wanted to travel westward. The old man warned him against it and gave him a cap with two hawk's feathers and told him to wear it wherever he went. On the hill the youth met four men painted like a snake's trail from the mouth down to the legs and from the eyes down the arms. One said, "Here is the man who was reared where the sun rises. His name is Iron Hawk. What has brought you here?" The boy said that he was looking for a wife. They all went on together and came to a lodge where human bones were lying about outside. An old woman came out leaning upon a cane and called to the girls inside to come out and see her sons-in-law. With the walking-stick she could kill whatever she touched. So she invited the men to approach and all four of the painted men she struck as they passed her and killed, and she tried to kill Iron Hawk but could not and when she turned he shot at her with a blunt arrow and broke her backbone. Then he brought out the four girls and went to each of the four men and took him by the arm and raised him up. He gave them the four women and bade them come to him when he called for help. These four men were the Lightnings. The old woman was one of the Rock People whom the Indians call Ukce'ġila (Petrified bones) and who do all sorts of harm on the earth. These he charged them to kill wherever they saw them.

Peeping over the top of the next hill he saw a great village. As he turned toward a lodge he met a man dressed in yellow with a quiver made out of the skin of a mountain lion. The man said, "You are the man reared where the sun rises. What are you after?" The youth said he was after a wife. Now in the great lodge of the village there lived a young woman and her sister whom many men courted but none had won. In the bottom of a pit was to be seen something that looked like a great dish but was in reality wampum shells. Anyone who secured the shells would have the woman. So Iron Hawk and the yellow man agreed to try for them together and take the two women. The yellow man said they must first undress, then he caught the boy's left wrist with his right hand and shouted "Go!" The boy jumped, but the yellow man sprang back and let the boy go down alone. Then he left him in the bottom of the pit, put on his fine clothes and went away to the village. As the boy stayed there crying an old woman looked down and saw him, let down a rope and pulled him out. When he came out his handsome clothes were gone and he was an ugly-looking boy. The old woman and her husband took him to her lodge and she gathered up the yellow clothes also and took those along.

Food was scarce in the village. The youth sent the old woman to the village to get some sinew. When she asked for old pieces, a woman brought her some fine sinews. The youth twisted them into rope and showed the old woman how to make snares with slip-knots which he hung all about inside the lodge. Then they went outside and when they returned, they found ducks, chickens, all kinds of birds caught in the snares. The youth bade them clean the birds and save the feathers. Then he sent his grandmother to bor-row a kettle. She demurred, but when she went, she met the same woman, who, when she heard what the grandchild wanted, gave her the biggest kettle in the camp. They gathered all the feathers into the kettle and carried it to the creek and upset it into the water and said, "Come alive so that all the people may eat you in future." Just the same birds came alive,—ducks swimming, birds flying as before. Then they went back to the lodge, cooked up the plucked birds and invited all the people to come and eat. The first one to come was the yellow man, who called himself Iron Heart. All were glad when they had feasted.

The boy told the old man to get a grape-vine stock and the old woman to soak a piece of rawhide without the hair. Out of the hide the old man cut around, cut around, and cut a long strand with which he tied the vine into a hoop and netted it, leaving a hole in the center. The youth tied some buffalo hairs through the hole with sinews and told his grandmother to hold up the hoop and say "*Pte ro cinca*," that is "Four-year-old buffalo," and make a motion to throw the hoop but not to throw it (until the fourth time). She repeated these words and made three motions and the fourth time she threw it and he shot through the hole and there lay a four-year-old buffalo.

The next morning the old man (the "yellow man" mentioned earlier) announced that a red fox was to run through the village early in the morning and a red eagle would fly over it at night and whoever shot them was to have their skins hung on his lodge. Just at sunrise came the fox. The old man shot at it, missed it,—something caught at him and made him miss, he said. The boy prepared to shoot but he told the woman to pull out its hair as fast as she could for some one would take it from him. Sure enough, when he shot it some Indians came and took away the skin. At noon came Red Eagle right over the lodge. The man missed again, said he caught the end of his blanket. The boy shot it and the woman pulled out a handful of feathers before the Indians came and took it away.

Now came the sister of the woman in the big lodge to ask for food. They treated her kindly and sent her back with meat. She came again crying because her sister had scolded her. She had come to marry the youth because the woman had heard that it was he who had killed the Red Fox and the Red Eagle. She invited him over to the lodge to live with his wife.

He told his grandmother that the woman must first pronounce his name Iron Hawk before he would go. When she called him he told her to go on and he would follow. He rolled on the ground and turned into a buffalo, followed the woman and made a dash at her. She stepped aside and he sprang through the lodge. When she came to the lodge to call him again he was a boy as before; when he followed her he was a buffalo—first a calf, then a young buffalo, then older, finally a big buffalo. This last time she came she said, "Iron Hawk, I have come after you!" He urged her not to be frightened. Now he came like an old buffalo with the horns almost worn off. "That is the Messiah! he can transform himself into anything," they said. The woman fell upon the buffalo's head. The buffalo turned into a youth and where the nose had struck there was blood on his nose.

The wife's sister had scorned the two and called them "lousy."

She was now to have the fox's hide and the eagle's skin hung upon her lodge in order to win honor among the people. The youth also prepared to hang upon his lodge what he had taken from the skins and put away in bundles. When the trophies were brought out for the sister's lodge they were nothing but a coyote's hide and a black crow. When the stranger's bundles were opened which the grandmother had kept for him, they drew forth a whole fox hide and an eagle's skin. Now Iron Hawk bade the grandmother take the yellow suit—leggings, shirt, blanket, cap—to the other lodge and demand from Yellow Spider his own clothes. She obeyed, saying, "Iktomizila, my grandson told me to bring these here and ask for his own clothes." The next morning before sun-up she returned to her grandson's lodge and there in the bed lay the finest-looking man she had ever seen. He dressed himself in his own clothing and went outside and she summoned the people to see him. The sister held her hand over her eyes, ashamed to see the kind of man she had obtained and the fine man her sister possessed.

It was in the summertime. The youth took his wife into the country and told her to roll and she turned into a buffalo and he turned into a buffalo too. Each took a different way and scattered hairs all over the country, then they turned into human beings again and came back home. In the morning men reported the whole country stocked with game. Five young men at each end of the village went through the camp and picked up all the arrows and he and his wife with these ten men went out to chase the buffalo. The wife turned into a buffalo by rolling and went through the herd and then circled four times about the husband and turned into a person again. The buffalo followed her. The ten men kept the youth stocked with arrows while he shot down the buffalo as fast as they came around him, then he told them to pick up the arrows and cut out the buffalos' tongues. Afterwards he sent the village men to butcher the animals. For the grandmother the people provided without his asking. Each brought him a little dried meat and some pounded meat. They made him a tent also of twenty skins such as a wealthy Indian lives in.

When his wife became pregnant he took her out into the country beyond the hills. She rolled and became a female buffalo and bore a young bull calf which turned into a child to whom they gave the name of Red Calf. She brought him out each day to the hill where he was born. In four days he was able to run about. Iron Hawk gave to this son the four arrows that had been made for himself and the gray cap and told the lad of his grandfather Meadowlark whom he was to think of if ever he needed anything.

One day he asked his wife to go swimming with him, but she excused herself until she had finished cleaning a hide, so he went alone. On the other side of the creek a woman called to him to help her across. He turned into a buffalo, swam across and told her to catch hold of his hair and swim across. She said she might lose hold and be drowned. He said she might ride on his back, but she objected that he might shake her off. At length he allowed her to ride on the small of his back with her head against his withers. Half way across the woman grew great wings and carried him off through a hole in the sky. When his wife came to seek him Iron Hawk had disappeared.

The grandmother appealed to Yellow Spider to recover Iron Hawk, but he did not wish to find him and gave the woman a push. She said, "Remember that what you wish for him will be done to you if ever Iron Hawk comes back."

Red Calf now bade his mother to take him to the spot where his father had disappeared and leave him alone there. The boy put on the cap that his father had given him and wished to his grandfather that he might find his father. The cap turned the boy into a hawk and he saw the buffalo's track on one side of the river and the woman's on the other. So he flew to the middle of the channel and there in the middle was a whirling wind. This was his father's trail. He followed it to the sky and went through the hole in the sky to a country where was a village which was the village of the birds called Ski'bibila. A man challenged him and told him that his father had been carried through that way. He went on to the village of the Ikpi'sapa or "Black Breasts," and they too said that his father had passed that way. Again he went on to the village of the "little birds that live among the sunflowers." They told him that his father had been there but had been carried beyond. In the next village he met a man all painted up called Hupuwangli (a grey-colored swallow that lives in the pines). He told Red Calf that his father had been taken further. A fine looking fellow called Bluebird came up (in the next village) and said the same. In the next village he met the Red Woodpecker, Canruruyaca (Wood burnt red). In the next the bluebird in the pines called Wazi'zitkala; in the next, robin, Śiśo'ka. Through all these villages his father had passed. The next was Crow village and here too his father had passed through. In the next village he met a man with a breach-clout that hung behind—a man painted white in patches and with scabby eyes. This was Magpie.

As he was leaving the magpie country he met a person who warned him against a little man on the hill who was dangerous. He came to a village between the fork of two creeks. An old woman took him home for the night and told him that tomorrow he might get liver to eat; for a man reared under the sun had been brought there in the shape of a buffalo by a person picked out to capture him, and the next day he was to be killed. The next morning the announcer called all the people together to see the captive who at noon was to be killed and his meat divided. The Calf went also, although the old woman protested that the people were dangerous and could kill all whom they touched. The father recognized his son. There was a Rock Woman fastened to his loins so that he could not move. The boy shot a sharp arrow and the Rock Woman burst to pieces and the father set out running as a buffalo and the son flying as a hawk. When they came to the little man on the hill Red Calf shot him also. The people cried "Let him go! he will kill us all!" He too was one of the mystery people. It looks as if he belonged to the Rock People.

The two passed back through all these bird villages to the last bird village and here the birds had been considering what to do when they came back in order to return Iron Hawk to earth. So they got all the different kinds of wood from the trees and made a great nest and all the birds let him down in the nest through the hole to earth. When they got there they first saw the father-in-law on a hill and he summoned the people, who welcomed them gladly. Yellow Spider too pretended to be pleased, but the grandmother told what a push he had given her and the boy began to beat him with a dirty lodge-skin until he turned into a black spider and ran away. He and his wife were to be seen afterwards with a lot of young ones on their backs.

Soon after Iron Hawk got home a man stood outside his lodge and said, "Iron Hawk, come out: I want to talk to you!" So he went out. The man said, "There is a man in trouble out there to the west. He told me to come and get you." As Iron Hawk was picking up his weapons the wife objected, but the son helped him, saying, "He will come back again." Iron Hawk went with the man. They came to a place where there was a fine lodge. Inside was a man sitting with his blanket over his head. (The man said) "Over here there is a big river and a man came from over the other side of the river and scalped me and went back. You are the only man on earth who can help me." Iron Hawk put on his cap and turned himself into a hawk and flew to the big village. People were gathered about the center of the village. Approaching he saw the man's scalp hung on a pole in the center. Everyone had gathered to see it. Now the people went to play shinny, and Iron Hawk flew to the scalp and carried it away. The people pursued, but one man cried, "You'd better let him alone. That is Iron Hawk. He can do anything!" He brought the scalp back to the lodge and said, "Grandfather, I have the scalp." As directed, he soaked the scalp in water and put it on the man's head; after he got it nicely placed he held it until it stuck just where it had been before, (The old man said) "Now, grand-child, you see some ropes hanging about here? These represent horses. I am a maker of horses. Choose one for yourself." Just at the right was a rather poor hair rope. Iron Hawk took that one. The old man said, "That is the chief horse—a small horse, but the right choice." He sent Iron Hawk to the horses and told him to put the rope about the horse that was the same color as the rope. There were fine-looking horses in the herd but only one that matched the rope—not a fine horse but bay-colored. He approached, and when the horse saw the rope it nickered. Iron Hawk put the rope about its neck and led it to the old man's tent. The old man said it was the right horse—it was not handsome but was the first horse he had made. "In the country you come from everybody is going to have a horse and the first herd will be bay-colored, later there will be different colors." Iron Hawk was directed not to look backward until he had reached his home. When he got there the lodges were still standing but not a soul was in sight. He looked back and saw clouds of dust coming and thought it was a storm. From a hill to the east he saw a boy running toward him. This boy was his son. He told Iron Hawk that when the people saw the great dust coming they had fled, fearing some danger, but he had returned in spite of the warning of the people when he saw a man come into the village, for he thought it was his father. (Out of the cloud of dust) horses came into the village, the whole space was covered with horses. The people came back to the village. Iron Hawk gave the young men ropes and they caught horses until each family had four horses apiece. He told them that hereafter they could use the horses to pack their things in moving. The horses left over he kept for himself.

First Iron Hawk made buffalo, then he made horses. From that time the Indians have chased buffalo on horseback.

Iron Hawk now sent his son to his grandfather Meadow Lark to report his condition—that he was chief of a band of Indians and had horses and that the horses were coming west. He told Red Calf if he was ever in trouble to call upon the Lightning People and they would help him. Red Calf came to a hill outside a village. Here was a woman all dressed in yellow. She told him that he must stay with her four nights before entering the village. She showed him a little lodge outside the camp where she lived. Inside he heard a child crying. Within was a young boy nursing a child. The boy told him that his sister had had the child by a man she had been with four nights: now she was gone with another man. The child was crying and fussing. Red Calf shot a red-tailed deer, got a little piece of the liver and put it on the child's tongue, and it stopped crying. He took the skin of the heart, boiled the inside hoof cut to the first bone and made soup, filled the bladder and left a hole for the child to suck. So the child was fed until it got strong enough to sit up. The mother came back, whipped the child and took away the food and went off. Red Calf got another deer. He bade the boy hang up the hoofs and dry them (Indians use the hoofs for necklace and armlets as rattles.) The child got to running around and the boy took his nephew to the hill outside the village and proclaimed his name as "Rattling Hoof" from the ornaments of hoofs which were hung about him. The woman came (and abused the child again). Red Calf sent the boy and the child to a big tree where there was a nest. He called for a lightning-storm to do away with the people in the village. Only the brother-in-law and the child remained. This was the Mountain Lions' camp. They were human beings in the story, but mountain lions scattered out from those who were left in the village.

Red Calf went on now to his grandfather's house, taking the child. The old man was complaining that Iron Hawk had promised to come back and was not there. He welcomed Red Calf and the child Rattling Hoof. He recognized the cap Red Calf wore. He took him to the lodge where he had nursed his father. A small bird outside called "He back!" It was the Śkibibi. In the spring of the year this bird talks Sioux and says "Did he come back!" but at no other time of the year. Another bird is called "T'iblo'!" (brother)— "Killdeer" the white people say. Meadowlark asked after his father and Red Calf gave the message that he should move west where his father was. But the old man said his life was in danger from a man, wife and son who lived in a deep lake over behind a great hill. So Red Calf called to Lightning and all night there was a storm. In the morning the lake was dry and the man, his wife and son lay on the side of the hill. These were the petrified people—the mysterious Rock People. Up to that time they had killed the birds, now the birds scatter out all over the country.

Appendix II

In her introduction to the Left Heron section of James R. Walker's *Lakota Myth* Elaine Jahner describes Makula's stories as "distinctive for their dramatic inventiveness, evidenced by the wealth of detail with which he embellished the tales" (103). Much of Makula's structural and descriptive technique can be readily appreciated in translation. The Lakota language versions have additional dimensions that future interpretations are likely to evoke. In her bilingual *Dakota Play on Words* from the Boas Collection of the American Philosophical Society (MS 30, X8a.12), Deloria transforms Makula's verbal brilliance into what literary criticism appreciates as "texture." The following reprint may serve to alert readers to similar possibilities in *Dakota Texts, Iron Hawk,* and the next volume in this series, *Ella Deloria's* The Buffalo People.

"Dakota Play on Words"

(That's what I call these small bits which are related as incidents, intended to amuse. This practice of pretending to mistake the meaning of words is common in some quarters. Not exactly puns, in this case, I don't know what to call them really. Their character is quite obvious from these little stories.) [1]

1. Kola Makula niun un han wawihahayeke? Agna ite eyeśni ece-ia canke takunl eya canśna heceya eye s'e leyeca'.

2. Tohunwel canpagmiyan ogna yankin nan ocanku okiżata wan el ya ke'.

3. Yunkan okażaya kin ot'inś kośkalaka wan nażin nan wikiyuta ohitiyela śkan canke ena pataka ke'.

4. "Huhin, taku le toka kehin nan śicawacin wiluta huwo?" eya ke'. Iyopeye s'e.

5. Eyaś kośkalaka kin he tunśkaku canke heya ke': "Lekśi, Toktuka huwo? El omayagnakin nan wicoti kin heciya amayala oyakihi huwo?" eya ke'.

6. Makula lecehcin canśkokpa opapun kin icanyan iyotakin nan ohanglegleya ayuta nan heya ke':

7. "Ho, eya aciyinkte kin he eś ito owakihi ye lo. Tka ek'eś nitanka nihanka ca okiniś nitke nacece lo. Ca tokeniś ciyuhakteśni iteke, niyecinkala keś ekta hiyali yo.

8. "Ekta ocignakinkte kin hehanyan owakihiśni ye lo." eya ke'.

9. Wana ekta iyali nan iyotaka canke yahanpi nan ke un ekta ipi yunkan yutintan iwicacu canke inażinpi yunkan lecehcin igluhomni nan heya ke':

10. "Tuktetu hca ca le la yacin huwo?" eya yunkan "lena keś mayuhpa yo, lekśi," ake kośkalaka kin eya ke'.

11. Yunkan Makula ake iśikcin s'e ayuta nan heya ke': "Hunhunhi, otawat'e-śice lo. . . . . Lecaś ociciyaka wan, nitke ca ciyuhaśni ye lo. He le wimacahcala nan mahunkeśni kin tokeśke hinskatanka ataya ciyuhpinkta he? Wan, niyecinka keś glicu wo, ektan yuhpapi yacinke!" eya ke'.

12. Akeś ti ożula takożakpaku, cinca nan eya hecel takuwicaye kin ahiyunka ke'.

---

1. Ella Deloria's introductory note

13. Yunkan wana wosnipi eyaś tuweni iśtinmeśni, woglaka-
hanpi ke'.

14. Ho, egna takożakpaku wan wana eya winyan-tankaka ca
hingnaku kici kal catkuta pikiyapi canke heciyatanhan akeśna
heya ke',

15. "Taku, hinhanna kinhan wakaġeġe-mninkta un, tokeśke
mninkta huwe," lehicita eya ke'.

16. Hcehanl tożanku wan iś eya kal hingnaku kici pikiya ca el
gliyunka ke', tankal i nan.

17. Ake eya ca, "Tunwin, hinhanna kinhan iś'eya le wakaġeġe-
mninkte, Tokśa . ." eye kin hehanni, "Tożan, k'imayakiya oyakihi
he?" eya ca, "To, cin he tokaka," eya yunkan hecena iyuśkin
it'a ke'.

18. Nan woglakapi eyaś el nunġe yuześni, akeśna "Hn, cewinś
mitożan tanyan k'imakiyinkte ke!" eyahan ke'.

19. Wanaś wanżikżila iśtinmapi nan; enana wana gopahanpi
eyaś hecena heyahan canke ohanketa Makula heya ke':

20. "Wan, eyaś henala eyin nan iśtinmi ye, wana le hancokaya
ye. Taku cewin canpagmiyan k'inkta wan iyuśkin ke!" eya ke'.

21. Akeś tohantuka wan kakena canpagmiyan sapa wan teca ca
ogna yahan ke'.

22. Kal tonakel witaya ahitipi canke el wicokanhiyaya inażin ca
wok'upi nan wana ake iyali yunkan wanżi heya ke':

23. "Ciye, ate ogna yankelakta keye lo, owakpamnita iś eya
waśicu okiye-yinkta ca," eya ke'.

24. "Ho, cin iś iye kin," eya canke wana wicahcalala wan sakye
kitun nan cancanyela ula nan hektatanhan iyalila ke'.

25. Nan le t'at'apike un hececa canke tokeśke iya ca, ksin s'e
ayuta nan heya ke':

26. "Cinkś, lel mat'in?" eya yunkan Makula heya ke',

27. "Wan, tuktetuka keś t'a yo, ekta canpagmiyan sapa cinke;
le teca nan tawayapi ca wicayakiluśicinkte lo," eya ke'.

28. Hmun sekse wawihaya ke'.

29. Eyaś śica wicahcalala k'un nah'unśni eyap ca itohomnimni
hiyayin nan tohanl kat'eyetanka iyotaka ke'.

Free Translation

1. How amusing was my friend, Makula, when he was alive! And he had such a trick of looking solemn, it was hard to realize when he spoke that he was only joking.

2. Once he was riding in his wagon-box and approaching a fork in the road.

3. And there in the exact angle made by the parting roads a man was standing and gesticulating at him with such vigor that he came to a sudden stop.

4. "Well, of all things, what do you think you mean by signalling with such frantic effort?" he asked, in such a way as to appear to be scolding him.

5. But the young man who was a nephew to him replied, "My uncle, how about it? Can you give me a lift and take me to that encampment yonder?" he asked.

6. And Makula leaned over the edge of the wagon-box and sized him up, measuring him by running his glance down the man's entire length and breadth, and then he replied:

7. "Well, now, as far as my taking you there goes, that I can do; but as for lifting you, you appear to me as a tall, large man, apparently you are heavy. So you are beyond my strength to lift you, obviously. Why don't you climb in of your own accord?

8. "To lift you up and place you in the wagon would be beyond my ability."

9. When the man had climbed in, they started out and drove on and arrived at the place he had indicated; whereupon he drew in his reins causing the horses to halt, and turned himself about in this manner as he sat, and said:

10. "And just where precisely do you wish to go?" he asked, so the man replied, "Right here will do; just put me off here, my uncle."

11. And again Makula, as though with great disgust, looked upon the man and said: "Well, well, well, aren't you the limit. . . . I have just finished telling you, you are too heavy, I cannot carry you. I am old now, and feeble, just how do you expect me to lift

all of a thing as big as you? Why, climb out yourself, under your own power; why must you be lifted out?" he said.

12. At another time one night all his relatives, his grandchildren and his daughters and relatives of that kinship class, all arrived and put up for the night in his tipi.

13. Everyone had retired, the light had been blown out, and still nobody slept, for there was conversation going on.

14. Now, amidst all the talking, there was one, a granddaughter to him, a woman now of mature years, who with her husband had her bedding laid in the honor-place; from her bed she would remark from time to time:

15. "Dear me, I wonder how I can get to the sewing society meeting tomorrow?" This she said frequently.

16. Just then one who was her niece, and who also with her husband had her bed in yonder part of the tipi, reentered the room, having gone outside.

17. Again the woman exclaimed, so she answered her, "My aunt, tomorrow I also am going to the sewing society meeting, so I will . . ." but without letting her finish, she went on, "O, my niece, can you drive me?" she asked, so, "Certainly, why not?" she replied, and then the woman was "tickled to death."

18. And so, paying no attention to the substance of the conversation, she would say again and again to herself, "O my, how nice that my niece can drive me!"

19. And by the time, one-by-one, the company had dropped off to sleep and some were already snoring here and there, still she kept on remarking in that manner till Makula could stand it no longer.

20. "That's enough now, say no more, and get to sleep, it is already midnight . . . Never have I known anyone to go into such ecstacies over the prospect of pulling a wagon" (as a horse. See notes on this.)

21. At another time, I don't know just when, he was going out in a certain direction in a brand new buggy.

22. He stopped for the noon meal at a place where a few families had recently camped together, and after eating, he was

now climbing back into his vehicle when one of the men spoke to him.

23. "Elder brother, my father wants to go in your wagon, he says; he too wants to confer with the white man," he said.

24. "Very well, that's up to him," he replied, and now the little old man came leaning on a staff, and shaking with old age he climbed into the back.

25. Now he was like the extremely old, he was feeble in every way, and he talked in a peculiar manner, so now, looking at him with squinting eye, he said:

26. "Son, may I die here?" he said, so Makula replied to him:

27. "Why, die anywhere, why must you pick out a buggy to die in; it is new, and it belongs to somebody; you don't want to use it ill for the owner," he said

28. At that everyone roared, like a great humming sound.

29. But the poor thing, the old man was deaf as deaf can be, so, oblivious to it all, he turned himself round several times, and at last succeeded in seating himself somewhere, settling down as if there for all time.

Notes

a. *ite,* face; *eyeśni,* to say not.
The phrase in colloquial Dakota means "with a straight face," as a man may look serious while saying something funny or in fun.
cf. *iteśniyan,* "Really?" or "Actually".
Examples:
Iteśniyan yuś'inyemaye', He actually frightened me.
Wana miglustan', I am through; I have finished (my work; my stint; my course).
Iteśniyan? Oh, really? Indeed!

b. *s'e lececa,* in colloquial Dakota is often pronounced like *s'e leyeca.* There is no such word—*leyeca.*

c. *ognaka,* to lift and place something in a container, may also be used to mean to give someone a lift in your vehicle. That is what the man wanted, but Makula amused himself by taking it to mean the first; that is, that he, the driver, should get down and pick up this good-sized man and place him literally into the wagon box, the container.

d. *yuhpa* is to take down something that is placed high; something heavy. Ex. If I take down a towel or a pencil from the top shelf, reaching high to do it, that is not *yuhpa*, but *icu*, to take. Only such a thing as a heavy suitcase, a large bundle, a load of some sort. *Wayuhpa*, to take things down, also means to unload, as freight.

But *yuhpa* is also used in a secondary meaning, to give the idea of letting or putting somebody off, as a streetcar puts me off at a given spot. The conductor does not haul me off, but the same word is used.

e. *taku!* Pronounced as *takooooooooooooo!* The last *u* is held long, to indicate bewilderment, wondering, etc. It is close to "Dear meeeee!"

f. *k'inkiya*, to cause (as a horse) to carry on the back. Also means, to cause horses to draw, as a wagon. Also, in the case of a passenger, to cause him to be drawn, with him for the lead. *k'in*, to carry on the back.
The pun is obvious, I think. The woman meant, "How nice that my niece can cause me to be a passenger, drawn along." Makula pretended to take the word to mean, "How nice that my niece is going to hitch me to a wagon and cause me to drag it." *Sapsapa k'inwicakiye'*, He had a black team; he was driving a black team. *Waota k'inkiye'*, He had a big load (on his wagon). *ota*, many.

g. *canpagmiyan*, wagon; *sapa*, a black one, i.e., a rig, a buggy. For a long time, a black buggy was considered the finest in elegance; a lumber wagon being the clumsy but usual means of transportation.

h. *kitun*, to use on one's person; to wear on one's body, as a hat or other garment. *tun*, to have on, acquire; take on; give birth to, etc. *ogle*, coat; *wapostan*, hat; *wapaha*, warbonnet; *hunska*, leggings; *ipiyaka*, belt; (*ipiyak-kitun*); *aopazan-kitun*, to wear a feather or other ornament in the hair; *owin kitun*, to wear earrings; *sakye kitun*, to use a cane; *istamaza kitun*, to wear glasses. *kic'un*, to put on what belongs to one by right; cf. *un*, to wear.

Note: Practically all the above nouns may be used with *kic'un*, just as well. In which case a specific garment or other object is indicated. As *ogle k̇itun,* he was "coated." *ogle k̇ic'un',* he was wearing his coat; he put on his coat. Except *hunsk̇a,* leggings, which always requires *k̇itun,* or better, *ok̇itun. hunsk̇a k̇ic'un* is possible but not idiomatic. This goes also for *hunyak̇un,* stockings. But *wase,* face paint, always takes *k̇ic'un,* not *k̇itun. wase k̇ic'un';* He wore face-paint. *k̇itun* is often contracted to *tk̇un,* but *k̇ic'un* is never contracted, *k̇c* is not a cluster.

i. *Mat'in,* may I die? is what the old man who spoke almost unintelligibly on account of his infirmity, seemed to say. What he meant was, *mank̇in,* may I sit? But Makula takes it the wrong way on purpose. *mat'a,* I die; *mank̇a,* I sit, from *yank̇a,* he sits.

Orthographic Notes

Most contemporary readers and writers of Lakota are more familiar with the orthography developed by Buechel than with that of Deloria. Ivan Star Comes Out's column in *The Lakota Times* (December 25, 1990), quoted here in the introduction, typifies the spelling and punctuation of modern Lakota. The newspaper includes no diacritics for obvious technical reasons. Recent scholarly books, such as the James R. Walker series published by the University of Nebraska Press (1980, 1982, 1983), and William K. Powers's *Sacred Language* (University of Oklahoma Press, 198) have included minimal diacritics, specifically ś (sounds like English sh), the gutteralized ḣ, and the glottal stop '.

In *Ella Deloria's Iron Hawk*, as in the preceding book in this series, *Deer Women and Elk Men: The Lakota Narratives of Ella Deloria*, I have modified her orthography to accord with the current predominance of the Buechel system in schools, colleges, and general use. Deloria's orthography may be examined in her books, *Dakota Texts* and *Dakota Grammar* (see Works Cited).

The first few units of *Iron Hawk* exemplify most of the changes.

Deloria's Spelling:

This Edition:

wióhinapᶜe, hécᶜeś, oyáte, wicᶜótᶜi.

Deloria provides the syllabic accent for every word. I have removed these accent marks, since they are already known to most speakers and because in most cases Lakota words are accented on the second syllable.

cį, wą.

The subscript hook, nasalizing the preceding vowel, is here written simply as n, in line with current practice, *cin, wan.*

ekta, oyate.

Deloria does not mark medial ċ, k̇, ṗ, ṫ. Since the Lakota sounds do not correspond to the English pronunciations of these letters, I have marked them as Buechel does, *ekta, oyate* (see pronunciation list below). When the consonants are juxtaposed, the second receives the medial pronunciation while the first is aspirated: *ekta, etḣiya.*

wiohinapᶜe, hecᶜeś, wicᶜotᶜi.

Deloria marks the aspirate sounds of c, k, p, and t with a diacritic (ᶜ) taking up a separate space above and following the preceding letter. Since the aspirates c, k, p, t are more common than the medial pronunciations of these letters, I have left them unmarked, as Buechel does. The first word of *Iron Hawk* in the present text is *wiyohinape*, not *wiohinapᶜe*, while the second last word in the first sentence is *wicoti* rather than *wicᶜotᶜi.*

b.lihecapila   Deloria employs a period in "clusters of sonants" to indicate "a very weak articulation of the following vowel" (*Dakota Grammar* 5). The period also marks a slight pause between the consonants. I have removed these periods throughout, since most readers will not recognize their purpose: *blihecapila* rather than *b.lihecapila*.

The following diacritics mark sounds that may be found in the opening units and throughout this edition of *Iron Hawk*:

When ḣ is gutteralized, it has a dot above it:
wicaḣcalala (unit 2).

When ġ is gutteralized, it has a dot above it:
naġalġatela (unit 8).

When ċ sounds like g in gentle, it has a dot above it:
ċisċila (unit 2).

When k̇ sounds like g in give, it has a dot above it:
k̇ici (unit 2).

When ṗ sounds like b in bill, it has a dot above it:
isanṗ (unit 3).

When t sounds like d in day, it has a dot above it:
ekta (unit 1).

Unmarked c sounds like ch in chair:
wicoti (unit 1).

When ś sounds like sh in ship, it has an acute accent mark:
heceś (unit 1).

When ż sounds like Russian zh or French j, it has a dot above it:
lużahela (unit 7).

Unmarked s and z correspond to the same letters in English:
ahiyokas'in (unit 5), *imak̇iblezinkta* (unit 16).

Works Cited

Ambrose, Stephen E. *Crazy Horse and Custer*. New York: Doubleday, 1975.

Beckwith, Martha Warren. "Mythology of the Oglala Dakota." *Journal of American Folklore* 43 (1930): 339–439.

Belden, George P. *Belden, the White Chief: Or Twelve Years Among the Wild Indians of the Plains, From the Diaries and Manuscripts of George P. Belden*. Ed. James S. Brisbin. 1872, 1875; rpt. Athens: Ohio UP, 1974.

Black Elk. *The Sacred Pipe*. Ed. Joseph Epes Brown. New York: Penguin, 1971.

———. *The Sixth Grandfather*. Ed. Raymond J. DeMallie. Lincoln: U of Nebraska P, 1984.

Buechel, Eugene, S. J. *A Dictionary of the Teton Dakota Sioux Language*. Pine Ridge, South Dakota: Red Cloud Lakota Language and Cultural Center, 1970.

———. *A Grammar of Lakota*. Rosebud, South Dakota: Rosebud Educational Society, 1939.

———. *Lakota Tales and Texts*. Ed. Paul Manhart, S. J. Pine Ridge, South Dakota: Red Cloud Lakota Language and Cultural Center, 1978.

———. *Wowapi Wakan Wicowoyake Yuptecelapi Kin*. New York: Benziger Bros., 1924.

Bushotter, George. "Teton Myths." Ed. and trans. Ella Deloria. ca. 1937; MS 30 (x8c.3), Boas Collection, Philadelphia: American Philosophical Society.

Cash, Joseph H. and Herbert T. Hoover, eds. *To Be An Indian: An Oral History*. New York: Holt, Rinehart and Winston, 1971.

Clark, Ann (Nolan) and Emil Afraid of Hawk. *About the Slim Butte Racoon. Paha zizipela wic'iteglega kin*. Lawrence, Kansas: Haskell Institute Printing Department, 1942.

———. *Brave Against the Enemy: A Story of Three Generations. Toka wan itokip ohitike kin he*. Lawrence, Kansas: Haskell Institute Printing Department, 1944.

————. *The Grass Mountain House*. Illus. Andrew Standing Soldier. Lawrence, Kansas: Haskell Institute, U.S. Bureau of Indian Affairs, 1954.

————. *The Hen of Wahpeton*. Illus. Andrew Standing Soldier. Lawrence, Kansas: Haskell Institute, U.S. Bureau of Indian Affairs, 1954.

————. *The Pine Ridge Porcupine. Wazi ahanhan pahin k'un he*. Lawrence, Kansas: Haskell Institute Printing Department, 1941.

————. *Singing Sioux Cowboy Reader*. Lawrence, Kansas: U.S. Indian Service, 1947.

————. *There are Still Buffalo. Nahaȟci pte yunk onpi*. Lawrence, Kansas: Haskell Institute Printing Department, 1942.

Collier, John. *Indians of the Americas: The Long Hope*. 1947; rpt. New York: New American Library, 1975.

Culin, Stewart. *Games of the North American Indians*. 1907; rpt. New York: Dover, 1975.

Deloria, Ella. "Camp Circle Society." Unpublished manuscript. Pierre: South Dakota State Archives.

————. Correspondence with Franz Boas (1927–1934). MS 31, Boas Collection. Philadelphia: American Philosophical Society.

————. *Dakota Grammar*. 1941; rpt. Vermillion, South Dakota: Dakota Press, 1982.

————. "Dakota Play on Words." MS 30 (X8a.12), Boas Collection. Philadelphia: American Philosophical Society.

————. "Dakota Tales in Colloquial Style." 1937; MS 30 (X8a.16), Boas Collection. Philadelphia: American Philosophical Society.

————. *Dakota Texts*. 1932; rpt. New York: AMS Press, 1974.

————. *Dakota Texts*. Vermillion, South Dakota: Dakota Press, 1978.

————. "Dakota Texts from the Minnesota Manuscript." 1941; MS 30 (X8a.17), Boas Collection. Philadelphia: American Philosophical Society.

————. "Legends in Santee Dakota." 1934; MS 30 (X8a.29), Boas Collection. Philadelphia: American Philosophical Society.

————. Letters and miscellaneous materials in Dakota from the Minnesota manuscript. 1941; MS 30 (X8a.20), Boas Collection. Philadelphia: American Philosophical Society.

————. "Old Dakota Legends." 1937; MS 30 (X8a.21), Boas Collection. Philadelphia: American Philosophical Society.

————. "The Sun Dance of the Oglala Sioux." *Journal of American Folklore* 42 (October–December 1929): 354–413.

————. "Teton Myths" (the George Bushotter collection). MS 30 (X8c.3), Boas Collection. Philadelphia: American Philosophical Society.

————. *Waterlily*. Lincoln: U of Nebraska P, 1988.

Densmore, Frances. *Teton Sioux Music*. 1918; rpt. New York: Da Capo, 1972.

Dorsey, James O. *A Study of Siouan Cults*. 1894; rpt. Seattle: Shorey, 1972.

Farber, William O. "Representative Government: Application to the Sioux." *The Modern Sioux: Social Systems and Reservation Culture*. Ed. Ethel Nurge. 123–39.

Hassrick, Royal B. *The Sioux: Life and Customs of a Warrior Society*. Norman: U of Oklahoma P, 1964.

Hiett, Louise. Interviewed by Steve Plummer. 8 July 1971. Tape and Transcript no. 0690. Vermillion: American Indian Research Project, South Dakota Oral History Center, University of South Dakota.

Hyde, George E. *Spotted Tail's Folk: A History of the Brulé Sioux*. Norman: U of Oklahoma P, 1974.

"In the White Man's Image." Writ. Christine Lesiak. *The American Experience.* PBS, WGBH Educational Foundation, Boston. March 1992.

Jahner, Elaine. "Cognitive Style in Oral Literature." *Language and Style* 15 (1982): 32–51.

Krupat, Arnold. *For Those Who Came After: A Study of Native American Autobiography.* Berkeley: U of California P, 1985.

Lyford, Carrie A. *Quill and Beadwork of the Western Sioux.* 1940; rpt. Boulder, Colorado: Johnson, 1982.

Macgregor, Gordon. "Changing Society: The Teton Dakotas." *The Modern Sioux: Social Systems and Reservation Culture.* Ed. Ethel Nurge. Lincoln: U of Nebraska P, 1970. 92–106.

Mails, Thomas E. *Fools Crow.* New York: Avon, 1979.

———. *Fools Crow: Wisdom and Power.* Tulsa, Oklahoma: Council Oak Books, 1991.

———. *The Mystic Warriors of the Plains.* New York: Doubleday, 1972.

———. *Sundancing at Rosebud and Pine Ridge.* Sioux Falls, South Dakota: Center for Western Studies, 1978.

Makula (Breast), also known as Hokacatka (Left Heron). Welcoming ceremony for John Collier, Commisioner of Indian Affairs, at Pine Ridge, South Dakota, 1932. Holy Rosary Mission Series 1, Box 2. Milwaukee: Department of Special Collections and University Archives, Marquette University.

Mallery, Garrick. *Picture-Writing of the American Indians.* 2 vols. 1888–89; rpt. New York: Dover, 1972.

Markoe, Glenn E., ed. *Vestiges of a Proud Nation: The Ogden B. Read Northern Plains Indian Collection.* Burlington, Vermont: Robert Hull Fleming Museum, University of Vermont, 1986.

Marriott, Alice. *Saynday's People: The Kiowa Indians and the Stories They Told.* Lincoln: U of Nebraska P, 1963.

Marrowbone, Ben. Interview. Videocassette. 25 August 1980. Oglala Lakota College Archives.

Mekeel, H. Scudder. "Field Notes of 1931, White Clay District, Pine Ridge Reservation, South Dakota." Department of Anthropology Archives. American Museum of Natural History, New York.

Mooney, James. *The Ghost Dance Religion and the Sioux Outbreak of 1980.* 1896; rpt. Chicago: U of Chicago P, 1965.

Murray, Janette K. "Ella Deloria: A Biographical Sketch and Literary Analysis." Unpublished dissertation. University of North Dakota, 1974.

Nurge, Ethel, ed. *The Modern Sioux: Social Systems and Reservation Culture.* Lincoln: U of Nebraska P, 1970.

Powers, Marla N. *Oglala Women: Myth, Ritual, and Reality.* Chicago: U of Chicago P, 1986.

Pond, Samuel W. *The Dakota or Sioux in Minnesota As They were in 1834.* 1908; rpt. St. Paul: Minnesota Historical Press, 1986.

Powers, William K. *Yuwipi: Vision and Experience in Oglala Ritual.* Lincoln: U of Nebraska P, 1982.

Prucha, Francis Paul, ed. *Americanizing the American Indians:* Writings by "The Friends of the Indian" 1880–1900. Lincoln: U of Nebraska P, 1978.

Rice, Julian. *Black Elk's Story: Distinguishing its Lakota Purpose.* Albuquerque: U of New Mexico P, 1991.

———. *Deer Women and Elk Men: The Lakota Narratives of Ella Deloria.* Albuquerque: U of New Mexico P, 1992.

————. "How the Bird that Speaks Lakota Earned a Name." *Recovering the Word: Essays on Native American Literature.* Eds. Brian Swann and Arnold Krupat. Berkeley: U of California P, 1987. 422–45.

Riggs, Stephen Return. *Dakota Grammar, Texts, and Ethnography.* Ed. James O. Dorsey. 1893; rpt. Marvin, South Dakota: Blue Cloud Abbey, 1977.

Sandoz, Mari. *These Were the Sioux.* New York: Dell, 1961.

Schusky, Ernest L. "Political and Religious Systems in Dakota Culture." *The Modern Sioux: Social Systems and Reservation Culture.* Ed. Ethel Nurge. 140–47.

Standing Bear, Luther. *Land of the Spotted Eagle.* Lincoln: U of Nebraska P, 1978.

————. *My People the Sioux.* Lincoln: U of Nebraska P, 1975.

Star Comes Out, Ivan. "We can retain our language in written form" in "Lakota Eyapaha" column, *The Lakota Times,* December 25, 1990.

Useem, Ruth Hill and Carl F. Eicher. "Rosebud Reservation Economy." *The Modern Sioux: Social Systems and Reservation Culture.* Ed. Ethel Nurge. Lincoln: U of Nebraska P, 1970. 3–34.

Vestal, Stanley. *Sitting Bull: Champion of the Sioux.* Norman: U of Oklahoma P, 1980.

Walker, James R. *Lakota Belief and Ritual.* Eds. Raymond J. DeMallie and Elaine A. Jahner. Lincoln: U of Nebraska P, 1980.

————. *Lakota Myth.* Ed. Elaine A. Jahner. Lincoln: U of Nebraska P, 1983.

————. *Lakota Society.* Ed. Raymond J. DeMallie. Lincoln: U of Nebraska P, 1982.

————. *The Sun Dance and Other Ceremonies of the Oglala Division of the Teton Dakota.* 1917; rpt. New York: AMS Press, 1979.

Williamson, Thomas. *The Books of Exodus and Leviticus, trans. from the Hebrew into the Dakota Language.* New York: American Bible Society, 1869.

Williamson, Thomas S. and Stephen R. Riggs, trans. *Dakota Wowapi Wakan. The Holy Bible.* New York: American Bible Society, 1914.

Wissler, Clark. "Costumes of the Plains Indians." *Anthropological Papers of the American Museum of Natural History* 17.2 (1915): 38–91.

————. "Decorative Art of the Sioux Indians." *Bulletin of the American Museum of Natural History* 18.3 (1904): 231–78.

————. "Societies and Ceremonial Associations in the Oglala Division of the Teton Dakota." *Anthropological Papers of the American Museum of Natural History* 11.2 (1912): 1–99.

————. "Some Protective Designs of the Dakota." *Anthropological Papers of the American Museum of Natural History* 1.2 (1907): 19–53.

Index